KILLING FREUD

*Twentieth-Century Culture and the
Death of Psychoanalysis*

For Clara and Chloe

KILLING FREUD

*Twentieth-Century Culture and the
Death of Psychoanalysis*

TODD DUFRESNE

continuum
LONDON • NEW YORK

Continuum
The Tower Building
11 York Road
London SE1 7NX

15 East 26th Street
New York
NY 10010

www.continuumbooks.com

First published 2003 by Continuum

British Library Cataloguing-in-Publication Data
A catalogue record for this book is available from the British Library

ISBN 0-8264-6893-4 (hardback)

Typeset by Kenneth Burnley, Wirral, Cheshire
Printed and bound in Great Britain by Biddles Ltd, www.biddles.co.uk

Contents

Introduction   vii

Part I Suggestion and Fraud in the Age of Critical Freud Studies
1 The Strange Case of 'Anna O.': An Overview of the
  'Revisionist' Assessment   4
2 Rhetoric, Representation and the Hysterical Josef Breuer   26
3 Critical Readers of Freud Unite: A New Era for
  Freud Studies   35

**Part II Selected Memories of Psychoanalysis: History, Theory,
  Politics**
4 Freud and His Followers, Or How Psychoanalysis Brings
  Out the Worst in Everyone   53
5 Jacques What's-His-Name: Death, Memory and Archival
  Sickness   72
6 Gossip, Fiction and the History of Psychoanalysis:
  An Open Letter   84
7 The Politics of Representing Freud: A Short Account of a
  Media War, This Time With Feeling   87
8 Funny Business: The Cartoon Seminar of Jacques Lacan   93
9 Going to the Dogs, Or My Life as a Psychoanalyst,
  by David Beddow   101

Part III Cultural Studies in Psychoanalysis: Analysts at Play, Working

10 Psychoanalysis on Thin Ice: Jones and Figure Skating
    (with Gary Genosko)   114
11 Psychoanalysis, Doggie Style   136

Part IV Interview

12 Psychoanalysis, Parasites and the 'Culture of Banality'
    by Antonio Greco   150

Part V Coda

13 Crisis, Death and the Futures of Psychoanalysis   164

    Notes   179
    Acknowledgements   196
    Bibliography   198
    Index   207

Introduction

The Deaths of Sigmund Freud

Scholars, medically trained doctors, journalists and former patients have long objected to aspects of Freud's creation. Hardly anyone claims that Freud was right about everything – which is, of course, fair enough. Beginning with Freud himself, psychoanalysis has been characterized by constant revision and amendment of the original program. Freud may not have gotten everything right, we tend to think, but obviously he didn't get everything wrong either. And so we hang on tight to precious bits and pieces of Freudiana, of which we can include some of Freud's most famous theories and techniques: the unconscious, regression, repression, the death drive, transference, free association, dream analysis and the couch.

At the same time, there is little agreement about what Freud got right and what he got wrong. Let's just admit the obvious – namely, that Freud, during the course of fifty-odd years as a theorist and a therapist, in more than twenty-three volumes of collected works, and in a correspondence that is estimated to be at least 35,000 letters long – let's admit that Freud was bound to get *something* right. I am reminded of authors like Erich Fromm and Max Horkheimer who argue, for example, that the death drive theory may have been very wrong, but it was at least a correct recognition that people are aggressive. Or of authors as different as Herbert Marcuse and John Updike who argue that the death drive is an accurate reflection of the horrors of the Holocaust. But, really, do we need Freud to tell us that people are aggressive? Do we really need the overblown theory of the death drive to explain the rise of Nazi Germany? I think not.

So why do we keep referring to Freud as though he was essentially correct about human psychology when, arguably, he was trivially or incidentally correct? There are, no doubt, many good reasons for this ongoing, albeit vague, allegiance to Freud, but I'll mention only two here. First of all, I think Freud gets cited out of habit, and a bad habit at that, or – what is almost the same thing – out of intellectual hubris. Masters by association, we are encouraged by a culture of theory to rub our intellectual projects against Freud or, even more likely nowadays, against 'Freudians' like Jacques Lacan. This state of affairs is in fact most obviously true among theorists of the French persuasion, where a reference to Lacan in their work operates like a leaf of radicchio in an otherwise mundane garden salad. The second reason Freud still gets cited across the literature has to do with the culture of therapy, a plague spread throughout the Western world, but which is especially virulent in the urban centres of the United States, Canada, England, France and Argentina. If this therapeutic culture is more dangerous than the theoretical one – and no doubt it is, at least for individuals – it is only because it is a horribly botched theory in practice. One need only think about the recovered memory fiasco and Freud's historical role in it all, as exposed so publicly in *The New York Review of Books* by that scourge of institutional psychoanalysis, Frederick Crews.[1]

In both theoretical and therapeutic cultures, feelings are easily hurt and egos are easily bruised by no-nonsense critics that comprise what I call the field of 'Critical Freud Studies'. After all, social or group identity is fundamentally at stake – which is to say, some version of The Cause is at stake. Theorists have written books (or 'texts', depending on your theoretical persuasion) and have thus staked their reputations on the ongoing viability of Freud, however much his thought (or 'spirit') has been perverted. The same can be said of some historians and biographers. In the meantime, therapists *and* patients are motivated to maintain their allegiance to some version of Freud on pain of becoming social outcasts: priests, mediums and quacks on the one side, malingerers, neurasthenics or just plain hysterics on the other.

Given the stakes for participants still committed to the contradictory cultures of psychoanalysis, I realize that the work that follows is at times cold-hearted. It couldn't be otherwise. For it is my contention that our continued allegiance to Freud – based largely on our motivated disinterest in the latest intellectual, cultural and social histories of psychoanalysis – is every bit as sentimental and superstitious as a rabbit's foot dangling on a key chain. So sentimental and superstitious that I would, to take just one example, draw a line between the old machine metaphors that once made us think of the body in terms of heat, waste and energy, but also of coolant; Clausius's and Lord Kelvin's ideas of entropy; the physician's mistaken belief that we should bleed the overheated body; and later, their belief that we should purge the overfull bowel, for example, with the warm and mildly laxative waters of Karlsbad; or surgically alter, with Elie Metchnikoff and others, that very same bowel for the sake of efficiency; or dream and dream, then talk and talk until we got all the bad thoughts 'off our chests', purging with Freud our 'overheated' imaginations, bleeding off the unused energy of our memories, discharging the waste products of our baneful existence, and functioning like a machine or, at least, like a well-oiled machine is supposed to function: compulsively, repeatedly, constantly. Of course the Luddite in Freud disliked this Machine Life and thus dreamt of the ultimate constancy that comes once life is turned off and silenced: namely, death.

And so, to put it as plainly as possible, we most certainly do not need Freud to help us describe the world – inner or outer. If, on the other hand, there is a use for Freud and psychoanalysis, it is as a cautionary tale or, if you prefer, as a case study of a modern politico-religious movement having just about run its course. In the wake of its demise, we are left the urgent task of picking up the remaining pieces and making sense of it all – most especially for an educated lay public with an abiding interest in Freud or at least Freudiana, but also for certain professional readers of Freud, from therapists to intellectuals, who have never bothered to acquaint themselves with the latest critical thoughts about psychoanalytic history, theory and culture.[2] Against this regrettable culture of motivated disinterest, *Killing Freud* is issued as a provocation and call to scholarly debate.

Critic as Agent Provocateur

Freud is reported to have once said to a patient that 'An analysis is not a place for polite exchanges'[3] – something he repeats, more or less, in his papers on technique. When it came to fantasy, sex, money and so on, Freud insisted as a fundamental rule that the patient, but also the analyst, speak candidly. The truths of psycho-analysis are, for this reason, typically dark, brutal, rude and anti-social. However, the seductive bad manners of psychoanalytic exchange are not merely a principle of good clinical practice, but has itself become a veritable culture, if not a worldview: a culture, however, that looks suspiciously like a Hobbsean state of nature where one's inevitable human folly is just more ammunition for a neighbour's analytic acumen.

If, as critical readers, we are expected to respect the principles of this peculiar culture, we must not be afraid, in turn, to play by the house rules. We must not be afraid to provoke, or to be provoked in turn. On the other hand, a critic must never take these rules too seriously, since the game is already rigged in favour of the house. The famous logic of 'heads I win, tales you lose' means that critics of psy-choanalysis are subject, in advance, to the (by now very tired) counter-charge that they protest too much and, thus, suffer from a bad case of resistance. Obviously silence in the face of this form of intellectual blackmail is a coward's game. And so I try in *Killing Freud* not to shrink from being as blunt or cruel as the truth demands. Yet at the end of the day this means something simple and, I assume, uncontroversial: first, I recount those basic facts that analytic historians of psychoanalysis have chosen to forget or ignore, and draw out their implications; second, I critically explore the connection not only between revised and official histories, but between history, theory, gossip and institutional politics; and third, I follow psychoanalysis into the margins of everyday life, for example, unpacking Ernest Jones's psychoanalytically inspired love for figure skating. These three approaches in *Killing Freud* may be considered provocative or impolite only to the extent that analysts, analysands and their band of cronies don't want to hear about them – to the extent, I suppose, that partisan interests get lampooned and embarrassed by straight talk and revelations.

In this respect I want to emphasize that this is not just another gloom-and-doom book about the crisis, death or decline of psychoanalysis. Not exactly. This work is ultimately intended as a joyous, Nietzschean-inspired *celebration* of the death of psychoanalysis as a viable methodology for intellectuals and therapists; a celebration that is long overdue and happily announced. And thus in what follows I often adopt a light and, I hope, a humorous touch, as when I discuss Freud's late love of dogs, provide a short open letter to my colleagues about the Freud Archives, and write a cheeky first-person fiction about the history of psychoanalysis. In these respects the lost cause of psychoanalysis inspires a wandering through the sometimes tantalizing, and sometimes bizarre, margins of the field – quite as one would happily inspect the contents of a large and untidy flea-market. How so? Depending on your mood, with amusement, horror, detachment and a sense of wonder.

The book is designed to be read from beginning to end, although little harm will be done by those preferring to skip about and enjoy the celebration in their own way. To help orient such readers, however, I have provided short introductions to each section of the book. The death of psychoanalysis has not only given us an opportunity to re-read Freud's life and work with the benefit of distance, but to turn that distance into a truly healing experience: to learn from, and even laugh at, the vagaries of human folly. Yours and mine.

PART I

*Suggestion and Fraud in the
Age of Critical Freud Studies*

Colleagues, friendly and otherwise, often marvel at the energy critics devote to debunking or demystifying the various histories of psychoanalysis. The conversations usually go something like this: If you think so little of psychoanalysis, then why invest even more time on the lost cause? The implication of this question is that only partisan thinkers (such as 'successful' patients, analysts and intellectuals) are expected to produce works on psychoanalysis. Thus the critic is at best perceived as a gadfly or nuisance, and at worst as a destructive, angry, bitter person – possibly a failed patient, analyst or intellectual.

The truth is that critics do not have to justify the act of criticism; nor need they apologize for not providing a 'constructive alternative' to their damning conclusions. That is not their job. Neither does it follow that critics are necessarily bitter and humorless souls bent on destroying the precious illusions of others. I have often found just the opposite. So-called 'Freud-bashers' are just as interested in psychoanalysis as Freud-boosters, though obviously for different reasons. Both parties can easily agree that psychoanalysis deserves our continued attention, not only because it has irrevocably influenced intellectual life and culture in the twentieth century, but because the efforts of Sigmund Freud are nothing short of awesome. Freud produced a massive body of work that in turn inspired an entire industry. Surely anyone wandering the stacks of a research library in the vicinity of BF173, the books cataloguing psychoanalysis, will be impressed by the collective effort of it all. Just how we make sense of it is another matter, and that is where the acrimony begins.

The following three chapters attempt to make sense of the early history (sometimes erroneously called the pre-history) of psychoanalysis. The first chapter examines in some detail the recent 'revisionist' interpretation of the ur-case of psychoanalysis, 'Anna O.'. The basic charge that critics have made is stunning and, if true, dire for the future of psychoanalysis: Freud knowingly bent the truth about this foundational case to suit his ever-changing (political and theoretical) needs. In short, critics claim that the case is an utter fraud. The second chapter examines Josef Breuer's under-appreci-ated theoretical contribution to the *Studies on Hysteria* (1893–5), arguing that Breuer's ambivalence toward his (and Freud's) theories is instructive, and demonstrates that he was a more cautious theorist of hysteria than Freud. The third chapter announces, largely by way of a discussion of suggestion (i.e., undue influence) in psychoanaly-sis, a new era of 'Critical Freud Studies', a new scholarly mood that has recently gained ascendancy in the field.

The guiding thought behind these three investigations of the early history of psychoanalysis is this: if the foundation of psycho-analysis is indeed faulty, then the rest of the building is not only shaky, but deserves to be abandoned, broken-up and buried.

1 The Strange Case of 'Anna O.': An Overview of the 'Revisionist' Assessment

How can you stop worrying and start living?

Some have argued that talking is the first step, an idea that is at least as old as the confessional, but which received its medical and scientific christening only with Josef Breuer and Sigmund Freud's *Studies on Hysteria* in 1893–5. Cathartic talk has since become a credo of all psychotherapies, including even that form of therapy known as Self-Help. Apparently the best way to change your life is to find someone who will listen to you talk about your life problems. In this way, so the story goes, disturbing ideas that have been pushed aside can be confronted and defeated anew; to wit, what was repressed and unconscious can be made conscious. As Breuer and Freud put it, talking 'brings to an end the operative force of the idea which was not abreacted in the first instance, by allowing its strangulated effect to find a way out through speech'.[4] Or as another advocate of the talking cure suggests:

> Psychoanalysis is based, to some extent, on the healing power of words. Ever since the days of Freud, analysts have known that a patient could find relief from his inner anxieties if he could talk, just talk. Why is this so? Maybe because by talking, we gain a little better insight into our troubles, get a better perspective. No one knows the whole answer. But all of us know that 'spitting it out' or 'getting it off our chests' brings almost instant relief.[5]

Interestingly enough, this last nugget of enlightenment was given, not by an analyst, but by none other than the author of *How To Stop Worrying and Start Living*. I mean, of course, the irrepressible Dale Carnegie. Although, Carnegie submits, 'No one knows the whole answer' to the riddle of cathartic talk, its efficacy has often seemed to us unassailable; as he says, 'all of us know' about the power of words, and of 'talk, just talk'. Breuer and Freud already said as much in their 'Preliminary Communication' of 1893–5: 'Linguistic usage,' they write, 'bears witness to this fact of daily observation by such phrases as "to cry oneself out", and to "blow off steam".'[6] Carnegie's brand of enthusiasm was borne of this kitchen psychology, and was typical of post-war American attitudes about mental health. At that time most of us believed that neurasthenic disorders, from mild neuroses to shell shock, could be successfully treated by some form of talking. In this respect, what began reasonably enough as a tentative theory of repressed energy and its cathartic discharge (or 'abreaction') became an entrenched cultural belief and, in some circles, an established scientific fact.

Actually, though, and this is important, Carnegie wasn't even right to claim that no one knows the whole story of how talking works its magic. True, few of us are taught the whole story, and even fewer care to hear it. Instead the partial story of the talking cure has been embraced as just another piece of common sense; so common that not many have felt sufficiently compelled to weigh the historical evidence, or think about the scientific merits of the talking cure and, along with it, the theory of the unconscious. As Breuer himself wrote in 1895, 'It hardly seems necessary any longer to argue in favour of the existence of current ideas that are unconscious or subconscious. They are among the commonest of facts of everyday life.'[7]

In what follows I outline the history of this everyday understanding, unpacking the relation between Breuer's Anna O. and the discourse of dual or split consciousness inherited from hypnotism by way of Franz Anton Mesmer's theory of animal magnetism. To this end I review and, to a modest extent, clarify and augment one stream of the 'revisionist' assessment of Anna O., the direction of which is determined, rather surprisingly, by a debate that raged in the late 1880s and early 1890s between the physiological explanation of hysteria advanced by Jean-Martin Charcot and the psychological explanation advanced by Hippolyte Bernheim and some others. After that I review the revisionist critique of Freud's use and abuse of Breuer's Anna O., a critique that raises disturbing ethical questions about the founder of psychoanalysis. By way of conclusion I indicate briefly what is left of psychoanalysis in the wake of the revisionist assessment of Anna O.

Hypnosis, Dual-Consciousness and 'Anna O.'

> With every day, and from both sides of my intelligence, I thus drew steadily nearer to that truth, by whose partial discovery I have been doomed to such a dreadful shipwreck: that man is not one, but truly two.
>
> (Robert Louis Stevenson,
> *The Strange Case of Dr. Jekyll and Mr. Hyde*[8])

It is generally acknowledged that the talking cure of 'Anna O.' is the founding story of psychoanalysis. In its traditional rendering, the story marks the beginning of a heroic venture that ends with Freud's discovery of unconscious, sexually charged and socially unacceptable, mental processes. Much of this history is obviously a myth, as even partisans of psychoanalysis now admit. But few are sufficiently cognizant of just how mythological that story is or, if they are aware, tend to embrace myth itself as the psychic ground zero of our shared social reality – as good an example of circular thinking and psychoanalytic double-talk as any.

The identity of Anna O. was revealed by Ernest Jones in the first of his three-volume magnum opus, *The Life and Work of Sigmund Freud*. There we learn that Anna O. was in fact Bertha Pappenheim, a well-known social worker and feminist activist.[9] This was a genuine surprise to everyone, since the trail-blazing Pappenheim is quite unrecognizable from Breuer's description of the hysterical

Anna O. The greatest surprise, however, occurred in 1972 when Henri Ellenberger revealed the existence of Breuer's original case report of 1882,[10] as well as a short follow-up report written by a Dr Laupus. Armed with these documents, Ellenberger quietly dropped a bombshell on psychoanalytic studies, concluding that 'the famed "prototype of a cathartic cure" was neither a cure nor a catharsis'.[11]

In the years since, commentators of all stripes have debated the true meaning of Pappenheim's hysteria, with retrospective *paleodiagnoses* ranging from the organic (e.g., tuberculous meningitis or epilepsy) to the psychological (e.g., depression or multiple personality).[12] Unfortunately, and yet so typical of psychoanalytic studies, relatively little revisionist work has been done to advance the *critical-historical* efforts initiated by Ellenberger. In fact some commentators, such as Toronto psychotherapist Adam Crabtree, have continued to repeat the questionable claims of the published case study as though Ellenberger never found the original report at all.[13] Still others continue to provide retrospective diagnoses that fail to convince, in no small measure because they tend to be too precious or contrived to survive the cut of Occam's Razor – the principle that demands we always favour the simplest explanation available.

Fortunately there are exceptions to these trends. Easily the most compelling and comprehensive revisionist assessment of this case has been ventured by philosopher Mikkel Borch-Jacobsen in *Remembering Anna O.: A Century of Mystification*. Borch-Jacobsen's 'scholarly thriller' (so says the back cover) turns on the sensation that Danish stage hypnotist Carl Hansen created at Vienna's famous Ringtheatre in February of 1880.[14] Although Hansen demonstrated the usual stunts known to magnetists of an earlier generation – for instance, the induced catalepsy of the 'human plank' – his tour through Germany and Austria generated renewed interest in hypnosis and hypnotic phenomena.[15] His performance created a substantial fuss in the media and drew some notable scientists out of the woodwork, including Gustav Fechner, Wilhelm Wundt and Moritz Benedikt.

In this respect the German-speaking scientific community was following a French fashion grounded in the works of Charles Richet and Jean-Martin Charcot, and propelled by such eminent philosophers and literary figures as Henri Bergson and Paul Valéry.[16] Of course, however much debate hypnotism engendered, such lavish attention automatically lent a kind of legitimacy to stage performers like Hansen, cloaking the occult aspects of hypnosis under the cover of science and enlightenment. The cover, to be more exact, of positivistic physiology.

It was precisely in this light that Josef Breuer – who knew something about hypnotism and was friends with key figures in the debate about its relative merits, including Benedikt and Franz Brentano[17] – began to take hypnotism more seriously in his own medical practice. But if Breuer was willing to experiment with these 'new' ideas, Pappenheim herself was only too happy to play along in what she openly called her 'private theatre'. Breuer tells us that Pappenheim, a well-educated woman of twenty-one years, was something of a day-dreamer; a propensity she indulged by placing herself in light hypnotic states, what she referred to in French as 'absence', and in English as 'time-missing' and 'clouds'. Although chaffing under the conditions of her Orthodox Jewish upbringing, Pappenheim never complained – apparenty because she loved and revered her father.[18] According to Breuer, Pappenheim's 'states of abstraction and dreaminess'[19] so typical of her private theatre were 'a permanent factor in her mental life',[20] a factor, moreover, which supposedly predisposed her to hysteria. Like Charcot and some others of this time, Breuer believed that 'the semi-hypnotic twilight state of day-dreaming, auto-hypnosis, and so on',[21] was a necessary precondition of hysteria. It followed, therefore, that hypnoid states often 'grow out of the day-dreams which are so common even in healthy people and to which needlework and similar occupations render women especially prone'.[22] Accordingly Breuer and Freud argue, following at this point the work of German psychiatrist Paul Julius Möbius, that 'the basis and *sine qua non* of hysteria is the existence of hypnoid states'.[23]

By the end of 1880 Pappenheim's private theatre was populated with hysterical symptoms. To many critics, however, these symptoms seem determined by a confluence of three related factors: cultural expectations, medical expectations and play-acting by the patient. Not incidentally, both Breuer and Pappenheim loved the theatre – that is, the blood and guts theatre of professional actors and actresses – and were inclined to take its lessons seriously; lessons that including the Aristotelian idea of catharsis as popularized by Jacob Bernays in the Vienna of the 1880s.[24] Accordingly, Pappenheim *tragedized* her feelings[25] in ways already mapped in Aristotle's *Poetics*: namely, 'with incidents arousing pity and fear, wherewith to accomplish its catharsis of such emotion'.[26] In a language well-known to her contemporaries, Pappenheim thus suffered, for example, from aphasia coupled, rather stereotypically, with amnesia.[27] As Mesmer's follower, the Marquis de Puységur, had already described in the 1780s,[28] and as stage hypnotists like Hansen had exploited for dramatic effect years later, Pappenheim would lapse into a 'twilight state' or *condition seconde*[29] wherein she could speak only English; later she would have no memory of that state. About these symptoms Borch-Jacobsen is categorical: Pappenheim exhibited 'symptoms that, feature for feature (intractable contractures, localized anesthesia, posthypnotic amnesia, positive and negative hallucinations, visual disturbances, aphasia and so on), resembled those produced during Hansen's staged demonstrations'.[30]

Breuer's explanation of Pappenheim's myriad of complaints is also well in-keeping with expectations derived from the stage and, more generally, from a culture that encouraged belief in mysterious, apparently unconscious, forces at work in the mind; a culture relatively well-versed in the magnetic treatments of an earlier generation. For instance, Breuer treated Pappenheim for what is calculated to be more than 1,000 hours,[31] a remarkable length of time only from the perspective of the typical family practice of the 1880s, but not unusual when compared to treatments conducted by mesmerists years before.[32] And like those cases of mesmeric illnesses during the early 1800s, Pappenheim engaged in a 'bargaining therapy'; the sort of self-directed therapy that was hard to reconcile with the 'authoritarian use of hypnosis' popular in the 1880s.[33] In fact, Pappenheim's symptom language borrowed heavily from what historian of medicine Edward Shorter calls the 'first wave of hypnotism', namely, the self-directed exhibition of motor symptoms under the influence of contemporary beliefs about catalepsy and somnambulism.[34] Shorter notes that the 'second wave' began in 1880, at which time Hansen's old-style performances were translated into the language of positivistic science.[35] It was, therefore, from within the mesmeric tradition that Breuer, like Alfred Binet and Pierre Janet, was able to describe Pappenheim as exhibiting 'two selves, a real one and an evil one which forced her to behave badly'[36]; or again, that she 'was split into two personalities of which one was mentally normal and the other insane'.[37] For mesmerism was a tradition steeped in the discourse of dual consciousness, which was later embraced by theorists of hypnotism, hysteria, and also psychoanalysis. As Breuer writes, 'it seems to us, as it does to Binet and Janet, that what lies at the centre of hysteria is a splitting off of a portion of psychical activity'.[38]

From the case study it is clear that Pappenheim's hysteria was related to her father's illness, which also began in July 1880. No doubt hysteria provided an alternative to this dismal reality, which included 'sick-nursing', if not a way for Pappenheim to set aside her consuming worry for her father.[39] Breuer, however, focused almost exclusively on how 'sick-nursing' promotes a distracted and hypnoid state,[40] and basically ignored the compensatory benefits provided by Pappenheim's hysteria – even in the wake of her father's death on 5 April 1881. At that point, and not surprisingly, Pappenheim's symptoms multiplied, culminating with half-hearted attempts at suicide. In particular, she became angry with her mother and brother, who had shielded her from knowledge about her father's death from a peripleuritic abscess. As Shorter rightly suggests, 'Instead of grieving as is customary in Western society, with tears and sadness, Anna O. proceeded to raid the pool of then fashionable symptoms for new kinds of illness behaviour.'[41] Not unlike Mr Hyde, Pappenheim's 'evil' or 'insane' self began to engage in all sorts of theatrics. For example, she no longer recognized or understood certain people, chief among them her *mother and brother* – a very convenient expression of her hysteria, to say the least.

Ten days after her father's death we learn of a humorous episode involving none other than Richard von Krafft-Ebing, later author of *Psychopathia Sexualis* in 1886. Claiming that she was unable to recognize anyone but Breuer, Pappenheim totally ignored Krafft-Ebing, whom Breuer brought along for a consultation on the case. Of this bizarre visual disorder, the incredulous Breuer writes, 'It was a genuine "negative hallucination" of the kind which has since so often been produced experimentally.'[42] Krafft-Ebing, who was to become an esteemed professor of psychiatry at the University of Vienna, seems to have been less convinced. Brandishing a needle he poked Pappenheim until, Breuer writes in the case report, she 'felt it and cried out'.[43] And then, for good measure, he lit a piece of paper and blew the smoke in her face. In 1895 Breuer writes, 'She suddenly saw a stranger before her [!], rushed to the door . . . and fell unconscious to the ground.'[44]

Pappenheim flew into a rage when her 'trance' was broken by Krafft-Ebing, and then became extremely anxious. As ever, Breuer remained oblivious to the most likely cause of his patient's anger – a trait that even informed readers, such as Albrecht Hirschmüller, have continued to share. For it is unlikely indeed, as Breuer and his apologists say, that Pappenheim's rage and anxiety was occasioned by her diabolical second state, or 'by the presence of a stranger'.[45] On the contrary, Pappenheim's state of mind was in all likelihood occasioned (recalling Occam) by her failure to maintain the illusion of a second state – and, along with it, the appropriate host of bizarre symptoms – in the face of Krafft-Ebing's justified scepticism and subsequent provocation.

Even so, one doesn't have to be a great sceptic to realize that Breuer and Pappenheim engaged in a classic *folie à deux*: the doctor coached and the patient performed. Surely it is no coincidence that

Pappenheim became a chronic bed case only *after* Breuer's first visit in which he diagnosed her 'extremely intense cough' as hysterical.[46] Just as damning is the fact that Breuer's outline of the so-called 'latent' stage of the hysteria, from July 1880 to 11 December, was a *retrospective reconstruction* distilled from months of Pappenheim's own daydreams. 'One may wonder', with Ellenberger, 'how Breuer could take at face value all the revelations of the hypnotized patient when he expressly notes that she "gave distorted accounts of what had irritated her during the last days".'[47] Or as Adolf von Strümpell had already remarked in his critical review of *Studies on Hysteria* in 1896:

> I wonder about the quality of materials mined from a patient under hypnotic influence. I am afraid that many hysterical women will be encouraged to give free rein to their fantasies and inventiveness. The attending physician can easily be put into a very slippery situation.[48]

Breuer, however, was so caught within the logic of his theatrical role that he was unable to know the truth when he heard it (certainly a problem when ostensibly conducting a *talking* cure, which is to that extent based on *listening*). For, as he admits in the case study, Pappenheim eventually confided to him that 'the whole business had been simulated'.[49] In short, Pappenheim was a typical hypnotized subject: as she herself recognized,[50] she played the game and watched, as though removed at a distance, one mad scene after another.[51] The good doctor was, however, unwilling or unable to face the implications of this monstrous possibility, which he undermined with his overdetermining belief in dual consciousness. Here is how Breuer explains away Pappenheim's clear admission of simulation, that is, of play-acting:

> Many intelligent patients admit that their conscious ego [*condition primes*] was quite lucid during the attack and looked on with curiosity and surprise at all the mad things [*seconde*] they did and said. Such patients have, furthermore, the (erroneous) belief

that with a little good-will they could have inhibited the attack, and they are inclined to blame themselves for it.[52]

In other words, in the confusion of first and second states, Pappenheim could not have known the truth about her essentially divided self. Breuer thus turned a disconfirmation into a piece of evidence that, naturally, reinforced his original assumptions.

Following in the tradition of the early James Braid, the English surgeon who coined the word 'hypnosis', as well as Charcot and his own friend Benedikt, the physiologist in Breuer held fast to the assumption that hypnosis and hysteria were at bottom organic problems, and not merely psychological ones. As Borch-Jacobsen puts it, 'Something real had to be behind it [i.e., the parade of symptoms] – something physiological, inaccessible to the hysteric's conscious will.'[53] Moreover, it was owing to this positivistic inheritance that Breuer felt obliged (or perhaps entitled) to pepper his case study with assurances that Pappenheim was 'completely unsuggestible'[54]; that is, the problems of psychology did not impact on her treatment. And what were his assurances? The list isn't very long, or convincing: Pappenheim's 'sharp and critical common sense'; her 'will power'; her truthfulness and trustworthiness; the intimacy of her revelations; the banality of her recollections and the detail with which they were embellished; and, similarly, the supposed complexity of the narratives.[55]

It is already rather telling that Breuer returns again and again to the problem of suggestion – so much so that, if there is any double or doubling in this case, it is the overlapping of Breuer's theoretical preconceptions with those of suggestion. Most telling of all is his plain admission that all the assurances in the world cannot dispel the suspicion that suggestion may have contaminated his treatment of Pappenheim; everything, as he says in the case study, 'may very well be explained by suggestion'.[56] By the early 1890s Breuer and Freud certainly understood this problem, and in their 'Preliminary Communication' of 1893 they took a small step to defend themselves. While their findings, they argue, may seem the result of expectations reinforced by suggestion, 'This, however, is not so. The first case of this kind [i.e., of cathartic discharge of a pathogenic memory] that came under observation dates back to the year 1881, that is to say to the "pre-suggestion" era.'[57] So much, then, for the criticism of a later, suggestive, era; criticism which, we are supposed to believe, cannot apply to Breuer in 1880. In the case study Breuer *nonetheless* feels obliged to offer a final assurance, and toward the very end pulls out a trump card, his own reputation, which we know was great indeed. In the second last paragraph the famous doctor reassures us:

> I have already described the astonishing fact that from beginning to end of the illness all the stimuli arising from the secondary state, together with their consequences, were permanently removed by being given verbal utterance in hypnosis, and *I have only to add an assurance that this was not an invention of mine which I imposed upon the patient by suggestion.*[58]

Breuer has, he says, 'only to add' this final assurance, which evidently underwrites the others. But for good measure he immediately adds that the events, in any case, 'took me completely by surprise' – as though that little detail settles the question of suggestion. Far from it, Breuer's surprise goes hand-in-hand with his (however understandable) naivety concerning Pappenheim's symptoms, which he coddled and fed even as he quite literally put a spoon to her mouth at supper, allowed her to stroke his hand to reassure, and actively encouraged her to talk about her fantasies morning and night for months on end.

Breuer's naivety about hypnotic phenomena can be plausibly traced to Charcot's physiologically based view of hysteria and hypnotism. This is important because we know that Charcot was mistaken. Recall that Charcot had dismissed the Nancy School criticism that suggestion played a contaminating role in his use of medical hypnotism with hysterics. For if hypnosis was an artificial hysteria, as Charcot believed, and if hysteria was itself physiological, then it followed logically that hypnosis was also a physiological phenomena.[59] Both hysteria and hypnosis, in short, followed 'iron laws' that were discoverable by science. Thus it makes sense that only people predisposed to hysteria (that is, only weak or sick people) could be influenced by hypnosis. Consequently, the possibility of suggestion not only wasn't a problem for Charcot, it was in fact a ready measure of a patient's constitutional fortitude. Or again, hysteria, like suggestibility, was for Charcot a *given*, a matter of hereditary disposition, while all social contact, including hypnotic treatment, was understood merely as an exciting agent or *agent provocateur*. Hysteria was, therefore, incurable, a verdict that reflected Charcot's own dim view of humankind.[60]

The upshot? It was under Charcot's influence that Breuer made his most basic, albeit mistaken, assumption about Pappenheim: she was *a priori* 'unsuggestible' because she was already hysterical, already an entranced and unstable subject, when he arrived on the scene in late November of 1880. Which is simply to say, from Breuer's perspective, that he quite literally arrived on the scene (one could say, 'always already' arrived) *after the fact*, namely, after the 'incubation period' of her illness. As Breuer put it, 'The great complex of hysterical phenomena grew up in a condition of complete latency and came into the open when her hypnoid state became permanent.'[61] The plant called hysteria had, in short, finally sprouted from the fertile 'soil' of Pappenheim's increasingly divided state of consciousness.[62] It is true, moreover, that Breuer arrived on the scene innocently enough as a *physician*, and not as a *psychiatrist*; part of his 'surprise' with Pappenheim was the perceived need to switch gears from doctor of the body to doctor of the soul. And this is precisely why he invited his psychiatrist friend Krafft-Ebing to consult on the case.

The theory of incubation also neatly explains why it was that Pappenheim's family members were totally unaware of Bertha's private theatre and, along with it, her many 'latent' symptoms in the months leading up to her confinement in bed.[63] Of course, for critics this explanation sounds like a convenient rationalization. According to a simpler explanation, there was absolutely nothing, no-thing, for the family to notice because the symptoms didn't exist until *after* doctor and patient had assumed their respective roles. As Borch-Jacobsen puts it: 'All the evidence of the "incubation period", far from preceding the treatment, was the product of progressive hypnotic coaching, and of what Bernheim would call a decade later a "retrospective hallucination".'[64]

The story of Charcot's unfortunate influence on Breuer is also, and more spectacularly, true of Freud.[65] The twenty-nine year old Freud studied with Charcot at the Salpêtrière in Paris from October 1885 to late February 1886, and always considered him a master.[66] 'No other human being,' Freud once wrote of Charcot, 'has ever affected me in the same way.'[67] Freud's own turn away from neuro- to psycho-pathology was largely made possible by this experience, so much so that he always sided with Charcot against his many critics, from Joseph Delboeuf to Bernheim and the Nancy School, on the burning question of hypnosis and suggestion.[68] Like Breuer, Freud claims in the *Studies* that 'I may have called up the [hysterical] state by my suggestion but I did not create it, since its features . . . came as such a surprise to me.'[69] Or, as he had already written in 1888, hysteria '. . . is of a real, objective nature and not falsified by suggestion on the part of the observer. This does not imply a denial that the mechanism of hysterical manifestations is a psychical one: but it is not the mechanism of suggestion on the part of the physician.'[70] Freud repeats this last claim even more forcefully in 1896, stating that suggestion 'is a *pathological* psychical phenomenon which calls for particular conditions before it can come about'.[71] Like Charcot, Freud in other words concludes that the responsibility for suggestion is not on the side of the *therapist*, but on the side of the *patient*, that is, on the side of *auto*-suggestion and hereditary disposition.

The early Freud was heavily invested in the organicist interpreta-tion of hysteria, although one would never know it from the years of hagiography surrounding Freud and psychoanalysis; a hagiogra-phy that neatly explains how someone like Dale Carnegie, among many others, could claim in 1944 that we don't know the whole story of how talking is cathartic. It is, however, plain that Freud's informed critics at the turn of the century knew perfectly well that the mysterious products of the 'talking cure' – including what we would now call recovered memory – were in all probability the result of a suggestive therapeutic regimen. That is, the results were a reflection of expectations revealed during therapy. As Eugen Bleuler put it in a review of 1896, the apparent cures by catharsis recounted in the pages of *Studies on Hysteria* 'are based quite simply on suggestion rather than abreaction of the suppressed affect'.[72] Or as John Mitchell Clarke more diplomatically put it in his 1896 review, we must bear in mind that 'in studying hysterical patients, the great readiness with which they respond to suggestions . . . may be the weak point in the methods of investigation' used by Breuer and Freud.[73]

The crux of the problem is that few people remember the substance of these early criticisms of Breuer and Freud, or care to hear that these critics were in fact right. This is of course a strange state of affairs, since the critique of Breuer and Freud owes everything to the famous debate between Charcot and Bernheim over the aetiology of hysteria; a debate long ago decided in favour of Bernheim, rather than on the side of Breuer and Freud's Charcot.

It follows that Karl Kraus's satirical quip that 'psychoanalysis is the disease of which it purports to be the cure' holds equally true of Breuer's treatment of Pappenheim. For if Breuer was able to remove anything at all through the technique of cathartic talking, it was the technique itself as it was unwittingly introduced by him and his patient over months of 'treatment'. Or as Borch-Jacobsen nicely puts it, 'The first symptom of Bertha Pappenheim's hysteria was Breuer's diagnoses of it.'[74] For this reason Shorter is absolutely right when he concludes that Pappenheim suffered from 'nothing' except a 'desire to communicate psychic distress in physical terms'.[75] In other words, she sommatized her emotional problems in the socially sanctioned ways available to educated, middle-class, Jewish women living in Vienna at the turn of the nineteenth century: namely, she spoke the symptom language of the hysteric.

As such the 'O' in Breuer's case study of Anna O. reveals itself as a big zero; a nothing, just the same, out of which Freud fashioned the foundation for a therapy that conjured patients and followers as though, indeed, they were rabbits pulled from a hat.

Confabulation and the Politics of Being Second

> *Mephistopheles.*
> Draw, then, your circle, speak your magic spell
> And serve a bumper of the secret juice.
> *Faust* (to Mephistopheles).
> Nay, tell me, why this queer parade of antic,
> This gibbering witch-craft, running wild and frantic?
> For I have known and hated, long enough,
> The charlantry of this senseless stuff.
> *Mephistopheles.*
> That's slap-stick, man, for laughter and delight.
> Why be so sober-sided and sedate?
> This hocus-pocus is a doctor's right,
> To guarantee the dose will operate.
>   (Johann Wolfgang von Goethe *Faust*, Part I[76])

The centrality of the Charcot/Bernheim debate for understanding Breuer and Freud's physiological interpretation of hysteria is mostly ignored or misunderstood today. Commentators continue to believe that Charcot, Breuer and Freud are notable for their psychological interpretation of hysteria, whereas the credit should in fact go to Bernheim.[77] A key part of this puzzle is the timing of Charcot's later, more psychologically oriented publications, and Breuer and Freud's *Studies*. Charcot became interested in the subject of hysteria in 1778, only two years before Breuer's treatment of Pappenheim, and more than a handful of years before he published his findings. It was, more to the point, only in the years *following* Breuer's treatment of Pappenheim that Charcot proposed a theory of trauma according to which hysteria is caused by dissociated memories. And so historians have had no reason to doubt the claim that Breuer and Freud came to their conclusions – the most famous of which, that

'*Hysterics suffer mainly from reminiscences*'[78] – quite independently of Charcot, although they published their results much later.

Revisionists like Borch-Jacobsen, influenced by the work of Edward Shorter and others, encourage us to rethink this old assumption. Borch-Jacobsen, for example, argues that the gap between supposed discovery and its communication is rather telling, and can be traced to ambition and professional rivalry. Quite unlike Hirschmüller, who tends to soft-peddle the facts, Borch-Jacobsen frankly accuses Breuer and Freud of injecting the theme of memory into the case study of 1895 in a bid to establish their priority with Charcot – and with other investigators such as Delboeuf, Binet and Janet.[79] It was, as he says, a 'self-serving revisionism that was anything but innocent'.[80]

We have plenty of reasons for doubting Breuer and Freud's claims to originality, and for accepting Borch-Jacobsen's challenging conclusion. As Ellenberger first discovered, not only does Breuer fail to emphasize memory in the original case report, but he does not even mention the word 'catharsis' there – the supposed hallmarks of his treatment and the cornerstone of Freud's later 'discoveries'. We have, therefore, no reason to accept the claims of 1895 that Pappenheim recalled actual events from one year earlier during her cathartic treatment. For again, while this remarkable feat is well in-keeping with claims made during magnetic illnesses of yesteryear, it does not appear in Breuer's original report on the case. Borch-Jacobsen therefore surmises the following: 'what Bertha had been reproducing with such stunning accuracy was not the *events* of the preceding year but rather the *stories she told Breuer during her trancelike states*'.[81]

But certainly most damning of all is the fact that Pappenheim's treatment was a total disaster. The truth is that Breuer failed to cure Pappenheim and was forced to institutionalize her in a fancy Swiss sanatorium,[82] where she was treated for an addiction to morphine and for a number of chronic ailments.[83] Chief among her complaints was a case of facial neuralgia – a painful organic condition that Breuer, yet again, altogether neglects to mention in the case study of 1895. What was the opinion of Dr Laupus of the Bellevue Sanatorium? 'As regards her mental health,' Laupus writes, 'in the unmotivated fluctuation of her moods the patient displayed genuine signs of hysteria.'[84] About one year after her institutionalization at Bellevue, Breuer apparently confided to Freud's wife, Martha, that he wished Pappenheim would be 'released from her suffering' by dying.[85]

What is astonishing is that although Breuer, first, failed to cure Pappenheim, second, was in all likelihood responsible for her drug addiction (to morphine) and, third, was heavily burdened by her years of suffering, he and Freud presented the case in 1895 as a triumph of the 'talking cure': that is, the cathartic narration of repressed memory. Hirschmüller goes to almost desperate lengths to rationalize Breuer's actions, and is to a very limited extent success-ful.[86] Yet however much we sympathize with Breuer's good intentions during Pappenheim's treatment, it is hard *not* to impute 'base motives' to his and Freud's dubious portrayal of the case in *Studies on Hysteria*.

That the case of Anna O. became the basis upon which Freud developed the theory and practice of psychoanalysis was ensured by one more, possibly malicious, step: over the years Freud spread gossip about Breuer's fear of Pappenheim's love transference during the treatment.[87] The story, a version of which is appended to the case as an editor's footnote in the *Standard Edition*, goes something like this: having fallen in love with her physician, Pappenheim claims to be pregnant with his child; Breuer's wife, already jealous that Pappenheim consumes all of her husband's time, attempts suicide; in turn, Breuer and his wife flee to Venice on a second honeymoon, leaving Pappenheim behind, and conceive a very real child of their own, named Dora. According to legend, Breuer's failure to confront Pappenheim's love transference (which lay behind the hysterical pregnancy) was parleyed by Freud into a vic-torious understanding of the hidden, which is to say unconscious, truth of neurosis: namely, repressed sexuality and, along with it, the analysis of transference. As loyalist historian Peter Gay would contend as late as 1988: 'The psychoanalytic process is a struggle with resistances, and Breuer's rejection of the elemental, shocking truths that this process may uncover is a plain instance of that maneuver.'[88]

While Breuer's 'maneuvers' certainly make for a spicy story, they were entirely fabricated by Freud and then eagerly repeated by motivated followers like Gay. As Ellenberger and others have found, not only is there no proof for the rumours in the original case report, but the chronology is all wrong.[89] As it happens, Breuer's daughter Dora, the apparent product of a second honeymoon, was actually born three months *before* her supposed conception in Venice.[90] More to the point, Breuer didn't flee his patient in horror, but took clear and responsible steps to ensure her care at the sanatorium. He also did not flee from cases of sexually charged hysteria, as many Freudians have claimed; cases which were, after all, recognized as the norm rather than the exception. As Breuer himself argues at one point, 'it is perhaps worth while insisting again and again that the sexual factor is by far the most important and the most productive of pathological results.'[91] It cannot be surprising, then, that during the same month that he terminated his treatment of Bertha Pappenheim, Breuer not only did not flee the scene to Venice, but actually took on another patient who manifested hysteria coupled with the usual sexual overtones.[92]

Critics offer two explanations – one internal, the other external – for the all the gossip and misinformation spread about Breuer. First of all, and as Hirschmüller, Webster and Borch-Jacobsen all agree, the tale about Breuer's therapeutic failure reads like a *reconstruction* or interpretation made by Freud. Indeed, in the two published references to Breuer's trouble with Pappenheim's love transference, in 1914 and 1925, and in a private letter of 1932, Freud explicitly uses the language of 'reconstruction' to drive his point home.[93] As such, the rumours seem less based on the facts than on a motivated spin of the facts – yet another example of a retrospective illusion. The gossip, Borch-Jacobsen therefore writes, was 'Freud's fantasy, a pseudomemory meant to explain away, after the fact, the abysmal failure of the original "talking cure" [of Anna O.]'.[94] Or as Hirschmüller more simply concludes, 'The Freud–Jones account of the termination of the treatment of Anna O. should be regarded as a myth.'[95] The second explanation for the unchecked spread of gossip has to do with personal and professional reputations. Having already convinced a reluctant Breuer to publish the case study,[96] Freud could count on his silence in the face of the gossip. Breuer, after all, was a well-known and respected physician and would have hardly wanted his part in the fraud called Anna O. exposed. If so, cynicism was merely piled on top of cynicism. Why? Because Breuer and Freud were already brazen enough to publish the fictionalized account of Pappenheim's treatment, at least in part, because they knew that Pappenheim herself would never publicly contradict their version of events. For having become a well-known personality in the German-speaking world, Pappenheim could hardly afford to tell everyone that the 'talking cure' was in fact an elaborate lie. In other words, just like Breuer she had a reputation to uphold; she certainly didn't want the *true* story of her troubled, drug-dependent case history revealed any more than Breuer and Freud did. As Borch-Jacobsen puts it, Breuer and Freud thus 'banked on her silence while they made their theoretical fortune; one word from her would have been enough to blow the whole fraud sky high'.[97]

But it was Freud, the puppeteer, who made the most of every opportunity, out-manoeuvring his master Charcot, then Pappenheim, and finally his old friend Breuer. As critic and historian Richard Webster suggests, Freud used Breuer's authority to help establish his own; and then, having at last established his own authority, he under-mined this early attachment to Breuer to help establish his own originality.[98] What remains is a rather unflattering portrait of one man's drive to succeed at almost any price, including friendship.

Given the facts of the case of Anna O., it is not surprising that Pappenheim thought ill of psychoanalysis and, one suspects, of Freud. According to her friend, Dora Edinger, 'Pappenheim never spoke about this period of her life and violently opposed any sug-gestion of psychoanalytic therapy [for others].'[99] And surely, given the rather lurid facts of her seminal case, it is hard not to agree with her critical assessment. It is also likely that Breuer, who was basically a kind man, felt badly used by his younger, more ambitious colleague. Certainly by the time the second edition of the *Studies* appeared in 1908, he wanted nothing more to do with the book or with Freud's later 'discoveries'. In a separate Preface for the new edition Breuer writes: 'So far as I personally am concerned, I have since that time [of the first edition] had no active dealing with the subject; I have had no part in its important development and I could add nothing fresh to what was written in 1895.'[100]

Conclusion

More than most, Borch-Jacobsen has drawn the sorts of unflattering conclusions about Freud and psychoanalysis that others have politely avoided. In a lecture on Anna O., Borch-Jacobsen bluntly declares: 'In any field other than psychoanalysis, such false claims would be deemed downright fraudulent and would justify an immediate rejection of the theory supported by them.'[101] By way of conclusion, I want to continue in this spirit and spell out exactly what is left of psychoanalytic theory in the wake of the revisionist critique of its history. To this end I can think of three shibboleths of psychoanalytic thinking that should be discarded immediately.

First of all, the unconscious: there is no reason to hang onto a theory inherited from the dubious baggage of mesmerism and hypnotism (which has nothing to do with what is sometimes called the cognitive unconscious). Boogie-men and other unknown forces may make for excellent bed-time stories, but that does not make them true. As the case of Anna O. amply demonstrates, the myth of the unconscious is the direct result of a paranoid discourse bent on proving its own assumptions; a discourse, moreover, that not only provides a symptom language, but makes people sick because *of* it (or, if you prefer, according *to* it). For example, it makes people 'dig deep' until they find a dual consciousness that doesn't exist except as an outmoded theory of spirit possession. Or it encourages the recall of memories that are patently false – sometimes absurdly so, sometimes tragically so.[102]

Second, the talking cure: if there really is nothing in the unconscious but the discourses we have already swallowed – hook, line, and sinker – there is no point in engaging in a cathartic talking cure. For obviously the only things we will hear spoken about are the expectations (or so-called free associations) allowed for by the discourse of the unconscious. In short, we will hear an echo of what is called psychoanalysis (or mesmerism, animal magnetism, hypnotism, catharsis, etc.), just as the Catholic church found an echo of its doctrine in the spirit possession of past centuries. As Breuer put it in his 'Theoretical' contribution to the *Studies*, 'The split-off mind is the devil with which the unsophisticated observation of early superstitious times believed that these patients were possessed.'[103] For this very reason, though, the only 'foreign body'[104] worth spitting up is the circular discourse and suggestive double-talk that is psychoanalysis itself.

And third, repression: since there is no *place* that the repressed actually goes, no dissociated netherworld from which the subject is thereafter haunted, there is nothing to fear from 'repression' except, in Roosevelt's words, fear itself. In short, repression is just another myth of psychoanalysis. It must be admitted, moreover, that even the commonplace notion of 'repression' as *avoidance* is unfounded: quite simply, no one has ever fallen ill from an act of 'repression,' but only from the specialist discourse of repression that Freud popularized. Indeed, recent findings indicate that a dose of repression commonly understood – what Freud calls an 'ostrich policy,' the 'prototype and first example of *psychical repression*'[105] – may actually *precipitate* recovery from trauma. Ironically, that is, recent research indicates that those who talk endlessly about a trauma to a therapist are, in the long run, worse off than their stoical, talk-averse neighbours.[106] So much, then, for the deferred effect, *Nachträglichkeit*, of a repressed traumatic episode.

And so much for psychoanalysis.

It is, on the other hand, unlikely that true-believers will be convinced by the revisionist assessment of 'Anna O.' or, in fact, by any reasoned argument that is critical of psychoanalysis. That is the beauty of psychoanalytic 'reasoning': like that other oxymoron, 'psychic reality', psychoanalytic reasoning dictates that the truth is always and already *less true* than fantasy. Wielding this higher (or lower?) Truth of truth, the unconscious, it is clear that psychoanalysis merely re-enacts at an institutional level the old struggle of Jekyll and Hyde. Indexed by the slippage of the letters A/B and O/P, it is the very same struggle we find between the fictitious case of Anna O. and the true story of Bertha Pappenheim.

That said, those who haven't totally identified with the myths of Jekyll and Hyde, Bertha and Anna, may experience the revisionist assessment of psychoanalysis as a kind of trauma or nightmare. Ironically, they are the lucky ones. But just how they cope with this trauma, otherwise called the truth, is far from certain. If history tells us anything, especially the history of psychoanalysis, only one thing is certain: the hucksters will always be there to reassure us with a logic tantamount to a cliche overheard from a movie, a novel, comic strip, Dale Carnegie, or maybe from the great Mesmer himself. I can hear them already: *When I Count To Three And Snap My Fingers You Will Awake Feeling Calm and Rested – But Completely Unable To Recall Anything You've Just Heard* . . .

2 Rhetoric, Representation and the Hysterical Josef Breuer

Hippolyta [attending an inept tragedy]: This is the silliest stuff that ever I heard.
Theseus: The best in this kind are but shadows; and the worst are no worse, if imagination amend them.
Hippolyta: It must be your imagination, then, and not theirs.
Theseus: If we imagine no worse of them than they of themselves, they may pass for excellent men.

(William Shakespeare, *A Midsummer Night's Dream*
Act V, Scene 1)

When Josef Breuer and Sigmund Freud published *Studies on Hysteria* in 1895, they found themselves in the midst of controversy over the true aetiology of hysteria. It is well known that Breuer was a reluctant participant in this debate, and scholars have offered a host of competing interpretations to explain this fact. But no one, to my knowledge, has seriously entertained the possibility that Breuer's reluctance owes something to his own doubts about his and Freud's basic theoretical assumptions. Although openly a staunch advocate of the physiological perspective, which he inherited from Charcot and the Paris School, I believe that Breuer was haunted by psychology and the ideogenic perspective, which was widely associated with Hippolyte Bernheim and the Nancy School. Such ambivalence is best evidenced in his much ignored 'Theoretical' contribution to *Studies on Hysteria*, but is already found in his and Freud's 'Preliminary Communication' of 1893.

In retrospect, the debate about hysteria was decided when Charcot died in August 1893, at which time the findings of the Paris School were subject to almost immediate and universal criticism.[107] Formerly silent disciples began to tell tales of coaching and simulation, lending decisive support, first, to the critiques circulated by the Nancy School and by critics like Paul Julius Möbius, and second, to the psychological view that hysteria is a disease of representation, that is, of the imagination.[108] To complicate matters, Charcot himself became increasingly aware of the role of imagination in the production of hysterical symptoms. So much, in fact, had Charcot begun to retreat from a strict organicist, hereditary view of the 'iron laws of hysteria' that a pupil later declared, thick with irony, that the back-sliding Charcot had inadvertently become 'the star pupil of the Nancy School'.[109]

It was no doubt this sudden reversal of the master's fortune that embarrassed Breuer when colleagues like Adolf von Strümpell more or less directed the old Nancy criticism at the *Studies*: the criticism, namely, that their findings were contaminated by suggestion. Certainly the timing of the *Studies* couldn't have been worse. For although the organicist interpretation of hysteria, according to which lesions in the nervous system cause the symptoms, was hotly debated when Breuer and Freud published their 'Preliminary Communication' in January of 1893, it remained the guiding paradigm for most workers in the field. Breuer and Freud did make a point of acknowledging the dissenting opinions of Möbius and, indeed, von Strümpell, but only indirectly and in a passing footnote.[110] Here is how they indicate their debt:

In this preliminary communication it is not possible for us to distinguish what is new in it from what has been said by other authors such as Moebius and Strümpell who have held similar views on hysteria to ours. We have found the nearest approach to what we have to say on the theoretical and therapeutic sides of the question in some remarks, published from time to time, by [Moritz] Benedikt. These we shall deal with elsewhere.[111]

What is perhaps most remarkable about this footnote is the omission of Charcot's name, coming as it does after the famous conclusion that '*Hysterics suffer mainly from reminiscences*' – an idea that Charcot first forwarded with his theory of traumatic hysteria. But just as interesting are Breuer and Freud's two comments: first, that 'it is not possible for us to distinguish what is new from what has been said by other authors such as Möbius and Strümpell'; and second, despite the very difficulty just mentioned, that they identify their work most closely with Benedikt. In a last sentence they seem to indicate a willingness to work out these relations, or non-relations, 'elsewhere'.

The context of debate about the proper aetiology of hysteria determined this rather ambivalent footnote, and also the direction of Breuer's 'Theoretical' chapter of 1895. For at issue was precisely the difference between the ideogenic view of hysteria advanced by people like Möbius, and the physiologic view advanced by people like Benedikt.

Now, if Breuer and Freud are already careful to point out in 1893 that they accept some aspects of the ideogenic view of hysteria, it is only because they don't, in any case, believe that it supplants the basic physiological view. As Breuer argues in the 'Theoretical' chapter, ideas may play a greater role in the aetiology of hysteria than had hitherto been recognized,[112] but they are by no means the only, or even the most important, factor. In this respect both Breuer and Freud remain entirely loyal to the latter Charcot: that is, they recognize the emergent psychological or subjective perspective but do not abandon the physiological or objective one. This explains why Breuer and Freud don't bother, despite their stated intentions in the essay of 1893, to spell out their debt to their old friend Benedikt in the *Studies*: the stakes lie, literally, elsewhere.[113]

Attending to this elsewhere, Breuer argues that Möbius in particular 'tears in half the clinical unity of hysteria'[114] with his conclusion that all hysterical symptoms are ideogenic. And yet, even as Breuer reaffirms the physiological view, he hedges his bets by invoking the very limitations he dismisses out-of-hand as unproductive. This he does most strikingly in the rhetorical gestures that open and close the 'Theoretical' chapter in the *Studies*. Having opened with an apology about the use of psychological terms in his discussion, a use which seems to Breuer regrettable but also unavoidable, he pleads for 'the reader's indulgence' if he is unable to distinguish between his views on hysteria and those of his colleagues. On this topic of 'common property' he advances the following remarks or, better, proviso:

> no one who attempts to put forward today his views about hysteria and its psychical basis can avoid repeating a great quantity of other people's thoughts which are in the act of passing from personal into general possession. It is scarcely possible always to be certain who first gave them utterance, and there is the danger of regarding as a product of one's own what has already been said by someone else.[115]

The possibility of regarding an other's work as one's own is, Breuer suggests, a 'danger' – to begin with, the dangers of misappropriation or plagiarism.

This passage is, of course, a restatement of the claim already made in the 1893 footnote to the 'Preliminary Communication' (cited earlier), which later served as the first chapter to the *Studies*. But it is a restatement with a difference. For unlike the first appearance of this proviso, in which Breuer and Freud imply that the danger has something to do with the limited medium of a 'preliminary communication', Breuer now implies that the proviso has something to do with the field of hysteria more generally. We are left to wonder why, and it is to the debate about aetiology that we will find the answer.

Brimming with self-reflexivity, the passage first of all begs the question: Is Breuer having fun at the expense of his colleagues who, like Möbius, mistake the entire field of hysteria for the psychic part? Breuer does, after all, trace the danger in question not to the *physiological* view of hysteria, of which he and Benedikt are representatives, but quite pointedly to those who want to 'put forward today [their views] . . . about hysteria and its *psychical basis*' (my emphasis). In this respect, Breuer's remarks are indeed a pointed joke, but also a warning, to all those who claim that ideas alone cause hysteria. Why is that? Because ideas, even more so than physical dispositions, which are subject to the laws of heredity, are the common property of *all* conscious beings; ideas are just the sort of thing that intellectuals like Breuer tend to have on a regular basis. In short, ideas grease the slippery slope until it is possible to conclude, as Möbius does in 1888, that 'Everyone is, so to say, hysterical.'[116] Not incidentally, it was this very text of Möbius, '*Über den Begriff der Hysterie*', that Breuer and Freud note in passing in their 'Preliminary Communication' of 1893.

The danger that worries Breuer so much, and which determines much of his 'Theoretical' contribution, is the possibility that Möbius is correct, namely, that we are all hysterical. For, indeed, if we are possessed by the 'common property' called ideogenesis, cut off from any objective measure, stuck with only half the clinical picture – in a word, hysterical – then we must be forgiven, in advance, if we constantly mistake our thoughts and works for that of some others, or are forever confusing who it is that said what, and when it is that they said it. Or again, we must accept that we are always liable to mistake a public discourse for our own, implying that we may be dupes and playthings of suggestive forces beyond our conscious control. The physiologist in Breuer thus wags his finger at Möbius and other proponents of ideogenesis, declaring that 'I regard hysteria as a clinical picture which has been empirically discovered and is based on observation.'[117]

If Breuer opens his 'Theoretical' chapter with a discussion of the difference between the physiological and the psychological aetiology of hysteria, it is because only *difference* provides the rule against which hysteria can be relatively measured. In effect the physiology and psychology of hysteria define, if not counter-balance, each other. However, insofar as the ideogenic view leads to the conclusion that we are all hysterical, it does away with difference altogether, including, for example, the absolutely crucial difference between first and second personalities that we find so prominent in cases of hysteria in the 1880s and 1890s; cases, not incidentally, like Breuer's own Anna O. Having split in half the 'clinical unity' of hysteria, Möbius essentially destroys the very correspondence that makes everything sensible. In other words, he cuts off the ego from its alter, and makes of all existence a variation on the theme of the altered, or second, state.

Confronted by this labyrinth without exit, Breuer holds ever more tightly onto the physiological theories of Alfred Binet and Pierre Janet, who contend that the mind is actually split into two, *normally unequal*, parts.[118] Speaking for the sane among us, Breuer writes: 'In our cases, the part of the mind which is split off is "thrust into darkness", as the Titans are imprisoned in the crater of Etna, and can shake the earth but can never emerge into the light of day.'[119] Psychology, we are led to believe, may have discovered the hidden world of the unconscious, but it is physiology which grounds this discovery and, moreover, equips us with a means with which to control it; I mean, that is, the objective reality of our nervous system and the reason by which we come to understand this system. In this respect, the split or dual or multiple consciousness of the nineteenth century is a quintessentially modern consciousness, one capable of seeing the light of day because it is continuously held up against the reality of night.

Things are further complicated for Breuer, however, by the troublesome realization that even the physiological view of hysteria is fraught with danger. Janet, for instance, maintains the objective picture of hysteria, but weighs it down with the baggage of an inherited '*insuffisance psychologique*', or psychological weakness.[120] As such, Janet draws a picture of degeneracy that is almost as bleak as that offered by Möbius. Breuer therefore counters his clinical picture with another that is based, not on the so-called degenerates of the Salpêtrière in Paris, but on the cultured and wealthy elite who comprise his clientele in Vienna. These patients, Breuer claims, are clearly not degenerate, but are on the contrary plagued with 'an excess of efficiency'[121]; that is, their minds are *over*-occupied by thought, for example, by the trance inducing thought of sick-nursing. 'The overflowing productivity of their minds,' Breuer effuses at one point, 'has led one of my friends to assert that hysterics are the flower of mankind, as sterile, no doubt, but as beautiful as double flowers.'[122] Freud makes the same point in the *Studies*, and provides the guiding rationale for their joint rejection of Janet's description of hysterics as mere degenerates. In the case of 'Frau Emmy von N.' Freud outlines his patient's excellent character, and then adds: 'To describe such a woman as a "degenerate" would be to distort the meaning of that word out of all recognition. We should do well to distinguish between the concepts of "disposition" and "degeneracy" as applied to people; otherwise we shall find ourselves forced to admit that humanity owes a large proportion of its great achievements to the efforts of "degenerates".'[123]

Breuer and Freud could not have been more clear: Möbius and Janet are two sides of the same coin, both, ironically, having committed errors of excess; the first on the side of psychology, the second on the side of physiology. For both men do their part to undermine the clinical picture, if not reality itself, with theories that leave us mad or becoming-mad – hysterics or degenerates.

All of which brings us back to Breuer's opening remarks in his 'Theoretical' contribution to the *Studies*, his self-implicating joke about advocates of ideogenesis, which he repeats again at the end of that chapter. Speaking, with exclamations, of the inevitable 'lacunas' in his analysis, he makes a final allusion to Plato, and to the puppet theatre in which he, the earnest physiologist, not unlike the hysteric, is trapped:

Only one consideration is to some extent consoling: that this defect [i.e., lacunas in the presentation] attaches, and must attach, to all physiological expositions of complicated psychical processes. We must always say of them what Theseus in *A Midsummer Night's Dream* says of tragedy: 'The best of this kind are but shadows'. And even the weakest is not without value if it honestly and modestly tries to hold onto the outlines of the shadows which the unknown real objects throw upon the wall. For then, in spite of everything, the hope is always justified that there may be some degree of correspondence and similarity between the real processes and our idea of them.[124]

Breuer's surprising consolation is that we are stuck with this unfortunate situation – itself a repetition, if not an affirmation, of the bleak possibility that we are all hysterical. At best, 'the hope is always justified' that what we describe corresponds with reality; that the clinical picture is not just a shadow on the wall of a cave we cannot escape, but only describe as though it were the real thing.

The Platonic image of the unenlightened cave was a suitable refuge for the scientific Breuer, who insisted upon seeing hysterical phenomena in the clear light of day, even though he was dragged down, not just by the ideogenic theories of his contemporaries, but by the dirty language of psychology, and by language itself. Faced with a dangerous theory that postulates in advance the common property of hysteria, Breuer was forced to acknowledge a familiar limit; the same limit that Descartes, asleep and dreaming by the fire, outlined as his sceptical doubt about the existence of the external world. Moreover, Breuer demonstrates by his rhetoric and by his complex argumentation that these limits are very much alive to anyone interested in human or social relations. To this end Breuer admits into his text the sceptical doubt that he will not countenance, but cannot dispel: the problem of representation holds not only for the many theories of hysteria, but also for anyone playing the role of physician or patient. In this respect Breuer must have been haunted by Anna O.'s insistence that she made everything up, that she simulated her illness, and by the consequent possibility that physician and patient engaged in a tragicomic piece of theatre.

Plato's solution to this problem of unauthenticity lie along the path of a non-mimetic theory of representation, the path of the Forms; a theory of education that breaks with the trance-like sleep-walking he associates with the low-level 'poetic' representations of an oral culture.[125] Plato's Idealism, however, proved itself unequal to Breuer's clinical experience with patients, especially the patient known as Anna O.; a name, case, shadow, or representation that, as Breuer knew very well, had very little to do with the historical Bertha Pappenheim. On the contrary, cut off from the relative measure called, for convenience, historical reality, the literature on this patient has been more or less consigned to fiction or, if you prefer, to hysteria.

That Breuer in 1895 already understood this dilemma is supported by his closing nod to Theseus and *A Midsummer Night's Dream*, the meaning of which he doesn't spell out, but which goes something like this: what seems like tragedy may in fact be comedy, in which case Hippolyta, like Hippolyte Bernheim and the other critics, may be right. To wit, *Studies on Hysteria* may be 'the silliest stuff that ever I heard', its findings a product of Breuer and Freud's vivid imaginations. As an ironical play-within-a-play, Breuer's rhetorical treatment of ideogenesis thus underscores a problem idea, the circle of representation, that we continue to pose, necessarily, to ourselves: *if hysteria really is a disease of representation, then maybe representation is a disease of hysteria.*

No wonder the sensible Breuer, already a reluctant actor in the *Studies*, walked away from this hall of mirrors, this bottomless dream, and from Freud's project which, after all, never ceased to find deep meaning along the length of its own shadow. And no wonder the insensible Freud refused, kicking and screaming, to be dragged into the light of day by Breuer.

3 Critical Readers of Freud Unite: A New Era for Freud Studies

The roughly thirty-year decline of psychoanalysis as a viable theory, therapy and business can be inversely related to the growing vitality of critical works on Freud during the same period. As signposts on the intellectual landscape, names like Ellenberger, Cioffi, Swales, Sulloway, Macmillan, Roustang, Esterson, Crews and Borch-Jacobsen are emblematic of this vitality. For without forming a unified canon, their works set rigorous standards by which we can measure, often for the first time, Freud and his so-called discoveries. Arguably it is because of them that a century dominated by partisan scholarship, fuelled by ignorance, self-interest and greed, is finally over.

When exactly the tables turned on Freud and psychoanalysis is unclear, although credit can be given, ironically enough, to Ernest Jones. I say ironic because the publication of his three-volume biography of Freud in the 1950s was meant to squash critique under the weight of a comprehensive, definitive and official work. What happened, instead, was that the biography became a catalyst for sober reassessments of the history of psychoanalysis, beginning with Jones's own account. Perhaps not surprisingly, analysts themselves issued many of the first challenges to Jones's biography. As the lay analyst Theodor Reik is reported to have said of *The Life and Work of Sigmund Freud*: 'It's a good book. But there are two things that Jones doesn't understand. He doesn't understand the Jews, and he doesn't understand the Viennese. Jones is like a porter: he carries your bags but has no idea what's in them.'[126]

Jones had access to unpublished documents and was able to shed new light on Freud and psychoanalysis, but much of the biography is mean-spirited, hagiographic, or just plain wrong. His treatment of dissident analysts, such as Otto Rank and Sándor Ferenczi, is a case-in-point. Their conflicts with Freud in the 1920s and 1930s are cast in terms of pathology, their 'failing mental integration',[127] while Jones is left sitting pretty – the sad-but-wiser hero of the story. It was immediately clear to informed readers that Jones's condescending and self-serving portrait required major revisions. As a result, we have a tradition of Freud criticism that is loosely divided into a before-Jones and an after-Jones.

The first wave of after-Jones criticism begins, roughly speaking, with Erich Fromm's slim book of 1959, *Sigmund Freud's Mission*, and culminates with Paul Roazen's *Freud and His Followers* of 1975. But Cioffi's early work, along with Henri Ellenberger's 932-page labour of love, *The Discovery of the Unconscious* of 1970, easily represents the best of this first wave. Having trained in analytic philosophy (with A. J. Ayer, no less), Cioffi's work is not just a correction of Jones, but a precise investigation of Freud's wayward retrospections and theoretical claims. At the same time, his approach is not blind-sided by issues of testability or falsification, as we find in the positivistic interpretation of Freud advanced by Adolf Grünbaum – Cioffi's intellectual nemesis. Cioffi's engagement with psychoanalysis is more often attuned to the troublesome contradictions of Freud's arguments, the logic of which is not linear. To this end Cioffi consults all of the relevant texts available, carefully weighing Freud's later, sanitized version of events against his original statements. Consequently, his engagement with Freud in the late 1960s and early 1970s was not just years, but decades ahead of its time.

Of course the cost of being untimely is being ignored or misunderstood. Even today, apparently sophisticated researchers in the field remain unfamiliar with Cioffi's name, let alone his work. For this reason the collection of his essays from 1969 to the present is an event of the most welcome sort. To begin with, honest researchers will no longer be able to ignore his work, which was squirrelled away in far-flung sources. And, best of all, they won't want to: Cioffi's arguments are brilliant, witty and generally convincing. Without exaggeration, *Freud and the Question of Pseudoscience* is the most significant work of critical Freud studies to be published in years.

Two of Cioffi's essays also appear in *Unauthorized Freud: Doubters Confront a Legend*, an anthology of twenty critical works lovingly collected, abridged and introduced by Frederick Crews. Published for mass distribution by Viking, the book is intended to counter and correct decades of misinformation about psychoanalysis, beginning topically enough with the Freud exhibition mounted in late 1998 at the Library of Congress in Washington, D.C. Since the world's most feared critics weren't welcome to participate meaningfully in the exhibit, Crews has taken the critics to the people. The result is a devastating portrait of Freud and psychoanalysis by a diverse group of scholars, from Peter Swales to Stanley Fish, that is impossible to dismiss as 'Freud bashing' or worse.[128] 'There is,' Crews rightly insists, 'no team of "Freud Bashers" at work here.'[129] On the contrary, the contributors provide reasoned and measured arguments proving, I think definitively, what many still refuse to hear: namely, that psychoanalysis is a serious menace based on a top-heavy theoretical edifice, faulty premises, circular and self-validating arguments, methodological laxity, motivated self-deception, bad faith and lies piled upon lies for more than a century. Arguably Critical Freud Studies – appropriately capitalized to signal the new mood – has come of age, and it is well worth pausing to see what the new consensus is all about, as evidenced by the appearance of Cioffi's and Crews' recent books.

Who Seduced Whom?

Although mostly forgotten, sometimes conveniently, there have always been powerful critics of Freud and psychoanalysis. As Crews remarks, 'In the years before Freud rewrote psychoanalytic history as a fetching Promethean myth, he was received *more* sceptically than

in the six decades since his death.'[130] Even before Freud dropped the
Seduction Theory in 1897, a date usually cited as the beginning of
psychoanalysis proper, there were no shortage of naysayers. For
example, when Freud and Josef Breuer published *Studies on Hysteria*
in 1895, J. Mitchell Clarke, Adolf von Strümpell and Eugen Bleuler
wrote critical reviews in prominent psychiatric and medical journals.
Like many others of that era, Clarke, Strümpell and Bleuler worried
aloud that suggestion may have contaminated Freud and Breuer's
findings.

To their detriment, neither Freud nor Breuer worried much about
suggestive collusion, since they believed, following Jean-Martin
Charcot and the Paris School, that hypnosis and hysteria were
primarily organic affairs. As we learn from Mikkel Borch-Jacobsen's
important, second contribution to *Unauthorized Freud*, 'Self-
Seduced', Freud took Charcot's lessons to heart.[131] Most
significantly, Freud echoed Charcot by falsely concluding that
hysteria 'is of a real, objective nature and not falsified by suggestion
on the part of the observer'.[132] As it happened, it wasn't Freud but
Charcot's great adversary from Nancy, Hippolyte Bernheim, who
criticized the findings of the Salpêtrière and advanced the psychological explanation of hysteria. And Bernheim was correct, as
everyone admitted not long after Charcot's death in August 1893.

The implications of this old debate about technique and etiology,
significant parts of which we explored in Chapters One and Two,
lends itself to the sort of logical exercise taught in Philosophy 101.
It goes something like this:

1. If Bernheim's psychological perspective about hypnosis and
   hysteria was right and Charcot's organic perspective was wrong,
   and
2. If Freud was avowedly Charcotian in his views, then
3. Freud, like Charcot, was also wrong.

Unfortunately one doesn't necessarily encounter logical conclusions
in the psychoanalytic literature, where Freud is simplistically

lionized as the father of modern psychology. What is true, however, is a less auspicious fact: Freud escaped the verdict universally reached of his Master's findings. The mechanism for this sleight of hand is the story of the rise and fall of the Seduction Theory, which is to Freud studies what Area 51 is to UFO fanatics: namely, a matter of blind faith.

According to psychoanalytic folklore, Freud replaced his early, objectivist belief in the Seduction Theory with a psychogenic theory of repressed infantile fantasies of an incestuous nature. But this is Freud's own account of events, and we have good reason to believe that he cooked the books to make it palatable for the unaware, gullible and intellectually starving. The ingredients of this recipe are at the heart of Critical Freud Studies, including *Freud and the Question of Pseudoscience*, where Cioffi wages battle with Freud and Freud apologists. This focus is no accident, since the future of psychoanalysis is literally at stake in the interpretation of the Seduction Theory.

So what's all the fuss about? Once the debate about the true etiology of hysteria had been decided, and decisively so, in Bernheim's favour, no one wanted to be painted with the same brush that had permanently tarnished Charcot's once golden reputation. Well, almost no one. While cautious researchers counted their wins and losses, Freud invested ever more heavily in Charcot's theories; an under-appreciated fact goes a long way toward explaining why Freud, on the one hand, had complete confidence in his claim that dissociated (repressed, unconscious) memories occasioned by childhood seduction were pathogenic, while critics, on the other hand, routinely shook their heads in disbelief. As Borch-Jacobsen puts it, for researchers in the field 'it must have been patently obvious that Freud was simply repeating the errors of his "Master", Charcot'.[133] But blinded by his motivated ignorance of, or disinterest in, the problem of suggestion, Freud continued to dismiss the critics and, in 1896, published three essays outlining the seduction thesis.

In a contemporary remark to his friend Wilhelm Fliess, Freud tellingly compared his evolving theory to 'the medieval theory of possession'.[134] To this end Freud posited a relation between 'confessions [extorted] under torture' and the 'communications made by my patients in psychic treatment'.[135] He also ordered, and eagerly read, the infamous guide for ferreting out the devil, the *Malleus maleficarum* [*The Hammer of Witches*]. The incredulous Freud says at one point, 'I dream, therefore, of a primeval devil religion with rites that are carried on secretly, and understand the harsh therapy of the witches' judges. Connecting links abound.'[136] *Therapy?* It is no wonder the esteemed Viennese psychiatrist Richard von Krafft-Ebing declared, during a meeting of 1896, that Freud's Seduction Theory 'sounds like a scientific fairy tale'.[137]

For indeed it was. In 1897 Freud finally realized that the memories he extorted during 'therapy' were false, an instance of what researchers today call 'experimenter's effect'. In other words his earliest reports of success were in fact dismal failures.

It is worth mentioning in this regard that, while failure is never opportune, the Seduction Theory debacle exasperated an already delicate situation in Freud's life. First of all, Freud's professional reputation was still recovering from his foolhardy advocacy of cocaine as a cure for morphine addiction during the 1880s.[138] Second, Freud's treatment of wealthy Viennese women, such as the Baroness Anna von Lieben ('Frau Cäcilie M.' of the *Studies*), left many with the impression that he was a disreputable quack, less a physician than a magnetizer or magician.[139] Cioffi was among the first to understand the seduction episode perfectly: 'His critics, it seemed, were right. What a humiliation! Freud now put all his enormous resourcefulness into mitigating, if not entirely evading, this humiliation.'[140]

Freud's evasion of humiliation is otherwise known as the birth of psychoanalysis. For it is psychoanalysis, the theory of fantasy rather than reality, that allowed Freud to escape Charcot's depressing fate. Having quietly discarded the Seduction Theory, Freud began to perfect what was to become his 'Teflon status'[141]: the 'need to avoid refutation' that best characterizes psychoanalysis.[142] This assessment by Cioffi is shared by many critics today, including Crews who declares in his 'Introduction' that classical psychoanalytic theory is 'a perpetual motion machine, a friction-free engine for generating irrefutable discourse'.[143]

Critics like Cioffi and Crews are right to question the old dogmas, since a close reading of Freud's texts reveal numerous misconceptions about the Seduction Theory – all of which, not incidentally, were perpetrated by Freud himself. Consider two examples that are discussed by Cioffi, Sulloway, Borch-Jacobsen and Crews. One, Freud's retrospective claim that his early patients produced memories of seduction. This is simply not true. On the contrary, Freud originally insisted that the patients withheld belief in stories of seduction and had no feeling of recollection whatsoever. Freud insisted upon this fact, saying that the scenes of sexual trauma were merely helpful *visualizations*, because it was the crux of his defence against critics who claimed that he had produced false *memories*. And two, Freud's claim that he only reluctantly acknowledged the pathogenic role of sexuality. This claim is also false, and for three reasons: Freud demonstrated just such an awareness of sexuality in his early texts, beginning at least in 1893; he was intimately aware of the role of innate infantile sexuality as advanced by Wilhelm Fliess; and, in any case, the theme of sexuality was already well-established by the sexologists of the 1880s, and was a recognized part of the discourse on hysteria well before Freud's 'reluctant' discovery of infantile sexuality in the late 1890s. Once again compelled to stave off the charge of suggestion, Freud falsely invoked the surprise factor: memories of a sexual nature could not have been suggested because they were both clinically surprising and culturally taboo.[144]

Such is thus stuff of pseudoscience.

Cioffi therefore concludes that Grünbaum and Masson get the Seduction episode all wrong: Grünbaum, for misreading Karl Popper's work on falsification (among other things), ignoring the *ad hoc* nature of Freud's theory-building, and thus believing that Freud abandoned the Seduction Theory for scientifically legitimate reasons; Masson, for peddling the 'politically correct' nonsense that

Freud was afraid of confronting the ubiquitous truth of child sexual abuse. 'Freud's dereliction in moral courage showed itself,' Cioffi argues, 'not in what he abandoned but in what he insisted on retaining: the boast that he could reconstruct by psychoanalytic method . . . the lost years of childhood.'[145] With psychoanalysis Freud swept suggestion under the rug, and along with it any responsibility he had for his past failures. As he put it in 1925, 'I do not believe even now that I forced the seduction-fantasies on my patients, that I "suggested" them.'[146] As Cioffi therefore concludes, 'Freud, like the Emperor in the story, dealt with bad news by having the bearer executed.'[147] That bearer of bad news was his patients, each of whom paid the price for Freud's careerist disinterest in their emotional well-being.

In fact, Freud never regretted the confusion, let alone the pain and suffering, that his botched technique caused his patients during this period. Always a reluctant therapist, he would refer to his patients as a 'rabble' best suited for floating psychoanalytic research.[148] And Freud never came clean with his critics, either – or especially. Instead, he kept silent about his abandonment of the Seduction Theory for *eight years*, until the publication of *Three Essays on Sexuality* in 1905, having shared his change of heart with Fliess alone. Why does this matter? Because when Freud published his first papers on 'psychoanalysis', readers assumed that the results were still based on the Seduction Theory. And in a way they were, for at least three damning reasons: first, because Freud *never* abandoned the theoretical utility of his method for naming the repressed, but only the contents of what is repressed; second, because Freud began speaking about 'psychoanalysis' in March 1896, more than one year *before* he dropped the Seduction Theory; and third, because Freud was still relying upon the Seduction Theory as late as 1905, when he finally published his purported *clinical substantiations* of the theory in the 'Dora' case.[149]

With the 'discovery' of psychoanalysis Freud effectively obscured the fact that it was business as usual – only *better*. Having lifted a theory of innate infantile fantasy from the speculations of Wilhelm

Fliess, there was no more need to worry about the problem of suggestion. So much, then, for the annoying critics of psychoanalysis. And so much for reality, which fell out of the clinical picture altogether from that point onward.

Savant or Charlatan?

Readers of Cioffi's book may be surprised by the contribution from Grünbaum in *Unauthorized Freud*. For although Cioffi makes a decent case against Grünbaum in his book, repeatedly dogging him for a recalcitrant belief in the possibility of a scientific psychoanalysis, the Grünbaum of 'Made-to-Order-Evidence' is hardly less critical about Freud's claims than Cioffi. Take for example the technique of free association. Freud believed that the problem of suggestion could be side-stepped by interpreting the patient's associations as a free expression of an internal state. Freud, in other words, claimed that the analyst is a neutral observer because he or she is literally external to the workings of the psyche. Grünbaum, however, debunks the assumption that such associations are in fact free, arguing that they are invariably compromised by preconceptions brought into therapy by patients; by verbal and non-verbal cues, subtle or otherwise, made by the analyst; by the promptings or 'intellectual help' (as Freud put it) of the analyst; and by the analyst's selective sampling from the flow of associations.[150] Thus Grünbaum's arguments nicely dovetail with those made in the first section by Cioffi, Sulloway, Swales, Borch-Jacobsen and Crews.

Just as Grünbaum deflates the pretence of objectivity in Freud's technique of 'free' association, Sabastiano Timpanaro exposes concretely its staggering indetermination. In 'Error's Reign', Timpanaro argues that the associations found in a famous interpretation from *The Psychopathology of Everyday Life* of 1901 are totally arbitrary, a reflection of Freud's 'zeal for his own theses'.[151] In the analysis, Freud concludes that a travelling companion's associations to a forgotten word, '*aliquis*', lead inexorably to the determining fount of his anxiety: the idea that a lover may be pregnant. Yet the forgotten word, Timpanaro argues, could have been any word in the relevant sentence from Virgil: '*Exoriare aliquis nostris ex ossibus ultor*' ('Let someone arise from my bones as an Avenger').[152] The word '*exoriare*', for example, means both 'arise' and 'birth' – either of which, with the slightest imagination, could be thought to signify the pregnancy-anxiety attributed to associations with '*aliquis*'. Timpanaro's counter-examples are instructive: 'irrespective of rarefied epistemological debates' about falsification, the fact that any word can do the trick of Freudian determination means that the explanation 'has no scientific value'.[153]

In the third section of *Unauthorized Freud*, Crews gathers expert examinations of Freud's case histories and case studies from Allen Esterson ('Dora'), Joseph Wolpe and Stanley Rachman ('Little Hans'), Frank Sulloway (a cross-section), Stanley Fish ('Wolfman'), and David E. Stannard ('Leonardo'). Esterson's essay, for example, depicts Freud's mind-boggling irresponsibility with a young victim of sexual harassment, proving yet again that Freud hardly mended his ways in the years following his abandonment of the Seduction Theory.[154] In Sulloway's contribution we are reminded of the incredible fact that Freud neglected to present a successful therapeutic outcome until 1908. Yet even this case has no more merit than the famous 'cure' of Freud's Russian patient, Sergius Pankejeff, a.k.a. the 'Wolfman'. It is an embarrassment for psychoanalysis that this most celebrated of all analytic patients was in and out psychoanalysis for *sixty years*. When asked about his experience by an Austrian journalist, Pankejeff confessed that psychoanalysis had been a 'catastrophe' in his life. He also insisted that his shocking revelations not be published until after his death, since Kurt Eissler and the Sigmund Freud Archives were paying him what amounted to hush money.[155]

That we ever believed psychoanalysis could cure anyone is partly explained by Stanley Fish, who provides a compelling analysis of Freud's spell-binding rhetoric. His conclusion: the real 'primal scene' at work in the case of the Wolfman is 'the scene of persuasion'.[156] It is only too obvious that this scene has infected generations of readers, including some of the most self-consciously brilliant literary critics and philosophers. But Fish, like Cioffi and Borch-Jacobsen, is a marvellous exception, someone who demonstrates by example how true sophistication can operate in Freud studies.

The last section of *Unauthorized Freud* contains thoughtful contributions about the 'militant exclusiveness'[157] of the psychoanalytic cause: Ernest Gellner discusses the shackling of patients with transference; John Farrell discusses the effects of Freud's paranoia; François Roustang explores the wicked sectarianism of psychoanalysis; and Lavinia Edmunds presents the tragic story of Horace Frink, once Freud's favoured apostle in America. Each contribution is worth reading, and spells disaster for psychoanalysis, but Crews has saved the most disturbing of the bunch for last.

Although many will be unfamiliar with Frink's story, it resonates with other well-known tales of Freud's inept meddling in the sexual affairs of his followers. Like some other therapists, including some of Freud's closest adherents, Frink fell in love with a patient who, luckily, was a wealthy heiress but, unluckily, was already married. Just as unlucky: Frink was also married, had two children, and was tormented by depression. Frink was an established American psychiatrist, already thirty-eight years of age, when he began an analysis with Freud in 1921. Freud liked Frink, partly for his dark sense of humour, but also because he was a Gentile who, like Jones and Jung, would help 'prove' that psychoanalysis wasn't merely a Jewish science. Freud also approved of Frink's mistress, Angelika Bijur, whose money could grease the wheels of his fledgling publishing house. In this last respect, Bijur had already proven her worth by paying for Frink's analysis with Freud. And so Freud, without even knowing their respective spouses, recommended that Frink and Bijur ditch their partners and get married. Predicting their impending happiness, he threw in an ominous warning that if they didn't marry, the depressed Frink might become a homosexual.

The story gets worse. Although Frink was still battling depression, Freud announced his case complete and sent him back to America to arrange his divorce. Worried about Frink's wife, Freud later issued the following, by now all-too-familiar refrain: 'Tell her she is not to blame analysis for the complications of human feeling which is only exposed but not created by analysis.'[158] Freud also arranged that the unstable Frink be voted the next President of the American Psychoanalytic Association (APA), which he was in 1923. After two additional mental tune-ups with Freud, Frink married Bijur at the end of 1922. However, Frink began to suffer from guilt in addition to depression, a state that only worsened when his divorced wife died of pneumonia in May 1923. Long story short: Frink was deposed as leader of the APA, committed himself to a sanatorium on two later occasions, attempted suicide twice, was divorced by Bijur, was remarried, and died a troubled man in 1936. In short, Freud's self-interested meddling ruined three lives and wrecked havoc in a fourth. Understandably, everyone involved in the Frink affair developed a distaste for psychoanalysis. Bijur's cuckolded first husband captured the feeling succinctly in a letter to Freud in 1922, in which he asks: 'Great Doctor, are you savant or charlatan?'[159]

Cioffi asks a similarly blunt question of Freud in his most famous essay, 'Was Freud a Liar?', and at times in his book flirts with an affirmative answer. But he is wary of putting questions to Freud in such a stark, uncompromising way. In his first long chapter of *Freud and the Question of Pseudoscience*, 'Why Are We Still Arguing About Freud?', Cioffi rejects the 'fake antithesis' that impels us to choose between Freud the savant or charlatan, truth-seeker or liar. For Cioffi, such simplifications only play into the hands of Freudian apologists, who are then able, in apparent good faith, to dismiss as naive and conspiratorial criticism that they don't want to hear. 'The sceptic,' Cioffi rightly counters, 'does not require large-scale lying on the part of analysts to account for the consistent reporting of phenomena now conceded not to occur.'[160] So what explains a century of widespread belief in, and misinformation about, the history and theory of psychoanalysis? Cioffi points to experiments in social psychology, such as those conducted by Solomon Asch in the late 1940s and 1950s, which prove that objectivity can be compromised by the coercion and peer pressure of authorities. The very same pressures of suggestion that are evinced in Freud's own practice and in the movement at large, and which are discussed in Cioffi's and Crews's important books.

Unlike much of the literature on Freud, which snuggles up to its subject, these watershed books of Critical Freud Studies are courageous provocations that, frankly, redeem psychoanalytic studies as an intellectual pursuit. *Freud and the Question of Pseudoscience* is a hard-hitting, sophisticated and much-anticipated book on the history and epistemic status of psychoanalysis. *Unauthorized Freud* is effectively the first collective statement made by the best critics of the last thirty years. The publication of these two books in 1998 represent the arrival of what could be considered a new golden age of psychoanalysis; a time first announced, in retrospect, when Crews published his now famous essays on the bankruptcy of psychoanalysis as announced on the front pages of *The New York Review of Books* in November 1993 and December 1994.[161]

Such Critical Freud Studies are overdue reading for those erstwhile intellectuals, heads buried deep in the sand, who care nothing about facts and, consequently, know little about the troubled history of psychoanalysis. Their uncritical investment in Freudian theory suggests we revisit a forgotten lesson of Philosophy 101. It goes something like this: one, if critics like Cioffi and Crews are right and Freud is wrong, and two, if theorists today are avowedly Freudian in their views, then three, these theorists, like Freud, are also wrong. *Quod erat demonstrandum.*

PART II

Selected Memories of Psychoanalysis:
History, Theory, Politics

Active forgetting is a term Nietzsche coined to designate the human will that affirms itself by actively dispensing with memories that compromise its current existence. Unwittingly, no doubt, Freud often enacted this idea, actively willing into existence a theory and technique that simultaneously did away with theories and techniques that challenged its existence. Freud's clever manipulations of the past helped establish psychoanalysis as a legitimate therapy, a reputable science and a powerbroker across academic disciplines, in psychiatry and psychotherapy and in everyday popular culture. Freud was, in a word, Nietzschean – an uncommonly gifted man who, on the strength of his will to power, stamped the world in his own image.

It is left to those of us no longer entranced by Freud's will to assess what remains of the psychoanalytic Cause and to unravel and even recover the facts that complicate the official, often mythological, histories of psychoanalysis. And while this task requires us to examine the early myth-making history of psychoanalysis, it also requires us to attend to and expose that same impulse in the works of latter-day Freudians. The critic's task is therefore political and epistemological; political insofar as the politics of psychoanalysis have constantly formed and deformed official histories; epistemological insofar as the 'politics of knowledge' is an ever-present problem for all historians, including those who pride themselves on their objectivity. This latter consideration is a constant conundrum for researchers, one insufficiently appreciated among friends and foes of psychoanalysis. For if one hopes to avoid the pitfalls of a positivistic history, according to which we can indeed recover a completely true account of the past, one needs to recognize not just the limitations of other historians's efforts, but also the limitations of one's own efforts – even when, or especially when, writing as a critical or revisionist historian.

That said, there is no need for despair in the face of these problems. The first task is absolutely essential, and is far from exhausted: exposing partisan histories of psychoanalysis as particularly bad histories. It is just not true in this regard that any history goes, that every story is equal in the face of our limited knowledge. Some histories are more coherent and plausible than some others. Secondly, we must attend to those sceptical critiques, nowadays often associated with post-structuralism, that seem to compromise our claims to knowledge. And then we must assess their worth. Some forms of post-structuralism, like some histories, are more coherent and plausible than some others. Finally, I think we can benefit from more humour in the face of intractable historico-epistemological problems. Without necessarily finding timeless solutions to such problems, it is perhaps enough that critics foster a healthy amusement about one's own limitations as a critic. We may not be able to hold on to the truth, but that doesn't mean that we can't dance around it in interesting and productive ways.

To this latter-most end, I close this section with a cheeky fiction (and a nod of appreciation to novelists like D. M. Thomas); a fiction that has the merit of coming close to the truth on many fronts, as readers will see in the 'true' considerations of skating and dogs in psychoanalysis that follow in Section III. As Lacan liked to say, sometimes fiction comes closer to the truth than the bare facts, a claim that erodes, sometimes to good effect, the difference between literature and history. The section opens with a 'wild analysis' of gossip, history and theory in psychoanalysis. The general aim of this chapter is to force the collision of interests between characteristically ahistorical post-structuralists and characteristically atheoretical historians of psychoanalysis; more precisely, between the works of Jacques Derrida and Paul Roazen. Next I have included a brief open letter concerning the everyday limitations of archival work, specifically in the context of gossip. In the following chapter I explore the trouble that can ensue when Derrida single-mindedly uses the archive for the purposes of deconstruction. It is, I argue, a cautionary tale – one that has made me rethink the politics of deconstruction and, more generally, my own commitment to post-structuralist thought. In response to this reassessment, I attempt in the next chapter to address in the simplest language a paradigmatic instance of the politics of psychoanalysis at work today. The 'case study' briefly discussed is the much-misunderstood controversy concerning the Library of Congress Freud exhibition of 1998. In particular I discuss the media campaigning that spun petitioners on behalf of openness into close-minded, censoring, 'Freud-Bashers'. To help drive the point home about the current state of psychoanalytic politics, I provide in the next chapter a critical analysis of Jacques Lacan's thought at its most accessible: the cartoon guide *Lacan For Beginners*.

If theorists fail to recall the sometimes banal politics of knowledge, keeping their hands clean of gossip, history, public exhibits and lowly objects designed for mass consumption, it is in part the job of Critical Freud Studies to help them remember and, if at all possible, push fundamental questions about psychoanalysis. And that is the job of the essays collected in this section.

4 Freud and His Followers, Or How Psychoanalysis Brings Out the Worst in Everyone

You are not neurotic, but you can be in time.

(Sigmund Freud[162])

In a lecture for the *Collège internationale de philosophie* entitled 'What's Wrong With French Psychoanalysis?', historian of psycho-analysis Paul Roazen argued that proponents of the French Freud have forgotten Freud. And thus he bluntly asked, 'Where's Freud?'[163] Without by any means taking on the mantle of the 'French Freud', we will try in what follows to appease Roazen by recalling (or, as it were, conjuring) the historico-biographical image of Sigmund Freud. On the one hand, located as we are just beyond the closure of the 'psychoanalytic century', this should be a fairly simple affair. Indeed, it may be that Freud is precisely the ghost we cannot exorcise, despite our best efforts. However, and on the other hand, while Roazen makes an interesting and no doubt timely point, his question is obviously compromised by what is called essentialism. Suffice to say that Roazen's subject – the science of psychoanalysis, Freud himself – is no longer the self-evident or common-sense one of modernity. In fact, post-structuralism has taught us to be increas-ingly sceptical that there is or ever was a privileged access to the truth of Freud – *wherever* he might have been or still remains.

In what follows I want to attempt to both answer and problem-atize Roazen's question, in part by addressing the subject of psychoanalysis through a timely question of my own: namely, *Who's* Freud? At the same time, I explore the structural role that institutionalization and discipleship play in the invention, adjudication and transmission of Freud's science, effectively asking: *Whose* Freud? Between the who's/whose of these questions, I hope to reveal a Freud that is irreducible to any biographical or institutional closure, one that is, in effect, radically self-deconstructive. To this end I attempt to locate Roazen's own work, the 'Where's Roazen?' implicit within his indelicate question, alongside some current theoretical trends in psychoanalysis.

1.

Since it is biography that is in question here, even the truth of biography and its contested utility, we might begin by citing a fairly well-known passage from Freud. 'Alarmed by the threat' that Arnold Zweig is thinking of becoming his biographer, Freud responds:

> No, I am far too fond of you to permit such a thing. Anyone who writes a biography is committed to lies, concealments, hypocrisy, flattery, and even to hiding his own lack of understanding, for biographical truth does not exist, and if it did we could not use it.
>
> Truth is unobtainable, mankind does not deserve it, and in any case is not our Prince Hamlet right when he asks who would escape a whipping if he got what he deserved? [164]

Freud not only feared the inevitable distortion that results from the 'furor biographicus', [165] but feared that his science be reduced to a piece of his own subjective phantasying, less a dream-work than a nightmare.

In his 'elementary' introduction to psychoanalysis, Freud evokes the case of historical research against which he situates psychoanalysis. There he claims that the analyst, unlike the historian, 'does at least report things in which he himself played a part'. [166] However, Freud still begs the question as to whether the report in question has more to tell us about the analyst, than an event from someone's

repressed past. And of course the same problematic plagues historical research, at least insofar as the historian attempts to transcend
the limitations of a purely descriptive accounting of events, what
R. G. Collingwood disparagingly called 'scissor and paste' history, to
the unspoken motivation lying behind some past action. Thus both
psychoanalyst and historian are caught up in the questionable reconstruction of events to which they are by necessity outsiders.

Still, Freud had good reasons for distinguishing psychoanalysis
from the historian's uncritical depth or psycho-history. After all, a
psycho-history always risks mistaking fantasy for reality in precisely
the same way that Freud did before privately dropping the Seduction
Theory in 1897. To Wilhelm Fliess, Freud wrote of 'the certain
insight that there are no indications of reality in the unconscious, so
that one cannot distinguish between truth and [affective] fiction'.[167]
In contrast, the scientific historian has always been committed to the
literal, realist truth of the subject, since without it history would be
reduced to the production of fictions; from this perspective scientific
method is never just another tall-tale, but the privileged medium
through which interpretations claim objective truth.

We are thus confronted with two difficulties. First, we are no
longer certain that the distinction between contemporary historian
and past object can be bridged; that, for instance, the gap Collingwood (dis)solves or leaps by penetrating from the 'outside' of an
event to its motivational 'inside' ever occurs. Second, we cannot be
certain that there ever was or is an accessible 'inside', an essential
object or kernel of truth that becomes subject in the historian's
mind and objectified in his text, a subject for his readers. For as
François Roustang argues: 'Historical truth exists no more than do
the origins of the Indo-European languages. What exists are
delusions founded upon the supposition of its existence.'[168] Thus
confronted with the 'invention' of culture and history, the fact of
interpretation probably tells us more about the analyst than his
object. As Nietzsche first guessed, system-building is always 'the
personal confession of its author and a kind of involuntary or
unconscious memoir'.[169]

Consequently, the 'truth' of the subject is revealed as the invisible ghost which propels the modern historian's imaginary time machine.

2.

Though we will return to these problematics, these are not new suspicions and we won't dwell upon them too closely here. Instead we might profitably turn to John Forrester where he considers the 'four ways of breaching the membrane' which forms between analyst and analysand: namely, scientific communications, acting-out, telepathy and gossip.[170] In each case the contractual relationship upon which therapy is grounded is violated; in effect, representation as 'wild transference' leaks outside the office, beyond the couch. While Freud accounts for the first two breaches in security – the first being 'permitted', the second being 'expected' – he never comes to grips with the last two, which remain as non-theorized contaminants in the Freudian corpus. Forrester thus suggests that 'Gossip is the underbelly of analysis, telepathy its shadow.'

It is arguably for the same reasons that Freud never came to grips with biography: as a discourse outside the analytic fold it breaches the space or bond between analyst and patient and produces a public or wild transference. In fact, as a kind of *voluntary whispering* – in contrast to 'involuntary whispering', which is tied to issues in telepathy[171] – biography is not unconnected with 'hearsay', as Freud likened it, or even gossip.[172] But as Roazen rightly suggests, 'what seems gossip to one generation may be history to the next'.[173] Indeed, by reducing the already shaky foundations of biography to the level of gossip, the more orthodox followers of Freud have tried their best to silence dissenters and limit the breach that is biography. Steven Marcus thus rails against the 'idle gossip and chatter' in Roazen's early, controversial work, preferring instead those 'differences [that] have meaning for the history of the movement'.[174] Of course, we might reasonably ask what these so-called differences amount to and, more critically, who is in a position to judge them.

That supposed differences are reducible to an orthodox 'archeology' of psychoanalysis surely doesn't make them any more favourable.[175]

If Freud and his followers often reject biography as theoretically impossible or, at least, a show of bad taste (often 'American'[176]), it may only indicate the extent to which they have something to hide, minimize, sweep under the analytic rug. Yet we have to wonder: if biographical truth, the truth of the subject, cannot be had (even supposing for a moment, against Freud, that we deserve it) or verified objectively by historians of psychoanalysis, we might question the extent to which the science of psychoanalysis was or is possible.

For finally the same questions of (an implicit) psycho-history can be asked of (an explicit) psychoanalysis: Can the analyst–patient duo join forces and bridge the gap between (screen) memory and objective fact? And when they (think they) do, is the re-membered product any less invented that the historian's? In his *An Outline of Psycho-Analysis* and elsewhere Freud certainly admits that:

> we fill in what is omitted by making plausible inferences and translating it to conscious material. In this way we construct, as it were, a sequence of conscious events complementary to the unconscious psychical processes. The relative certainty of our psychical science is based on the binding force of those inferences.[177]

Leaving aside Freud's tireless assertion that anyone who disagrees with these constructions is lacking a deep enough understanding of psychoanalysis – as the inimitable Karl Kraus puts it, 'If I tell the analyst to kiss my ass, they tell me I have an anal fixation'[178] – or is really committed to the underbelly of hearsay and gossip, we are at least beginning to appreciate that Freud was dealing with highly dubious representations in his practice. Could it be, then, that the 'relative certainty' of psychoanalysis was based not on the 'binding force of those inferences', but upon the transference which bound the patient to the analyst? For as Fliess already suspected of Freud in late 1901, 'the reader of thoughts merely reads his own thoughts into other people'.[179]

Actually, in his attempt to break with hypnosis Freud confused the repetition of 'acting out' in the transference with remembering.[180] What, then, does the analyst–patient construction represent? Freud of course always maintained that 'we never fail to make a strict distinction between *our* knowledge and *his* knowledge'.[181] But if, further, the patient's transference onto the analyst is indistinguishable from good old suggestion and hypnosis – if, in other words, 'hypnotic suggestion had returned *into* psychoanalysis, *as* psychoanalysis'[182] – then analytic construction does not necessarily (or even likely) represent an actual (original) event at all. And so we have a situation where 'analyst and patient finally enter into the same cultural mini-universe . . . ; that is, their delusions, which are based on the same supposed historical truth, have become similar enough to communicate and found a mini-society'.[183]

In this respect, it is no accident that Freud recommended to Ernest Jones that 'the simplest way of learning psychoanalysis was to believe that all he wrote was true and then, after understanding it, one could criticize it any way one wished'.[184] But confronted with such 'Catholicism', as Joseph Wortis put it,[185] there was always the danger that Freud's student-patients would never emerge from the 'hypnotransferential tie'[186] that bound, and still binds, this delusional mini-society together.[187]

And no doubt Jacques Lacan only pushed this mad logic to its extreme when he declared that the goal of psychoanalysis was the creation of more psychoanalysts. As Stuart Schneiderman puts it, 'someone chooses to practice psychoanalysis because he cannot see himself doing anything else, because he cannot think of any other way to deploy his desire in terms of work'.[188] With this psychoanalysis has truly become 'an elegant solution to the problem of madness, since it amounted to dissolving that problem in the establishment of a society that was itself delirious'.[189] As Havelock Ellis liked to say, psychoanalytic logic was a sort of 'heads I win, tails you lose' proposition. This point is nicely captured by a story from

Abram Kardiner who once claimed to get 'nothing' out of his analysis with Horace Frink. In response Freud ironically responded: 'You did get something out of it . . . A little neurosis.'[190]

Hence the troublesome question: 'Is there an end to analysis, after all?'[191] Similarly, is there an 'outside' of the transference?[192] And if there is, who is in a position to end the analysis, to introduce what Jacques Derrida so wittily calls the '*tranche*-ference'?[193]

3.

A Spatially Enlarged, Solitary Solitariness: Psychoanalysis was inaugurated into the twentieth century with Freud's autobiographical and self-analytical *Interpretation of Dreams*. There Freud admitted that he had 'to reveal to the public gaze more of the intimacies of my mental life than I liked, or that is normally necessary for any writer who is a man of science and not a poet'.[194]

But why, then, should Freud's 'auto' be considered any less delusional, gossipy or different than the biographer's tall-tale? As Roazen was among the first to insist, 'The psychological system Freud created closely fit his personal peculiarities – demonstrating that the rise of psychoanalysis was far from a coldly neutral scientific advance.'[195] Consequently, and as Freud once admitted, 'It remains for the future to decide whether there is more delusion in my theory than I should like to admit.'[196] To be sure, Freud 'very much needed a "yes" from the outside world',[197] 'someone who would confirm him, comfort him, encourage him, listen to him and even feed him'.[198] And thus, as Roustang formulates it:

In these circumstances, how can he who either invents a new theory or renovates a theory prevent himself from wanting to share his findings, that is, to find a public who will applaud his sayings, which would no longer be delirious because others would share them? Delirium is the theory of the one, while theory is the delirium of several, which is transmissible.[199]

Or again, as Nietzsche succinctly argued long ago: '*Multiplication Table.* – One is always wrong, but with two, truth begins. – *One* cannot prove his case, but two are irrefutable.'[200] Following Freud in *Civilization and Its Discontents*, we need only add that the delirium 'of the one', of Freud's defiant 'hermit' turned fool or madman, often becomes transmissible in the 'mass-delusions' of a religion; in this case, the psychoanalytic religion. Unfortunately, and as Freud realized, 'No one who shares a delusion ever recognizes it as such.'[201]

Thus grounded as it is upon the subjectivity (or autobiography) of Sigmund Freud, the objectivity (or science) of psychoanalysis is, from (or at) the very beginning, severely compromised, split in two. At the same time, since Freud 'could not separate his creation, the theory of psychoanalysis, from himself',[202] and since it 'would be impossible to overestimate how much of himself Freud put into his work',[203] we are quite unable to justify *where* exactly that split takes place – assuming it does or should take place at all. In other words, and perhaps this is the crux of the matter, we are unable without considerable interpretive violence to distinguish once and for all the auto from the biography, the man from his science, the flesh from the word, the dream from its manifestation or, if you prefer, the self, psyche or psycho from the analysis.

Consequently, Where's Freud? And furthermore, Who is (and isn't) Freud? Whose Freud is it anyway?

4.

Stemming, no doubt, from the uniquely French preoccupation with the abyss in all its post-structural guises, many critics today emphasize the structure of this uncertain, split, double origin; and this, it occasionally seems, at the expense of the 'true' biographical Freud and his earnest biographers. Yet this abyss betrays an altogether different kind of madness than the one we usually consider. In the first place, it does not necessarily entail just another excursion into existentialism, which always remained a humanism. Rather, at its most rigorous the abyssal madness of post-structural thought refers to a contamination or mixing of boundaries that mark the outer limits of an inner dehiscence; a *double chiasmatic invagination of edges*, as Derrida colourfully puts it,[204] which undoes the purity of our scientific model, our logical law of non-contradiction, even as it points towards the impossible, the beyond, the mad as instituted *within* our rational categories of thought, 'inside' the dream of a synchronic, essentialized truth.

Despite, then, what appears the taming, normalization or institutionalization of psychoanalysis – its freezing in time, its timely death – we should not be too surprised to find at the heart of Freud's science a logic of madness or, from the other side, a madness of logic; a lively (de)logic that disrupts the singular subject of psychoanalysis and, with it, the possibility of its simple transmission from Freud to his attentive followers. If so, and here Roazen & Co. would have to agree, it is no longer possible to simply, naturally, that is, without pre-judgement and prejudice, foreclose in advance the choice between subject and object, Freud and analysis. For in what is not by any means a new formula, psychoanalysis *is* Sigmund Freud. By insisting upon this 'convergence' or 'mutual interference', not just of the unconscious and conscious forces in the production of manifest symptoms,[205] but of subject and object, autobiography and biography, psychoanalysis reveals itself as its own symptom or accident, a veritable slip of the old man's tongue. Kraus of course knew this and more when he coined the famously witty line in *Die Fackel*: 'Psychoanalysis is the disease of which it claims to be the cure.'[206]

In this way, we stumble upon a radical undecidability that exists both at the origins of psychoanalysis and in its multiple after-effects; an undecidability that exists along the borderline between its autobiographical 'inside' (subject as object) and scientific 'outside' (object as subject), and at the heart of that very inside, the irreducible *subjectobject*. Consequently, the invention or construction of psychoanalysis already implied its inevitable deconstruction, its circular logic exploded and transformed by the structure of the 'chiasmus'.

5.

Usually in the most vague and clumsy way this sort of troublesome complexity makes some think, no doubt a bit too quickly, that Freud was never much of a philosopher and, in any case, was more than a little neurotic himself. Indeed, that Freud was never properly analysed by a fellow analyst, that psychoanalysis originates in his incomplete self-analysis, has been for some of his followers an uncomfortable, regrettable and even forgettable detail. But let's not forget that on 14 November 1897, Freud sent a letter to Fliess, writing: 'True self-analysis is impossible, else there would be no [neurotic] illness.'[207] This rather pessimistic sentiment is not an aberration in Freud's thinking, and forty years later in his important 'Analysis Terminable and Interminable' he concluded that psychoanalysis itself, along with education and government, is an 'impossible' profession.[208]

Part of what is so unnerving about Freud's inaugural and interminable self-analysis is captured by Peter Gay when he rightly asks: 'How could Freud, no matter how bold or original, become his own other?'[209] How could Freud, in other words, create the distance of an Other through which psychoanalysis (and its mediating transference) was made possible? Or again, more simply, how did psychoanalysis happen (to Freud) before it was founded (by Freud)? This leads Alberto Ceiman, a Lacanian analyst from Mexico City, to propose the following paradox:

> Transference was discovered when the analytical setting had already been invented. Transference got there late. We have here a funny paradox: psychoanalysis only makes sense in terms of transference, however it was discovered after it was invented; at least this was the case for Freud and the Freudians.[210]

Transference, the emotional bond between analyst and patient, missed its appointment with itself; we might even say that it differed and deferred from itself, from the possibility of an original self-same.

Ceiman, however, is far too comfortable with the idea that this inaugural paradox can be restricted to 'Freud and the Freudians', as though the aporia shrinks rather than expands over time and space. After all, Lacan and his followers never resolved the paradox, but were only its most uncanny embodiment and (re)incarnation. Passing through Lacan, they were always just another link 'in a historical chain of training analyses that can be traced back, through a kind of apostolic succession, to the personal analytical interactions of Freud and his first disciples'.[211] Or, as Lacan put it near the end of his life, shortly after the dissolution of the École Freudienne: 'C'est à vous d'être lacanien, si vous voulez. Moi, je suis freudien.'[212]

As embarrassing as it may sound, we are beginning to grapple here with the possibility that psychoanalysis is a science that has yet to happen – even to itself – and is still being invented from out of the rupture of a 'non-origin which is originary'. And thus Derrida argues:

> If one wished to simplify the question, it would become, for example: how can an autobiographical writing, in the abyss of an unterminated self-analysis, give to a worldwide institution *its* birth? The birth of whom? of what? and how does the interruption or the limit of self-analysis . . . reproduce its mark in the institutional movement, the possibility of this remark from then on never ceasing to make little ones, multiplying the progeniture with its cleavages, conflicts, divisions, alliances, marriages, and regroupings?[213]

Once again, conditioned by its own certain uncertainty, how did psychoanalysis happen – if in fact it happened at all?

Like some others before him,[214] Lacan felt that psychoanalysis only became a method – a happening – for Freud's followers: 'Freud, for his part, did not apply a method. If we overlook the unique and inaugural character of his endeavour, we will be committing a serious error.'[215] For this very reason, though, Ellis wisely cautioned a young Wortis against a 'didactic analysis' with Freud in a letter of 14 September 1934. Ellis wrote:

About being psychoanalysed, my own feeling most decidedly is that it would be better to follow his *example* than his precept. *He* did not begin by being psychoanalysed (never was!) or attaching himself to any sect or school, but . . . always retained his own independence. If he had himself followed the advice he gives you, he would have attached himself to Charcot with whom he was working, and became a disciple, like Gilles de la Tourette, an able man now forgotten. If you are psychoanalysed you either become a Freudian or you don't. If you don't, you remain pretty much where you are now; if you do – you are done for! – unless you break away . . . To every great leader one may apply the saying of Nietzsche about Jesus: – There has only been one Christian and he died on the cross. There has only been one Freudian![216]

So true. The upshot is that we can no longer avoid asking what psychoanalysis means and for whom, since what we call Freud's creation has always been tied up with factors other than 'science'.

6.

Situated within its historico-political context, Freud's refusal to submit to an official psychoanalysis is perhaps less scandalous than it might seem otherwise. For, in the first place, and despite protests to the contrary, one can argue that Freud never *needed* to submit to an analysis. It is not only that he was his own analyst and best patient – as he put it, 'the most important patient for me was my own person'[217] – or that he was and remains the father of psychoanalysis. Of course, all of this is true and we can hardly underestimate its importance. More generally, though, Freud was able to escape analysis because he was always 'something of a scientific wildman', as Marcus admits,[218] his own heretic, the first and only orthodox but wild analyst.

Recall, though, that the training analysis was meant to screen, police, or exclude such heretical thoughts from the theory, practice, transmission and reception of psychoanalysis. It is therefore a great unappreciated irony in the history of psychoanalysis that Carl Jung, of all people, was the first to suggest to Freud that all future analysts be analysed[219] – that is, trained in accordance with the rules and regulations of a new and expanding institution. As Freud himself put it later, 'There should be some headquarters whose business it is to declare: "All this nonsense is nothing to do with analysis; this is not psycho-analysis".'[220] Hanns Sachs thus noted that 'It can be seen that analysis needs something corresponding to the novitiate of the Church.'[221] Or as Jones more romantically thought, psychoanalysis would require something along the lines of Plato's ideal Republic, with Freud as uncontested Philosopher King.[222]

A few years after Jung's fateful suggestion, Jones recommended to Freud's great delight that they form a 'secret committee' as a way of protecting the Freudian cause – only now from the immediate threat posed by Jung's desertion![223] Be that as it may, and as you might expect, these trained analysts proved generally more committed and domesticated, if less original, than Freud's earliest band of followers. For if anything the training analysis was less concerned with the objective truth of psychoanalysis – whatever that means – than with the truth of Freud and his interminable self-analysis. Or more exactly, the new institution was concerned with simultaneously maintaining *and* eliding the tenuous link or difference between these two realms. And this because Freud himself always walked that thin borderline, careful not to upset the balance in favour of the one or the Other, the self or the science.

Freud's role as an orthodox but wild analyst is echoed throughout the literature. For instance, he once told self-proclaimed 'wild analyst' Georg Groddeck that 'I myself am a heretic who has not yet turned into a fanatic.'[224] This sort of admission is worth keeping in mind when we hear our 'orthodox' colleagues – those more orthodox than orthodoxy it(him)self – bemoan some idiosyncracy of Freud's life and work, or when they dryly claim that Freud, alas, was beset by unresolved conflict. At the same time, I am not trying to make a large claim on behalf of Freud's conscious life or freedom from neurotic conflict. My claim is much more mundane: namely, that only Freud could get away with being Freud; that only Freud could transgress the rules of psychoanalysis with absolute impunity. For this reason, some of Freud's followers would say (or complain) that 'What was permitted to Jove is not permitted to an ox'.[225]

The law it(him)self, Freud was exempt from his own regulations concerning proper conduct and technique. For instance, and in no particular order, we know that Freud adorned his office with personal items, especially antiquities, sometimes allowed patients to live in his house during short analyses, lent them books and money, accepted money for institutional affairs, told jokes and 'chattered' during sessions, rapped on the head of the couch when irritated, gossiped about colleagues, nodded off to sleep, let his chows into the office, shook hands before and after each session, offered signed photos of himself, complimented patients on their clothing, invited some for supper, left the office to urinate and, of course, habitually smoked cigars during sessions. Such is the stuff of legends – or of mausoleums.[226] 'I told him,' Hilda Doolittle states of her first impression of Freud, '[that] his room had overwhelmed and upset me. I had not expected to find him surrounded by these treasures, in a museum, a temple.'[227]

We should also recall that Freud as a clinician could be idiosyncratic, judgemental and aristocratic; never a fan of the 'furor therapeuticus',[228] at times he considered people unworthy of analysis. And thus he once refused to continue treatment of an American patient, claiming he had no unconscious! To his friend and colleague Sándor Ferenczi, Freud wrote that 'Patients are a rabble'[229]; and to Sachs he once referred aloud to patients as *die Narren*, 'the fools'.[230] Elsewhere he simply remarked that 'In the depth of my heart I can't help being convinced that my dear fellowmen, with a few exceptions, are worthless.'[231] Or again, 'that most people are stupid'.[232] Erich Fromm thus concludes that 'Freud had little love for people in general.'[233] Arguably though, and this is revealing, it is this side of Freud that intellectuals still find so compelling, especially as it expressed itself through his late speculative works.

But in what Roazen first disclosed and describes as Freud's most 'wild' piece of analysis, Freud actually analysed his own daughter Anna between 1918 and 1921 and 1924 and1925. 'If it was a matter of heresy to treat a patient sitting up, instead of lying on the couch,' Roazen wonders, 'what did it mean to analyze one's own child?'[234] Interestingly enough, in later years some of Freud's followers – including A. A. Brill, Melanie Klein, Marianne and Ernst Kris and Anna Freud – would repeat this heresy by also analysing close friends and family members. Against the fact of such wild analyses, Roazen rightly suggests that 'all these squabbles about what constitutes proper psychoanalytic technique . . . are reduced to trivia'.[235]

Julius Tandler put it this way in a private memorandum of 29 November 1931: 'He [Freud] is a person who is only accountable to his own law, who lives according to its direction and cannot subordinate himself to rules.'[236]

7.

To Be the Law Itself: Let's try to be clear about this. Freud's attempt to be his own law was always tied up with his audacious bid, his wager to *be* the borderline between subject and object, an orthodox but wild analyst, a founding father who operates as the liminal condition making possible and impossible the circle of exchange that begins *and* ends with the Father analyst. Having said that, at the same time and in the same movement, this is also Freud's bid to escape the reciprocity of that very exchange, the *counter*, since his position can no longer be identified with either term in the opposition father/son, analyst/patient, sender/receiver. At least, it cannot be identified as such in any simple or unequivocal way.

We should probably be careful here since Freud is not really engaging, as Foucault dramatically put it in another context, in a 'wager that man would be erased, like a face drawn in sand at the edge of the sea'.[237] Rather what Freud points to is his 'right to an exceptional position'.[238] 'I discovered analysis,' Freud said; 'that is enough to excuse me.'[239]

But what is, and who occupies, this exceptional position? Parroting Roazen again, Where's Freud? Outside the exchange of transference/counter-transference, a position that is rigorously understood and non-positional, Freud-the-subject is not liquidated exactly,[240] but is from the outset *generalized as the fractured structure of psychoanalysis itself*, a sort of ghost in the influencing machine. To be the law, then, is to be this irreducible structure, the chiastic container of conflict, two in one; the simultaneous condition, in other words, of reason and madness beyond the confines of the law of non-contradiction. In turn, from out of this inaugural incompleteness is fashioned the grounds upon which all subsequent institutional and therapeutic successes sit – and inevitably slip.

As the method it(him)self, the very figure of Sigmund Freud defies capture and cannot be tamed or unified into a singular method, concept, word or name. And thus we are never encountering Freud, the subject (or victim) of some unobtainable or gossipy biography, but always 'Freud' or a multiplicity of little 'Freuds'; a differentiated and deferred X, a liminal something *sous rature*. Or again, between the original subject and studied object of Sigmund Freud lies a 'Freud' as *differance*, which is to say, a 'Freud' that is radically self-deconstructive. Psychoanalysis is thus pluralized.

8.

The Crapule That Surrounds Me: Defined from within the snare of a double bind, it is perhaps no accident that the politics of psychoanalysis have been both tragic and comic, suicidal and surreal. For how could the father *be* a heretic, a bastard and still keep the family peace? Or what is the same thing, how could a disciple *be* like the father, a heretic and still keep the family peace? 'For a man to be like Freud,' Roazen writes, 'meant finally for him to be original. Yet originality ended his usefulness to Freud.'[241] Such was, according to Thomas Szasz, 'Freud's overweening selfishness and vanity. His world [was] divided into two kinds of persons: those who are useful to the "cause" and those that are not.'[242] Or as Roustang contends:

'It seems that only two solutions were available: either to stay within the mainstream, which implies accepting a permanent allegiance to Freud, or to acting independently and find oneself rejected from psychoanalysis, to cease to count for it.'[243] Of course, Freud understood this dilemma well, once stating to a patient in the late 1920s that 'the goody-goodys are no good, and the naughty ones go away'.[244] Jung, who finally had enough of this, told Freud plainly that 'your technique of treating your pupils like patients is a *blunder*'. More to the point, he asked Freud: '*Who's* got the neurosis?'[245]

With the institutionalization of psychoanalysis, it is at last no wonder that Freud looked upon his disciples, following Jung, as 'slavish sons and impudent puppies'. For Freud was always the pack-leader: 'They take a bone from the table, and chew it independently in a corner. But it is my bone!'[246] Perhaps not unlike his dogs Jofi, Lün, Wolfi or Jumbo, Freud's psychoanalytic 'bestiary' demanded 'both obedience and innovation within certain boundaries'.[247] But once faced with his grow(l)ing creation, his primal horde, Freud had 'to ask what has become of the ennobling influence of psychoanalysis on its followers'.[248]

In fact, around this time Freud was beginning to realize a central, yet horrible, truth of psychoanalysis: 'I had learnt that psychoanalysis brings out the worst in everyone.'[249] His colleagues had become, as Freud himself reported, 'the crapule that surrounds me'.[250] Evidently the psychoanalytic Republic was not the refuge he might have envisioned. Even here, perhaps especially so, '*Homo homini lupus*' – 'man is a wolf to man.'[251]

9.

Moi, je ne suis pas une Freudiste: Never much of a disciple himself, Freud once declared (only to excise the remark in later editions) that 'there is scarcely any group of ideas to which I feel so antagonistic as that of being someone's protege'.[252] Instead, Freud the father was devoured in the totem feast he prepared for his disciples, a willing sacrifice to the science he embodied. For in his followers he might live on, paradoxically, as their unforgettable father–ghost, the signified space of death, the spirit of guilt, finally, the only-analyst-that-matters.

But like many innovators, Freud never wanted to be his own follower, an all too common 'Freudian'. As he once told Theodor Reik: 'Moi, je ne suis pas une Freudiste.'[253] Neither son nor father to himself, Freud's life and work thus reveals a most precious (though entirely open) secret: *Me, Sigmund Freud, I don't follow him/me*. Alienated from himself in this way, from the self-same, Freud was always his own impossible condition of psychoanalysis, his own Other (recalling Gay), what we used to call the abyss itself. Positioned in (or as) this unrepresentable space between, Freud therefore remains father *and* son, everywhere *and* nowhere, no one *and* everyone. As a result, one is quite unable to answer Roazen's timely though inherently logocentric question – Where's Freud? – except through a strategy of deconstruction, one whereby the proper name of Sigmund Freud is deferred and displaced as yet another in a list of undecidables. Here in this non-place – (w)here?! – one both can and cannot submit to, less forget, Freud's audacious wager to live on through his science. At least I can't; for if you haven't already guessed, I too am not a regular *Freudiste*.

But, then again, who really is – or isn't?

10.

Ce sont les mort qu'il faut qu'on tue. Finally, then, this modest act of parricide, this wild and hyperbolic analysis, has been unavoidable and only reflects a kind of faithfulness to the irreducible legends of Freud and his followers. As Ellis advised, it reflects a faithfulness to Freud's example but hardly his precepts. To this end I have only given Freud and his followers, our charming Prince Hamlets, the whippings they demand and deserve. For, as Borch-Jacobsen submits, 'Sometimes you have to kill your father to preserve his heritage. Sometimes you have to throw away the doctrine to find its "meaning".'[254] Or as Nietzsche's Zarathustra says, 'One repays a teacher badly if one always remains nothing but a pupil.'[255] With this in mind, even if psychoanalysis, like biography, has all along been committed to lies, concealments, hypocrisy, flattery and even to hiding its own lack of understanding, even if psychoanalytic truth doesn't exist, it has in any case been good for *something* . . .

Whittshhh.

5 Jacques What's-His-Name: Death, Memory and Archival Sickness

Just as Freud's theory of the death drive, first announced in *Beyond the Pleasure Principle* in 1920, undermines classical psychoanalysis from within, Jacques Derrida's deconstruction does its work from the inside of classical philosophy. It is perhaps not surprising, then, that Derrida returns again and again to Freud's death drive theory, which, on the surface at least, has the makings of a radical self-critique. And so the late Freud has a proto-deconstructive streak.

Or so the story goes. Naturally we are left to wonder if it is an accurate or fair story, or just a bed-time story told by deconstructionists for deconstructionists. To help formulate an answer to this question of fair or unfair interpretation – a political question – I will provide a cursory overview of the role of the death drive in deconstruction, and then get to the business of assessing the place of memory in the crypts we usually call museums and archives.

Deconstructive Cancer

Since deconstruction always operates from within a given structure or system of thought, be it psychoanalytical or otherwise, some commentators have described it as a parasitical practice. '[A]ll I have done,' as Derrida himself admits, 'is dominated by the thought of a virus, what could be called a parasitology, a virology, the virus being many things.'[256] Of course, the semiotic bar separating inessential parasite from essential host is far from determined or fixed in Derrida's work. For Derrida both displaces the assumed separation between parasite and host and affirms the absolute necessity of the excluded supplement; the one makes no sense without the other. The deconstructionist as parasite can just as usefully describe it as a kind of 'bastard' offspring of the history of philosophy. Once again, Derrida says as much – this time in *Glas*, an experimental work on Genet and Hegel – wherein he poses the crucial question of whether or not there is room for (the history of) Judaism, the excluded Other, within the developmental structure of Western Christianity in general, and in Hegel's work in particular. Derrida thus follows what he calls 'a bastard course' while asking a fundamental question: 'Is there a place for the bastard in ontotheology or in the Hegelian family?'[257] Arguably this is a guiding concern for Derrida, who happens to have been born a Jew in Algeria.[258]

The importance of Hegel's phenomenology for the strategy of deconstruction can hardly be underestimated, and is especially relevant given the various dialectical interpretations of Freud's dualistic thought that proliferate in the secondary literature. As Derrida repeatedly argues, deconstruction inhabits 'philosophical opposition, resisting and disorganizing it, *without ever* constituting a third term, without ever leaving room for a solution in the form of speculative dialectics'.[259] And thus, for example, Derrida exploits in Freud's *Beyond the Pleasure Principle* a speculative style of reasoning that appears to take logical steps but in fact goes nowhere. Since there is no resolution of conflict in *Beyond*, nothing is accomplished save for the analysis itself qua analysis – as a kind of work for its own sake. Or rather, as Derrida argues in 'To Speculate – On "Freud"', it is work for the sake of Freud himself, who is understood as conterminous with his creation. Freud thus represents nothing but himself in *Beyond*, and to that extent throws psychoanalytic objectivity to the wind: to do psychoanalysis is to 'do' Freud, a conclusion with rather dire political and emotional consequences for the followers of psychoanalysis. As Derrida nicely has it, Papa Freud pulls on the strings-sons (in French, *fils*) and attempts to make them do his bidding. He sends them to and fro, like puppets and playthings, thus performing (like an experimental artist) one of the most famous scenes in all of psychoanalytic literature: the fort/da game of his grandson, little Ernst. Such is Derrida's often sophisticated, playful analysis of the theory of 'repetition compulsion' as it was reformulated in 1920.

Derrida's deconstruction of Western metaphysics hinges on the problem of representation as correspondence without failure (i.e., without supplement, contamination or excess), as the ring or circuit that traditionally binds and separates, for example, master and slave, speech and writing, Form and substance, mind and body, signified and signifier, unconscious and conscious, thesis and antithesis, Being and becoming, etc. More exactly, Derrida deconstructs the idealized relation between these classical binary oppositions, and to undermine the various methodologies – be they dialectic, hermeneutic or psychoanalytic – that claim to mediate such opposition. Of course, interpretation as transcendence is an old story of 'good' versus 'evil', however defined: Plato drew his Divided Line, separating authentic truth from mimetic falsity, philosopher King from poet, in the erection of an ideal Republic; Descartes effaced sceptical doubt in the clear and distinct idea of the rational subject whose existence was guaranteed by self-conscious awareness, *cogito ergo sum*; Hegel ordered and resolved the conflictual history of thought, of *Geist*, through the cunning of a rational history made known to the retrospection of an Absolute Knower; Heidegger cleared an opening wherein the forgotten question of Being, and with it the ontological difference between Being and beings, lay unconcealed and thus recalled; and Freud cured the hysteric by bridging the gap between the repressed memory (or later, the wish) and the inexplicable symptom, the unconscious reality and the conscious illusion. In its various manifestations the history of Western philosophy is, in other words, a repetitious tale of the quest to ground truth in the transparency of a method somehow high above or deep below the surface of everyday life. And so the interminable debate about interpretation has always been entangled in a history of religion, religious feeling and 'ontotheological' presuppositions about human existence.

Derrida is the bastard philosopher in this melodrama, someone who disturbs its history from within; the bastard who might easily be mistaken for a cancer, if not, from the perspective of Anglo-American philosophy, the death knell of Western reason. Deconstruction thus has a strange affinity for Freud's unruly theory of the cancerous death drive. For, quite simply, both de-structure the system within which they operate.

If we accept the idea that deconstruction, like its famous neologism *differance*, is not a 'word', 'concept' or 'method' – at least not in any conventional sense – it is because such parasitology, in its most rigorous formulation, *has no content*. Instead, deconstruction is always dictated by the particular text in question and under erasure. From within the structure, Derrida de-structures. Metaphysics fails, or approached the other way around, deconstruction succeeds, because of the 'ultimate pretensions to self-foundation' found in metaphysical structures[260]; because of the pretension that a text can be a host without parasites, its health a reflection of its native purity. And so, like many, many other commentators, Derrida often recalls the strong impulse in Freud's work that rejects philosophy in order to protect its own originality as an autobiographical science. The papa stands alone holding all the strings.

If Freud tries to make psychoanalysis debt-free, that is, objectively true yet grounded in his singular subjectivity, Derrida is perfectly happy to be his dogged bill collector. At its best Derrida's deconstruction is a work of textual analysis that foregrounds and explodes the narcissistic conceit of *causa sui*, of the self-made man that Freud dreamed of being for his followers.

Of course, exasperated critics throw up their hands and ask what this strategy for reading texts leaves us with. If Freud is not the papa of psychoanalysis, the actual ground, then who is? What next for the (willing or unwilling) heirs of Freud? For his part Derrida has been very explicit about the affirmative aspect of this work, and has rather convincingly explained away the charge of being apolitical or nihilistic. Unfortunately, though, Derrida often flirts with a kind of self-referentiality that undermines his case, where unchecked self-reference can and does produce the appearance of a self-satisfied, self-absorbed, and even self-caused discourse – the very discourse of the self-made, self-sufficient man that Derrida usually deconstructs. And so the nagging problem of deconstruction and politics pops up yet again.

While self-indulgence isn't always a problem in Derrida's work, it can get him into trouble – the kind of *trouble de archive* found in his book of 1995, *Archive Fever: A Freudian Impression*. Although this book has the appearance of a ghost story, it is one in which Derrida never manages to conjure up the spirit of Sigmund Freud. Instead, and as I will now argue, the great critic of subjectivity conjures up little more than his own famous self. Let's turn to this work with an ear to the politics of the archive, and with an eye on Derrida's stakes therein.

Autoeconomy and the Anarchivic 'Beyond'

> Who wants to substitute him- or herself for Freud's phantom? How can one not want to, as well?
>
> (Jacques Derrida, *Archive Fever*[261])

That Derrida implicates his own subject position in his more recent, experimental works of deconstruction is by now a hallmark of post-modernist scholarship. At times this strategy is more or less successful, as in his 1980 essay, 'To Speculate – On "Freud"', briefly discussed above. But on occasion Derrida's self-involvement in the text being deconstructed is distracting and even self-indulgent. More to the point, the later Derrida seems less and less interested in the text in question than in repeating some old deconstructive insights, scoring points with other theorists, or even appropriating another's symbolic capital to himself. One of the most unfortunate aspects of this turn in Derrida's work is a renewed suspicion that deconstruction is not, after all, very attuned to politics in general, and to the politics of knowledge in particular. Or, perhaps more simply, it underscores the usual hazards associated with fame, including a bloated sense of self.

Archive Fever is in this respect a cautionary tale. Derrida notes at the outset that *Archive Fever* is the text of a lecture delivered at The Freud Museum on 5 June 1994, during an international conference called 'Memory: The Question of Archives'. What he does not mention, here or elsewhere, are the circumstances leading up to the conference. It is a familiar story: mired in debt, the Museum enlists the help of its well-connected French cousin, partisan historian Elisabeth Roudinesco, who embarks on a fundraising campaign in France. As a reward for her diligence, she is allowed to organize a conference at the Museum.

Now, there is obviously no shame in rallying the troops in a time of financial crisis, even when the cause is a dying one like psychoanalysis. What is shameful, however, is the Museum's record, first, with regard to memory and, second, with regard to its French cousins. It was only a few years earlier, from 26–8 October 1990, that the Program Director of the Freud Museum Sonu Shamdasani and his assistant Michael Münchow organized a colloquium called 'Speculations: Appraising Psychoanalysis, Philosophy and Cultural Studies'. Basically a Continental affair, the participants included Sarah Kofman, David Farell Krell and Mikkel Borch-Jacobsen. The Museum, though, was not impressed by the company, and just a few days later Shamdasani and Münchow were canned – along with Museum Director, Richard Wells. Subsequently the Museum, claiming ownership of the disowned conference papers, tried and failed to block their publication of the collected edition, *Speculations After Freud*. Given the Museum's deplorable record in these regards and others, its sponsorship of a conference devoted to memory is a trifle cynical, to say the least. Moreover, such cynicism reflects rather badly upon those intellectuals who, running blindly to the rescue, lend their names to the psychoanalytic cause without problematizing the censorship that promotes the everyday deformation of memory.

While the politics of the psychoanalytic archive can, with some effort, be read into Derrida's discussion of '*mal d'archive*', it is not really what his text on the archival sickness is all about. Early in

Archive Fever, Derrida explores the various techniques of information processing, from the postal system to e-mail, that produce even as they record information.[262] Similarly, Derrida is interested in how the psyche writes and is written, is archival and archived. To this end Derrida recalls the *Wunderblock*, a writing apparatus with which Freud substantiates or materializes the psyche, and which first caught his attention in an old essay of 1967, 'Freud and the Scene of Writing'. If Freud thinks that 'Man has, as it were, become a kind of prosthetic God',[263] Derrida insists that this is always already the case: the psyche is *ex-tendre* and essentially prosthetic. The archival psyche is also for Derrida, following Freud, problematized by a self-destructive force. To this end Derrida invokes his favourite text of Freud's, *Beyond the Pleasure Principle*, and the death drive theory announced therein. And thus in *Archive Fever* he argues that the archive is haunted by 'archive fever', which is to say, it is possessed by a death drive: 'the death drive is above all *anarchivic*, one could say, or *archiviolithic*'.[264] Just as there is nothing outside the text that can guarantee meaning, *il n'y a pas de hors-texte*, there is no '*meta-archive*'[265] that can prevent this fever. Alas, at the heart of the *arkheion*, an official house of records, sits an ex-house or, better, an out-house. Derrida as usual sets up shop in this (non-) space, and works to give the archive, and at times the reader, a splitting headache – maybe a fever.

Derrida's original lecture at The Freud Museum was called 'The Concept of the Archive: A Freudian Impression'. This is a more accurate title than *Archive Fever*, since Derrida has obviously produced a deconstruction of the *concept* of the archive – if not, in the spirit of grammatology, a 'general archiviology'[266] – and not, I think unfortunately, something about the everyday politics of the archive. Derrida doesn't *do* archival work, doesn't step into the Freud archives, read an unpublished letter, sneeze upon the dust, or choke upon the corruptions that are the bricks and mortar of the history of psychoanalysis. While there is no doubt that Derrida is aware of these old and ongoing scandals – his wife Marguerite is, after all, an analyst – he mostly recalls his own corpus in *Archive Fever*, thus making of the concept 'archive' yet another philosophically unde-cidable notion of deconstruction. As he puts it, 'the concept of the archive must invariably carry in itself, as does every concept, an unknowable weight'.[267] Needless to say, if 'every concept' is so com-promised, then why keep repeating this old saw with every concept that comes along? In any case, it is obviously business as usual in *Archive Fever*: Derrida adds the word 'archive' to a formidable list of 'undecidables' that already includes (in no particular order) *differ-ance, pharmakon, supplement, remainder, hymen, trace, écriture, marge, entame, parergon, gram, spacing, incision, reserve, blank, écart, envois, aporia, hinge* and so on *ad nauseum*. As provocative as this game can be, Derrida at times seems to *speak* the archive – ironically, given his famous critique of Foucault – and, worse, to speak *for* the archive.

It is true, and uncharacteristically so, that Derrida does pay sustained tribute to someone who happens to haunt archives. In fact, much of *Archive Fever* is consumed with archiving the effects of Derrida's own encounter with Yosef Hayim Yerushalmi's 1991 book, *Freud's Moses: Judaism Terminable and Interminable*. And actually the more interesting parts of *Archive Fever* consist of a long book review. Not surprisingly, Derrida's review is a deconstruction of Yerushalmi's position as a traditional historian and keeper of the archive. He is, for example, captivated by 'the joint [situated] between truth and fiction'[268] that Yerushalmi exposes when he closes his book with a fictional letter to Freud. 'I cannot imagine a better introduction to the question of the archive,' Derrida states, 'than the very stakes of this vertiginous difference [i.e., between truth and fiction].' Derrida's deconstruction: Yerushalmi's 'entire book is in advance contained, as if carried away, drawn in, engulfed by the abysmal element of the [closing, fictional] "Monologue"'.[269]

Of great importance to Derrida is Yerushalmi's discussion of whether or not psychoanalysis is a 'Jewish science' – an old, and sometimes racist, charge made against Freud.[270] While Derrida is sympathetic to Yerushalmi's argument that Freudian psychoanalysis is indeed a Jewish science, he is at the same time careful to endorse

Yerushalmi's passing remark that the very terms 'Jewish' and 'science' are not really assignable in any simple, *a priori* way. Derrida therefore 'trembles',[271] and rightly so, before Yerushalmi's contradictory claims about the supposed essence of Jewishness: on the one hand, the Jew is open to the future while, on the other, he is a keeper of the past. Yet if Derrida properly deconstructs the violent, presumptive metaphysics of 'the *One*' and 'the *Unique*',[272] he comes dangerously close to instituting this violence in his own name and autobiography at various places in *Archive Fever*. It is not just that Derrida speaks far too much about himself in this book – 'On a beautiful morning in California a few weeks ago, I asked myself a certain question, among many others'[273]; or again, 'By chance, I wrote these last words on the edge of Vesuvius, right near Pompeii, less than eight days ago'[274] – or tends to cite from his own work more and more often, but that he sometimes appears to speak to, and write of, no one but himself. Indeed, when archived by Derrida, Yerushalmi's question to Freud about the Jewish science sounds more like a question of, to, and for *Derrida* concerning the 'Jewish science' called deconstruction.

Why is that? Among other reasons, because this troublesome question posed to Freud by Yerushalmi (about the Jewish science) is a question that has been posed to Derrida, in his case by Jürgen Habermas – just as Yerushalmi's question of Freud was also once posed to Freud (in 1926) by Enrico Morselli.[275] This appropriation of the Other to the ends of deconstruction, which in my opinion is no longer deconstructive, is the very *coup de théâtre*, the dramatic twist, that Derrida recalls of Freud and then re-enacts himself, or for himself, as when he writes: 'Freud pretended to speak of someone else, of a colleague. (If I were to be immodest to such a point, doubly immodest, I would say that he did what I am doing in speaking of a colleague, Yerushalmi, while I am speaking of myself).'[276] In passages like these Derrida seems possessed by an evil genius that makes it impossible for him to distinguish between himself, the father of deconstruction, and Freud, the father of psychoanalysis. From a deconstructive perspective I have no trouble with this potentially interesting confusion. The '*trouble de l'archive*' only begins when Derrida-deconstruction looms over, above, and outside this Other, Freud-psychoanalysis. When this happens, the Derrida machine functions like an archi-prosthetic device that denies in advance the Other his or her otherness. But in this vein let's not ignore the simple fact that the father of deconstruction is *not* the father of psychoanalysis.

The dangers I am discussing are, I think, endemic to Derrida's later, more playful works of deconstruction – what Frank Kermode critically calls Derrida's 'ludic',[277] perhaps as opposed to lucid, writings. Derrida is no doubt aware of the charge. Having just cited a passage from himself in another essay on Freud, Derrida notes the following:

> If I quote this book [of mine], I do so because I find it included in the program of our encounter . . . Don't accuse me, therefore, of being, as you say in English, 'self-centered.' In truth I always dreamt of writing a *self-centered* text; I never arrived at that point – I always fall upon the others.[278]

Derrida's defence of himself is that there is no secure subject position from which he could possibly speak of, to, and for himself: the proper name of 'Jacques Derrida' is thus placed under the erasure of quotation marks. On the one hand Derrida is right. But on the other, this self-defence of the decentred self is just another trap – in part a contradiction, in part hypocrisy – that conveniently shuts down critique of Derrida even before it begins.

Whatever the value of this Derridean autoeconomy, which I often admire as intellectual *haute couture*, it is a scandal from the perspective of historical research. It is not just that autoeconomy tends to be as interesting as someone else's dream – namely, not interesting at all – but that this dream, even when it speaks of and for the Other, for example, for Freud and Yerushalmi, *is not history*. At best, and not to deny this intriguing possibility, it is telepathy, or fiction, or what Derrida calls the '*truth of delusion*'.[279] Yet with all due respect

for the figments of the deconstructive imagination, if Derrida wants
to turn a page on Freud and Judaism, he *surely* needs to open more
than one or two books in this regard. The restriction of his analysis
to Yerushalmi's archive (which quickly becomes his own) is tantamount to a suppression of the many other memories, books and
archives that also deal with Freud and Judaism.[280] French intellectuals are, of course, famous, or infamous, for dispensing with such
memories, otherwise called citations. It is a practice that can easily
slip into selective or even false memories. I am reminded here of
something David Bakan once told me when asked about his
landmark book of 1958, *Sigmund Freud and the Jewish Mystical
Tradition*. Without judging their credibility, let me submit his
remarks of 19 July 1996 to the public archive:

> So many people take and write with no acknowledgement. For
> instance, in this new book called *The God's Phallus*, the author
> Howard Eilberg-Schwartz has simply drawn, holis bolis, from my
> work. He has one reference to my work, where he cites some
> minor point. But I am not even listed in the Name Index. *Holis
> bolis* [chuckling]. There is a similar situation with the Yerushalmi
> [1991] and Rice [1990] books. Somebody ought to write a story
> about this: the Yerushalmi book is almost completely stolen from
> the Rice book, and the Rice book is stolen from my book.[281]

Still – better robbed than ignored! Bakan is at least right about this
much: stories must be told. For if memory is repetition, as Derrida
often insists, then we should probably repeat as many stories as
possible – including even gossip and tall-tales – when invoking the
relative merits and limitations of memory. And this brings us back
to the representation of psychoanalysis in Derrida's work, and to the
politics of the archive.

'Of course,' Derrida is careful to emphasize in his very first
footnote to *Archive Fever*, 'the question of a politics of the archive
is our permanent orientation here, even if the time of a lecture
does not permit us to treat this directly and with examples.'[282] How

convenient. To put it as frankly as possible, isn't the 'time of a lecture' without examples – permanently oriented towards indirection – a kind of empty, ahistorical and, worse, forgettable time? Derrida certainly spent a lot of timeless time delivering this uncanny lecture for the Freudian out-house. Time enough, no doubt, to *make* the time. For the sake of memory.

So Derrida's 'Freudian impression' is indeed impressive: it is a coin stamped on both sides, *yes, yes*, with his own image and signature. Appropriately enough, such 'doubly immodest' self-affirmation reminds me of an old yarn. When told that his book on Kant was not very good, Heidegger supposedly said that 'It may not be good Kant, but it is excellent Heidegger.' Similarly, and without putting words into Derrida's mouth, *Archive Fever* may not be good Freud, but it is excellent 'Derrida'.

Ho-hum. Yawn. We no longer need Derrida to 'do' himself, a practice that has become a bore for spectators. So maybe it is time for more fresh appraisals of Derrida's work – especially from specialists in the many fields in which Derrida sets up shop as an eager parasite. In the case of Freud studies, I would argue that he has made genuine contributions. However, that contribution is limited not only by Derrida's ahistorical methodology, but by his own more recent failures as a deconstructionist of the subject – beginning, unfortunately, with his own position as the great papa of deconstruction. In the end fame may prove to be the hardest nut of all to crack.

6 Gossip, Fiction and the History of Psychoanalysis: An Open Letter

n.d.

Dear Colleague,

If I often insist upon the role of gossip in the history (of the history) of psychoanalysis, it is not because the wild and prurient is more valid than the conventional views espoused by our orthodox colleagues. For although gossip is certainly more interesting than what sometimes passes as orthodox history, it is not for that reason any more legitimate or true. Just the same, gossip is valuable to the extent that it exposes a desire – an illicit desire, I think, that exceeds first, the clinical setting, second, the analytic community, and third, the history of psychoanalysis.

Now, if I ask you, as we say in English, 'to take my word for it', you can bet that I have a bit of gossip to recount. It has been suggested that this piece of desire – mine, but also that of some others – deserves to be circulated, even if we dispense with the protocols of proof, permission and copyright. And so here is my tale, one that touches upon the problem of fiction in the history of psychoanalysis.

Not long ago I procured permission from the Sigmund Freud Copyrights (SFC) to reproduce a postcard from Freud to Lacan for the cover of a collection of essays I was preparing. Upon this little postcard of 1933 – which I received from Peter Swales who, I was told, had received it from Jacques-Alain Miller, Lacan's son-in-law –

Freud briefly acknowledges the receipt of Lacan's dissertation. It was, as far as I knew, the only response Freud had given Lacan. However, an Archivist with the SFC informed me (9 May 1995) that Freud had, in fact, also written a long letter to Lacan on the same date as the postcard. Like the postcard, it made its first appearance in the French journal *Ornicar?*, though in a later issue in 1985. Since I had never seen or even heard of this letter before; I asked the Archivist to send me a copy; I also mentioned that the letter should be translated into English, and that I could probably track someone down for the job. Shortly thereafter I received a copy of the Freud–Lacan letter, which was duly stamped as a document of the SFC Archive. My helpful correspondent suggested (31 May 1995) that an English translation should be based upon the original letter, presumably written in German, and that I would have to locate this myself. Apparently the Archive was holding only the French translation of the letter from *Ornicar?*, which was authored by the Argentinean psychoanalyst Roberto Harari.

Freud's letter was very long indeed, at least in Harari's translation, covering more than seven pages with the kind of detailed commentary on Lacan that I didn't expect. After all, Freud didn't know Lacan, and had by this time withdrawn from close contact with his professional colleagues. Despite my surprise, which bordered on suspicion, I did not read the letter carefully; and, actually, since it came from the Archive, I immediately circulated it to a few interested colleagues. Consequently it wasn't until Mikkel Borch-Jacobsen contacted me that I learned that the letter was a fabrication; evidently, Harari admits as much in the letter's 'Epilogue'. Borch-Jacobsen, who once created a small scandal of his own with some fictional letters, was quick to remind me that the SFC had inadvertently passed off Harari's fiction as the real thing. So, shortly thereafter, I let Harari know that his literary efforts had found a distinguished place among the documents of the SFC Archive. For his part, Harari suggested that I record this little episode for posterity – hence this open letter.[283]

If embarrassment is at the heart of this tale, it is only because it is

echoed throughout the history of psychoanalysis as error, misrepre-
sentation, fiction and fraud. And this, I think, is quite unavoidable.
For how can we separate Freud's incomplete self-analysis from his
self-promotional histories? More critically, how can psychoanalysis
extricate itself from the fact that reality was given a secondary status
after Freud dropped the Seduction Theory in 1897? And to what
extent are the various histories, orthodox and revisionist, contaminated by these problematics? Who among us, finally, can tame the evil
genius of psychoanalysis?

If, as I would argue, there is no reasoning with this evil genius,
then there is also no extrication from this epistemological mess.
Consequently, it may be time that we found room within psychoanalysis for interminable disagreements over, say, 'the fictitious case
of Tausk contra Freud', Freud's affair with Minna, fake book reviews
of Freud's work and fictional letters. In other words we need a place,
even a committee, within psychoanalysis to serve and protect the
unwritten history of gossip, fiction, and wild biography.

To this end I recommend we consider the unsuspecting SFC
Archive.

Of course, since purists on both sides of the ideological fence will
balk at this idea, it would be best to keep this scandalous business
strictly between friends. For upon hearing of our gossip the SFC
Archive will only purge its records, leaving nothing of interest for us
to discuss in the future. So let us promise – for Harari's sake, and for
the sake of gossip – that our lips, like so many Freud documents,
will remain tightly sealed until sometime in 2020. And if anybody
asks us about Harari's fictitious letter, just tell them the original was,
well, *purloined*.

Yours Truly,

T. Dufresne

7 The Politics of Representing Freud: A Short Account of a Media War, This Time With Feeling

Since cancellation of an exhibit is the easiest response to bitter and heated controversy, cynics may be surprised that the Freud exhibit at the Library of Congress (LoC) ever happened. We have certainly grown accustomed to expect the worst of these affairs. After all, similar controversies about representation and inclusiveness toppled the 'Out of Africa' and 'Enola Gay' exhibits once planned for the Royal Ontario Museum and the Smithsonian respectively. And so a brief history of this rare and, indeed, happy turn of events deserves to be recounted, especially since the sparks that flew are likely to fly again whenever it is a question of representing Freud in a public venue.

The mostly quiet debate over the LoC exhibit took a fateful turn in December 1995, when it was abruptly 'postponed'. In what seemed a face-saving gesture, Librarian of Congress James H. Billington claimed that budget considerations alone had forced the postponement. Yet the timing of the announcement suggested otherwise, following closely upon the heels of criticism aired in the (now defunct) gossipy magazine of academic life, *Lingua Franca*. Already attuned to the sensationalistic politics of exhibits, the LoC decision was immediately picked up as fodder for the front pages of *The Washington Post* and *The International Herald Tribune*. Soon thereafter the debate deepened, media coverage widened, and positions hardened between friends and foes of psychoanalysis.

Called 'Sigmund Freud: Conflict and Culture', the exhibit was organized in three sections – historical, theoretical/practical and cultural – and was slated to include the display of Freudiana. In addition to including pop paraphernalia, such as snippets of *The Simpsons*, the exhibit promised Freud's couch, a selection of his antiquities, photographs, prints, films and original manuscripts and letters. Also organized were workshops for educators, a conference, and a catalogue of essays on Freud from over a dozen analysts and scholars, such as Peter Gay, Harold Blum, John Forrester and Michael Molnar. Initially projected for the Fall of 1996, the LoC exhibition promised to be the largest Freud retrospective ever mounted.

Critics charged, however, that the exhibit tables were unfairly loaded to favour Freud and psychoanalysis. They argued not only that the symposium excluded any real dissenting voices, but that partisan interests were manipulating the exhibit from influential positions behind the scenes. Dissenting voices gathered momentum after independent researcher Peter Swales, a well-known sleuth of psychoanalytic history, was excluded from the symposium; although Swales informally assisted the guest curator, Michael Roth, by providing advice and information for the exhibit, his brand of critical Freud scholarship wasn't welcome – at least in the light of day. In response, and despite their own obvious differences, an initial group of forty-two critics signed a petition against the exhibit – myself included. Ultimately the number of petitioners sat at over fifty. Among the signatories are included some of the most respected figures (historians, philosophers and analysts) in the field, including Swales, Mikkel Borch-Jacobsen, Frank Cioffi, Frederick Crews, Allen Esterson, Phyllis Grosskurth, Adolf Grünbaum, Robert Holt, Malcolm Macmillan, Frank Sulloway and even Freud's own grand-daughter, Sophie Freud.

The unfolding affair took a number of interesting twists during the following months. As controversy brewed, Borch-Jacobsen was belatedly invited to participate in the catalogue. Borch-Jacobsen, though, refused to play the role of token critic – or martyr. As a consequence, more than one scholar scolded Borch-Jacobsen for stoking the flames of discontent. In an e-mail response of 1 September

1995, Borch-Jacobsen defended himself against one such critic, arguing that Roth's seemingly neutral position was compromised by partisan interests. 'That Michael Roth,' writes Borch-Jacobsen, 'was not able to overrule the objections of his advisory panel [concerning Swales] was a clear indication that the real organizers of this exhibit were the representatives of the major orthodox psychoanalytic institutions (Freud Archives, Freud House, etc.). Like you, I have been working in this field for twenty years now, and I know what that means: BLACK LISTS. . . . I have no patience for that anymore, and if these people want to play that kind of game, I am not going to be a player. It is as simple as that.' As the acrimony escalated with every new phone call, e-mail message, letter, radio interview and newspaper and magazine article, names like Swales and Gay became convenient shorthand for all that is either good or bad about the current state of Freud studies.

While the exclusion of dissenting opinion was enough to make critics shake their heads, it was disturbing news about finance that impelled them to draft and sign the petition. Having agreed to match funds with the Sigmund Freud Society (SFS) in Vienna, the LoC committed itself to pledge approximately US$250,000; apparently the SFS garnered this sum from the Austrian government, which was eager to present its best face to the American public. In addition, substantial donations were pledged from a number of well-heeled patients of psychoanalysis, and by The Mary Sigorney Charitable Trust established in 1989 by the estate of Mary Sigorney to support various psychoanalytic activities. Recent funds have apparently come from 'private sources', in addition to the Lotte Kohler Foundation and The American Psychoanalytic Foundation. In short, it seemed to critics that exhibit organizers were buying themselves some desperately needed good press by washing their dirty-linen under the auspices of a public institution. As psychoanalyst Harold Blum rather bluntly put it at the San Francisco Congress of The International Psychoanalytic Association at the end of July 1995, the exhibit would appear 'under the virtual sponsorship of the United States government'. Aimed at an audience estimated at over one million, consumer confidence would presumably increase, and people would reconsider a therapy they had largely abandoned since the sixties.

For the record: petitioners had simply argued that a publicly funded exhibit should reflect a diversity of informed opinion about the legacy of psychoanalysis, rather than the narrow orthodoxy of a special interest group. Similarly, petitioners resented the attempt by partisan organizers to appropriate the symbolic capital of an august and (presumably) neutral institution to fit a private agenda and, indirectly, help line their own pockets. In this respect, many critics suspected that taxpayers in both Austria and the United States had been hoodwinked by the international psychoanalytic establishment. In an interview for CBC Radio, Swales thus likened criticism of the LoC exhibit to a form of 'consumer protection'. Still, the cancellation of the show in December 1995 was unexpected by everyone involved, including the critics. Despite the media hype, at no point did the petitioners demand the show's cancellation, or imagine that the organizers would make of the debate a veritable battleground for raising the profile of the exhibit.

It is certainly no accident that the LoC, which holds the world's largest collection of Freud materials, became the site of this media war. In exchange for a treasure trove of important historical documents from The Sigmund Freud Archives, Inc., the LoC has allowed Officers of that Archive to impose arbitrary restrictions on the subsequent availability of material. As a result, the public has long been denied access to those documents, parts of which are restricted until the fantastic date of 2113 (series ZR). In this way the LoC has become an unwitting accomplice to years of conservative censorship by the analytic establishment. It is in this context that scholars have for years reproached the psychoanalytic establishment for its flagrant disregard for historically objective, non-partisan scholarship.

Thus it was an unexpected irony to read that Roth, Elisabeth Roudinesco and some others were accusing the *critics* of the exhibit of censoring the free flow of information. The American Psycho-

analytic Association formed a 'Task Force to Monitor Freud Exhibit'
– what Frederick Crews calls 'a slander campaign' designed 'to depict
petitioners as enemies of free speech'. Crews and Swales in particular were singled out for attack, critics dressing up their *ad hominem*
attacks in the analytic garb of parricide, resistance, transference and
so on. In France the rhetoric was even less restrained – no doubt as
a consequence of their continued ignorance of critical work
published on Freud, mostly in English, over the last thirty years. In
France the petitioners were variously described as Freud bashers,
Nazis, ayatollahs and politically correct Americans. One reviewer
even described Borch-Jacobsen as a 'negationist', a loaded word
normally reserved for deniers of the *Holocaust*. Borch-Jacobsen,
naturally outraged, sent off a stinging retort that appeared in
Évolution Psychiatrique. Meanwhile, Roudinesco circulated to the
French intellectual elite a less than honest description of events in
the backwaters of ugly America; a description which doubled as a
petition against the original petitioners. Given this distorted
portrayal, 180 (mostly French) intellectuals signed Roudinesco's
petition, among them such luminaries as Julia Kristeva, Etienne
Balibar, Jean Laplanche and Jean-Bertrand Pontalis. As if things
couldn't get much worse for the exhibit critics, media venues such as
The New York Times began to hedge their bets with Roth and Co. –
all of which proved that a good news story, just like a dream, can be
subject to the most bizarre, if catachrestic, interpretations. Of course
these sorts of tactics, reminiscent of the McCarthy-era witch hunts,
did not shock anyone familiar with the history of psychoanalysis.
Such reversals have always formed the backbone of analytic interpretation within the psychoanalytic movement, where an
impeccable logical tradition of 'heads I win, tales you lose' has
become an almost unbeatable stratagem for dispensing with The
Enemy – all the while buttressing the lost cause of psychoanalysis.

   Yet it is precisely the advancement of the Cause that was at the
heart of the LoC debate, where psychoanalysis proved that it has less
in common with therapy and medicine than with politics and persuasion; and where inept doctors of the soul became adept and

mendacious spin-doctors of the media. Cast in a twilight where ethics becomes politics, the ironies multiplied to the point where the slanderous media spins by the analytic establishment themselves became the best reason for rethinking Freud and psychoanalysis. As always, *caveat emptor*, the Freudians continue to be their own worst enemies.

It should be admitted that minor adjustments to the exhibit were indeed made. While no critical voice was invited to the exhibit conference, three of the original petitioners were invited to contribute essays to the catalogue, which has since appeared: Oliver Sacks, Adolf Grünbaum and Frank Cioffi. But what has really changed as a result of the media war? Not much. Critical voices in psychoanalytic studies are tolerated only on the condition that they be ignored. In a personal communication, one critic put a recent experience this way: 'As the only speaker among two dozen who had anything negative to say, I was largely ignored or patronized. Typical comment: "I admire your courage." Translation: "You have your head up your ass, but at least you aren't afraid of the dark."'

And this translation rather succinctly, if bluntly, captures the spirit of the current debate about the legacy of Freud: Who has their head where and, better yet, why? As the 'Freud wars' begin to wane, I am guessing that this inherently political question will inform the judgement of posterity.

8 *Funny Business: The Cartoon Seminar of Jacques Lacan*

The addition in 1995 of Jacques Lacan to the pantheon of luminaries published in Icon Book's popular 'documentary cartoon' series must have raised a few eyebrows.[284] It is not just that Lacan theorized the impossibility of 'the subject supposed to know' only to be cast in that very role by his devoted followers – *Lacan est l'icône* – but also that, for Lacan, understanding never came so cheap. 'The mistake', as Lacan put it of television, lies in the very idea 'of speaking so as to be understood by idiots'.[285] The author and artist of *Lacan For Beginners*, psychoanalyst Darian Leader and illustrator Judy Groves, are aware of the discrepancy between holy writ and unholy reception, truth and screen. And so on the first page of the book, just opposite the credits, they place the following words in Lacan's smug-looking, cartoon-speaking mouth: 'Be wary of the image.'

Of course, such a brazen warning does nothing to stop the reader from venturing inside to take a look around. For in fact the warning is also an advertisement: like a curse etched large upon a Pharaoh's tomb, the ad appeals to the grave robber in each of us. Or, more exactly, the warning follows the dictates of desire, namely, the desire for the object of the other's desire – in this particular case, the desire to understand something about Lacan's desire through the veiled desire of some others. For me, then, it is this book – at once object *petit a* and short session – that drops into place between desire and its impossible fulfilment as *The Cartoon Seminar of Jacques Lacan*.

Golden Idols

Freud once said that 'The sand in almost every river contains gold, the question is whether there is enough gold to make it worth exploiting.'[286] What Freud, that old alchemist, reserved of his own desire he sublimated into the gold of psychoanalysis; a metal he steadfastly refused to cheapen with impurities, although not for want of opportunities. In the summer of 1924, the *Chicago Tribune* was apparently willing to pay Freud at least $25,000 to psycho-analyse two American youths, Leopold and Loeb, then on trial for murder.[287] And, in the following year, Hollywood producer Samuel Goldwyn offered Freud a staggering $100,000 to help write a film script for his studio. According to Ernest Jones, Goldwyn wanted Freud to 'cooperate in making a film depicting scenes from the famous love stories of history, beginning with Antony and Cleopatra'.[288] Freud wanted nothing to do with either scheme. Freud's distaste for American 'Dollaria' was similarly, though more seriously, reflected in his annoyance with the deviations of Carl Jung and Alfred Adler. Just as Jung was willing to exchange a piece of the libido theory for a slice of American pie, Adler sold Freud down the river with his counterfeit 'Individual Psychology'. Since psycho-analysis was a truth that demanded a high price in self-sacrifice and discipline, Freud wanted nothing to do with these sort of bargain-basement sales that, naturally, attract the vulgar hordes. Of his own speculative work *Beyond the Pleasure Principle*, Freud once dryly remarked: 'It is very popular, [and] is bringing me lots of letters and expressions of praise. I must have done something very stupid there.'[289]

Nonetheless, psychoanalysis is a business and, as such, has always demanded a steady stream of customers with which to float its ventures. For various reasons, Freud felt that capitalism was 'quite satisfactory', adding that 'the discovery of money was a great cultural advance'.[290] By the 1920s, Freud was at the centre of a multinational concern, having himself become what he calls 'a mere money-acquisition machine'.[291] His own reputation had become a commodity, a piece of symbolic capital, with which he and his followers could earn some much-needed interest. 'Business,' Freud laments to Jones, 'is devouring science.'[292] Furthermore, even as the theme of money littered Freud's personal correspondence, it polluted his relationship with patients who became benefactors of the cause. In the end, then, Freud may have hated 'American' commercialism, but he needed *someone* to swallow his bill of goods.

Lacan could be just as vitriolic as Freud about the hoary mob around him, including his totem brothers. And he could be impatient with the dirty politics of institutional psychoanalysis: better to sink the ship than set sail with a crew of bureaucratic rats. To this disagreeable pied-piper of the people, discipleship was an unseemly business. Of Lacan's followers, Daniel Bougnoux writes:

The procession of Lacan's followers is a march to the whistle. They travel and timidly pay to hear their gurus and, should they happen to write, churn out annoying literature. The world might change, but these people take no notice. Don't they ever get it? In this respect, the contrast is sharp between Lacan's sparkling intellect – his incredible cultural receptivity to the intellectual innovations of his time – and the incuriosity or mental restriction of his followers that verges on stupidity. Lacan, himself, certainly lamented this fact.[293]

Whether on television or on stage, Lacan never identified himself with the loving gaze of his audience: 'a gaze to which, in neither case, do I address myself, but in the name of which I speak'.[294] While Lacan reconceptualized psychoanalysis as a colonizing project of expanding desires, the low-brow 'idiots' were never an accepted part of the analytic high. As an absolute master, at least in France, Lacan didn't need or demand the money, the aggravation or the impotent gaze of the slave. Or rather, he took what he could and looked the other way: by the end of his life, Lacan had amassed a small fortune which included paintings and gold bars. Now, on the one hand, Lacan knew his Hegel well enough to realize that there was *simply no there there*, that is, no chance for identification with the mob. But, on the other, he knew which side his bread was buttered.

If Lacan's desire was always elsewhere, it was probably a function of the unique prestige accorded to intellectuals in France – a prestige dependent upon, and yet distanced from, the general public. Unlike Freud, a cloistered family man, Lacan was a Parisian socialite who felt most comfortable among the intellectual elite of his time. For this very reason, though, I doubt he would have found his own desire reflected in the pages of *Lacan For Beginners*. The book rather seems like a figment of an-other's populist imagination.

Although Lacan taught that ideas are produced and held communally, his own ideas have long since become valuable pieces of real estate. According to an old story, Lacan once dared his son-in-law Jacques-Alain Miller to transcribe and publish his densely baroque, yet extremely popular, seminars. Miller rose to the challenge and established himself as an excellent Plato to Lacan's Socrates. And while the resulting texts were as much his as they were Lacan's, 'Jacques Lacan' remained on the cover as a guarantee of authenticity, that is, as a brand name.[295] In the meantime, unofficial transcripts of the seminars began to circulate among disgruntled (real?) Lacanians, some finding their way into Paris bookstores. For many, of course, this rich underground economy was a justifiable response to Lacan's own rejection of the idea of intellectual property. However, such a generous (or tolerant) state of affairs disappeared with Lacan's death in 1981. After a legal battle with the *Association pour la Recherche et l'Establissement des Seminars*, Miller was awarded sole custody of the bastard seminars. As *Le Monde* reported in December 1985, and in caps: 'JACQUES LACAN "BELONGS" TO HIS SON-IN-LAW.'[296]

Fool's Gold

Even so, it is remarkable to find Miller's stamp even on this little cartoon book, as we learn in the 'Acknowledgements'. There is, I think, already something peculiar about including acknowledgements in a cartoon book; there isn't anything quite like it in the other books of this series. 'The approach to Lacan adopted in this book,' Leader writes, 'owes a great deal to the work of Jacques-Alain Miller. He has clarified and explained what is often difficult and apparently [huh?] obscure, and has stressed the historical consideration of the development of Lacan's thought.' At the risk of sounding (overly) facetious, it appears that Miller – the leader of the *École de la Cause freudienne* – is the other Leader of the *Cartoon Seminar*, while Leader is grist for the Miller. From my perspective as a critic, Leader demonstrates how biased the study of psychoanalysis remains today by supposing that Miller's position is a secure nodal point, a *point de capiton*, in this notoriously slippery field.

Tantalizing morsels of Miller's desire – at least as it has been transcribed by, or filtered through, Leader's desire – are scattered throughout *Lacan For Beginners*. For starters, the book is protected by copyright, though not without some hesitation. In addition to the copyright the reader is advised: 'The author and artist have their moral rights.' While I don't know what this qualification means exactly, it certainly doesn't undue the *legality* of copyright. If anything, and like the opening warning, the remark emphasizes the opposite: 'No parts of this book may be reproduced in any form, or by any means, without prior permission in writing from the publisher.' At the same time, special effort is made in a 'Note on the Text' to distinguish Leader's voice from Lacan's: 'This book is an attempt to expound the work of Jacques Lacan. The material contained in balloons is not quotation unless it is set within quotation marks. Likewise, the clinical examples are only Lacan's when this is explicitly stated.' Unlike Miller, Leader is apparently not willing to put words into Lacan's mouth and, in any case, *he doesn't have the right*. One hates, I suppose, to step on toes.

Like other books in this series, a list of primary and secondary sources available in English is also included for the beginner. A similar bias emerges as *Ecrits* translator Alan Sheridan receives an obligatory slap on the wrist, and we are urged onward to Miller's 'more accessible' *The Seminars of Jacques Lacan*. Among the rest, the

citation of two Lacan essays from *October* isn't surprising; an
adopted sister of Miller's journal *Ornicar?*, this American journal
was once a stronghold of Lacano-Millerian thinking. Among the
secondary texts listed is a book edited by Richard Feldstein *et al.*
called *Reading Seminars I and II: Lacan's Return to Freud* (1995).
This seems like a serious book, but it can't be an accident that Miller
is involved in the series within which it appears. Other favourites are
also listed, including two books by Slavoj Žižek – a great popular-
izer of Lacanian doctrine in America and someone associated with
Miller in the past. Meanwhile, important criticisms of, and com-
mentaries on, Lacan are quietly overlooked.

I have, however, saved the most cheeky example of partisan
politics for last. In his section on 'Biography' Leader purports the
following: 'Unfortunately, there is as yet no reliable, scholarly
biography of Lacan in either French or English. Elisabeth Roudinesco published *Jacques Lacan: Esquisse d'une vie, histoire d'un
système de pensée* [no source cited] in 1993, yet this book and her
*Jacques Lacan and Co.: A History of Psychoanalysis in France
1925–1985* (Free Association Books: London, 1990) should be
approached with caution, particularity in their questionable
accounts of historical issues.' In fact it is Leader's objectivity on this
matter that is questionable. For although Roudinesco is 'guilty' of
telling the story of 'Lacan & Co.' from her own perspective, it is
simply outrageous to cite her work only to dismiss it so easily. Of
course, Leader is unable to ignore Roudinesco precisely because her
work constitutes a clear leap forward in our understanding of
Lacan's life and work; like the Jones biography of Freud, it is a
valuable reference for any serious student working in the field. Consequently, the only thing that is truly 'unfortunate' here is the fact
that, alas, Roudinesco and Miller are personal and professional
adversaries. In this respect, it is humorous indeed to find Leader tip-
toeing around the publisher's name for Roudinesco's biography
Esquisse d'une vie – something he does nowhere else. It was only a
few years before that a public scandal erupted between Roudinesco
and Miller: apparently Miller strongly disapproved of the biography,

which was slated for his own publisher at Seuil. As a consequence, charges of censorship were bandied about, Roudinesco left her own post at Seuil, and the book was published by a competitor at Sayard.

Having flushed some of the dirt from out of the political margins of *Lacan For Beginners*, it is no surprise to find that the book's content reflects the surface prejudice of myopic desires. For instance, the role of surrealism in Lacan's life and work is minimized; Lacan is cast unproblematically as an analysand of Rudolph Loewenstein (one of the founders of 'American' ego psychology); and the 'variable session' is eagerly rationalized without measuring its limitations. And, as expected, Leader defers to Miller on a number of occasions – as when he minimizes Lacan's role as a structuralist, or repeats Miller's views on language and castration.

Leader also forwards the unlikely, if not absurd, view that Lacan's theoretical innovations always reflected his clinical concerns. This is a typical tactic among analysts worried about the practical side of things – no more so than in England, where the fortunes of psychoanalysis have been tied to the polytechnical schools. Leader, in fact, teaches psychoanalysis at Leeds and Brunel Universities. But psychoanalysis is neither a science nor an empirically driven enterprise: it is a humanistic endeavour at best, an exploitive cult at worst. For my money, Freud's 'discoveries' were projections seasoned with a dash of scientific preconceptions, most of which have been (conveniently) forgotten. Like other analysts after Freud, Lacan's innovations were mostly Freud warmed-over – with, mind you, a very serious dash of whatever intellectual fashion blew his way or fell into his lap.

I don't mean to demand more from a cartoon book than it can possibly deliver. Leader packs a lot of information into a short space, in a doubtful medium, about an obtuse thinker; as he says, he 'expounds' Lacan. But for this very reason *Lacan For Beginners* is too ambitious and ill-humoured for its own good *as a cartoon*. Unlike its natural counterpart, the sometimes delightful *Freud for Beginners*, this book is text-heavy and, worse, image-light: the drawings are dreary and tedious, while the cover doesn't begin to compare with the others of this series. In short, even though the idea of this book is comical, especially given Lacan's own views about the communicability of his work, the book itself is not very funny – not a very promising diagnosis for a cartoon.

The Golden Fleece

When told by Wilhelm Fliess that his interpretations were laughable, Freud responded by writing his serious Joke Book. As always, Freud was able to transmute a load of shit into a bag of gold with which to smack his critics about. Such was Freud's genius.

Yet in some ways Freud just didn't (or couldn't) get the joke, didn't understand the funny business called psychoanalysis. With his keener, more ironic sense of humour, Lacan confronted what Freud never could: that analysis didn't 'cure' anyone; that the goal of psychoanalysis was the production of more psychoanalysts; that analysis hinged on a speech act quite distinct from the 'truth'; that, alas, the tomb was empty. Thus, while Freud resigned himself to the limitations of psychoanalysis, Lacan exposed and revelled in them as a court-jester. Such was Lacan's genius.

Unfortunately, if Lacan himself knew that he knew nothing, among those who knew everything he became the one who knew most or, willy-nilly, knew best. So perhaps it was inevitable, after all, that the surrealistic Lacan would one day become a cartoon figure, his delirious seminars a very serious cartoon book. Bridging the worlds of psychoanalysis and popular culture, the *Cartoon Seminar* is a book for everyone and no one – or, if you prefer, for idiots and non-idiots. However, unlike the non-idiots Lacan called analysts, idiots at least know when they've been fleeced.

9 *Going to the Dogs,*
Or My Life as a Psychoanalyst

by David Beddow, M.D.,
with an introduction by Todd Dufresne

*In November 1989, I sent a number of questions to Dr David Beddow
about the history of psychoanalysis. I was particularly interested in some
rather murky details concerning Ernest Jones's 'Toronto Period'
(1908–13). Beddow, who was born in Toronto and practised psychoanalysis in New York and London, declined to answer my questions in
writing. Instead, he suggested that we meet at his family home on
Madison Avenue in Toronto, where he would be staying for part of the
following summer.*

*When I finally met Beddow he spoke at great length about his career
as a psychoanalyst which, he claimed, began with Ernest Jones and dogs
and ended with figure skating. He was extremely candid, sometimes
indiscrete, and seemed to enjoy conversing with an interested outsider. At
one point he lowered his voice to a dramatic whisper, leaned forward,
and recounted a scandalous (and frankly unbelievable) tale about
Jacques Lacan and Anna Freud. Beddow claimed that Lacan and Miss
Freud had a brief romance during the 1950s which cooled only when
Dorothy Burlingham discovered a 'love letter' from Lacan in a book on
Anna's night table. In her 'established role as jealous lover', Beddow
continued, Burlingham made a number of 'threats' until Miss Freud
broke off with Lacan.*

*According to one historian, Beddow was once laughingly referred to
in psychoanalytic circles as the 'imitation Freud'. And indeed, his
appearance seemed an uncanny semblance of the older, severe Freud we
find in grainy photographs and film footage. When we met on a swel-
tering summer day, Beddow wore an old-fashioned tweed coat, black tie*

on white shirt, dark round eyeglasses, and an impeccably trimmed grey beard under a fringe of short, grey-black hair. At eighty-one years of age, Beddow was intellectually engaging and alert but, physically, a bit fragile. Even so, I was shocked to learn of his death only three months later from lung cancer. But, like Freud, Beddow smoked cigars incessantly and was a self-confessed 'addict'.

Since Beddow mentioned that he had never produced an article on Freud or psychoanalysis, I was intrigued and a little surprised to hear that his niece found a number of his 'professional papers' in the Toronto home. When I visited, I found a desk drawer full of old photographs, receipts, tax returns, a small diary and more than a dozen yellowed letters. But I was most surprised to find a short manuscript entitled 'Going to the Dogs' which he dedicated 'For Ernest, July 12'. Apparently Beddow wrote the short account on the same day as our meeting.

As far as I know, 'Going to the Dogs' is Beddow's first and last attempt to narrate his encounter with Freud and psychoanalysis. For this reason alone his story assumes the retrospective significance of an important milestone in his intellectual and emotional life. The account itself is written with humour and perfectly captures the personality I was fortunate enough to meet. Other than a slight change of title and some minor corrections for grammar and spelling, I have transcribed his handwritten notes without modification or editorial apparatus.

*   *   *

Having approached the natural end of a long and rich life, some may judge me badly for isolating one period, one string of events, from the rest as especially noteworthy. And, to be sure, I hardly want to diminish the many characters, whether loved or hated, that populated my life and gave it shape and meaning. Yet the life of the mind is often punctuated by experiences that transcend and determine both what follows and, let it be known, precedes that experience. In fact I was never able to view the story of my life with the same eyes after my formative encounter with Freud and psychoanalysis. Still, for various reasons I have mostly kept this tale under my cap. These, then, are the first meandering thoughts of a reluctant but, finally, confiding Old-Man-Of-Analysis.

Actually, my lifelong reluctance to share this story is really the whole story, and can be traced to an unwieldy piece of cowardice on my part. Back when psychoanalysis was the therapy of choice throughout urban America, during a time when every major psychiatric hospital was run by an analyst, I was afraid no one would believe my story – or worse, that I would suffer reprisals from my orthodox colleagues. As any professional knows, it is nearly impossible to make a decent living outside the network of referrals available from friendly, like-minded colleagues. The return on an investment in sharing my modest story was very low indeed. And thus I have remained a coward for nearly sixty years – but one, to my small credit, with the means to support my family in relative comfort.

Yet this explanation sidesteps the inner mechanics of my cowardice, which was never exhausted by material considerations alone. For at the end of the day I was probably more afraid of my own thoughts than those of my orthodox colleagues. Even for an analyst, or especially so, it was difficult to face an experience that, on the one hand, made my professional life possible and, on the other, exposed its foundations to profound doubt. Although I am now retired, financially secure, in the last of my days, in short, beyond the reach of institutional psychoanalysis, this little confession still carries with it a grave price for an identity forged by the fire of analysis. But I have begun to speak, at last, of my formative analysis with the Professor at Berggasse 19 in Vienna, between September 1933 and July 1934.

Due to a number of coincidences, my exposure to psychoanalysis dates almost from the time I was born on 4 February 1909, in Toronto, Canada. My father, Dr Henry Beddow, knew Ernest Jones quite well and even worked as a psychiatrist at his Out-Patient Clinic on Chestnut Street. Jones had moved to Toronto in 1908, and was not then well-known as a follower of Freud. His Toronto Clinic, which was really a small house, was torn down years ago to make room for another concrete monstrosity in the Toronto core. According to my father, though, the Clinic was already less a house than a 'shack' when he began to work there in 1910. Surely this fact kept more than a few patients away. But the Clinic's financial prospects were especially compromised by Jones's unfortunate ability to alienate whomever he met, including colleagues who refused to send him referrals. But, to be fair, it is also true that Jones wrote numerous analytic essays during this period – essays that caused 'ripples' as my father put it, across traditional medical circles. In any case, my father was only needed for work on Fridays and on irregular occasions when Jones travelled abroad and lectured. However, at one point my father single-handedly maintained the Clinic for over three months. During this time Jones was preoccupied with a sexual abuse charge that culminated in an incriminating, if staggering, $500 bribe to the apparent victim. Although he protested his innocence, Jones was plagued by such charges throughout his career.

At some point, Jones and his common-law wife Loe Kann purchased a house on Brunswick Avenue and became good friends with my parents, who happened to live just around the corner. They became collegial enough, at least, that when Jones fell into trouble my parents lent him a portion of the money needed to 'stay out of jail'. Loe also lent money to this end, although it came with a conditional clause: Give up psychoanalysis, or else! Desperate, Jones agreed with Loe's demand but, as we know, quickly reneged on the deal. During happier times the group would frequent a downtown German club where they sang songs and drank spirits with the local folk. My father remarked that Jones liked to work on his language skills in this way and, anyway, preferred the sophisticated company of Europeans to that of the 'backward colonists' of Toronto. Jones hated Toronto.

Despite religious differences, Jones and Kann became my godparents when I was born. As a result, I was often left with 'Auntie Loe' for babysitting duties while my mother, Isabelle Beddow (née Chase), performed various tasks around town. During the winter,

'Uncle Ernest' would take me ice-skating on a pond near his house. Although I could barely walk at the time, let alone skate, Jones argued tirelessly with my parents that an early exposure to the charms of gliding effortlessly over the frozen pond would increase my self-confidence as an adult. My parents humoured Jones in all of this, and I would find myself perched in his arms as a thrilled, yet immobile, skating partner. I have a vague recollection of this, centring mostly on my mother's anxiety at seeing me in his arms while executing 'Grape Vines' on the rough outdoor ice. (As far as I know, he only rarely fell.)

Through Jones and his prescriptive 'psychology' of figure skating, I was introduced to his developing psychoanalytic views. Or, to put it more accurately, he discussed Freud's work with my father who would, in turn, inevitably use me as an analytic case study. Indeed, if it wasn't for my mother's strenuous objections, my father would have probably opened a psychoanalytic practice in Toronto; for in those days, it was a simple affair to become a psychoanalyst. Jones played another significant role in my psychological development, the effects of which were invisible for many years: he infected me with his own fear of dogs. Jones had been bitten by a dog in the field near his house and required stitching. Despite the fact that he and Loe owned a noisy little terrier, he began to complain repeatedly that dogs were 'stupid' and 'untrustworthy'. Then, with great dramatic flair, he would bare the corresponding scar to make his point.

I began my degree in medicine at the University of Toronto in 1926, at the tender age of 17. However, medical studies were a bore and I turned to electives in literature for greater stimulation. Through the great playwrights I cultivated my passion for psychology which, as I said, had long been kindled by my father's illicit interest in my 'psycho-sexual' development. Not unlike Freud's 'Little Hans', my father would quiz me about my mental states, dreams, random thoughts and so on. So Freud wasn't entirely new to me when I began to read him systematically as a disenchanted medical student. It was also during this time that I learnt much about my famous 'Uncle Ernest', who had long since returned to London where he held a pre-eminent position among English analysts. Although my parents lost contact with Jones and Kann, who broke up after leaving Toronto, my father suggested that I pursue Jones in London. While 'the Jones affair', as my mother called it, had placed a great strain on their relations, my father still liked Jones and admired his 'Herculean' efforts to conduct a self-analysis in Toronto. More importantly, my mother had softened her position on psychoanalysis over the years, becoming my greatest supporter. Thus, with my parent's blessing, I wrote a short letter to Jones indicating my interest in pursuing a career as a psychoanalyst.

Jones's prompt response was encouraging. In a letter of 2 June 1933, he wrote:

Many thanks for the good wishes from your mother and father, whom I think of often. Please send them my regards. And what a great pleasure to hear from my little nephew! So you have already graduated from medicine. Didn't I say that *skating* was the best education for you!! Incidentally, I have recently written a little book on the subject, and will give you a copy when we meet . . .

Unfortunately, I cannot take on another patient but will try to arrange for you an analysis with the Professor himself – if that suits you. This would be a most happy solution, and I know you will learn much from the source itself. Please let me know your thoughts in this regard.

Yours Always,

Uncle Ernest

The prospect of learning psychoanalysis 'from the source itself' was obviously irresistible to an ambitious young man. So on the next day I wasted no time and cabled my interest to Jones, along with a note of thanks for his efforts on my behalf. As you can imagine, the subsequent wait was torturous and, full of youthful impatience, I had already given up hope when I received a postcard from the Professor dated 27 July. The message was clear, if a bit spartan: 'Dear Sir; As you come so highly praised, I can spare time for you between the 18th of September and the end of May, 1934. However, I can only manage five days a week, rather than the usual six. You know my rate. Send your response immediately. Freud.' With my parent's blessing, not to mention their money, I set sail for England on 5 September 1933. Three days later I met Jones and his pleasant wife, 'Aunt Katherine', for a brief tour of London. On 11 September, I purchased a second-class ticket for the train to Vienna.

Luckily, Jones had already secured quarters for me in the Sühnhaus, where I moved in with one of Freud's former patients. Over the next months I became acquainted with a number of American doctors, including Joseph Wortis and Roy Grinker, both of whom were in analysis with Freud. And I would occasionally bump into such notables as Ruth Brunswick, Wilhelm Stekel and Giovanni Papini on the lovely streets of Vienna. Of course, in those days everyone used to sit in the cafes for hours at a time, leafing through local and foreign newspapers, making notes, exchanging gossip, discussing the dire political situation and, when all else failed, looking preoccupied and suitably eccentric. Every second week a small group of us would gather at the Cafe Astoria and discuss each other's cases over a hot cup of cappuccino.

But, shy and a little homesick, I mostly kept to myself. I walked all over Vienna, visited museums, studied German, read Freud's works over and over again, and recorded my reflections in a diary. On one occasion, while walking along the Ringstrasse, I even bumped into Freud and exchanged pleasantries. Life was very sweet. Or rather, and here the trouble begins, it could have been sweet if I didn't sour the experience with my growing insecurities. It may sound odd today, but as a young man I didn't feel neurotic *enough* for psychoanalysis. For in the game of 'one-downsmanship' that seems to frame analytic relations, my dog phobia hardly won the day against the lurid tales of sexual perversion that circulated in Freud's Vienna. To make matters worse, rumour had it that Freud once refused to continue treatment with an American patient – claiming that he had no unconscious! I quickly learnt that depth of sickness was a ready measure of emotional and intellectual worth for Freud and some of his followers. Consequently, I began to wonder when Freud would send me packing, tail between my legs, for being too superficial, too healthy, in a word, far too *Canadian* for the psycho-analytic sickness.

It is true that a helpful colleague, now famous, once consoled me with the suggestion that my little phobia actually disguised a 'latent bestiality', and that I could, after all, take 'refuge' in a well-earned sickness. While impressed, tempted, and a little flattered, I nonethe-less declined to pursue this most delightful solution to my worries. For, as it happened, I soon found solace in the small place Freud reserved for me in the pantheon of his great case studies: with a little chuckle, Freud began to distinguish me as his '*Hundmännerle*', literally his 'Little Dog Man'. In turn, and like any obedient student, I rarely stepped out from under the shadow of this nickname (a name, incidentally, that my old friend Jacques Lacan later re-chris-tened, with a characteristic twinkle in his eye, my '*collier de misère*').

For a long time I wore this psychoanalytic 'collar' with pride, not entirely upset that it was tied around my neck, attached to a leash, and held in check by Freud himself and the institution he found in his name. And indeed, to the extent that I remain afraid of dogs, this dog-tag has always followed, or preceded, me around. Mind you, this is not an entirely bad thing. I am perfectly aware that I owe to dogs my profession, my livelihood and that, for me, psychoanalysis was always 'going to the dogs'. But make no mistake: my fate was sealed less by my encounter with rabid dogs than with the conta-gious bite of Freud and his creation. For it wasn't until I began to read Freud as a medical student that my phobia took hold. Or, more exactly, my symptoms emerged shortly after my father began to reminisce aloud about my phobic Uncle Ernest's 'Toronto years'.

Of course, it didn't help that Freud himself was a great dog-lover by the time I met him in 1933. Like some other patients of this time, I was a bit shaken by the menacing growl that his dog Jofi greeted me with upon my first visit. Even so, her bad manners didn't prevent her from 'auditing', as Freud often put it, most of my sessions! On the first such occasion, Jofi scratched on the office door while I mused over my pathetic state. Never one to deny his dog, Freud immediately rose to his feet and invited her inside. As they settled into their usual spots, Freud rapped his knuckles lightly on the back of the couch and remarked comically: 'I can see the dog has evoked a strong reaction in you – which at least proves you weren't sleeping!' Over the next months, Freud would wax philosophical about his relationship with dogs whose company, I might add, he clearly valued over my own. In turn, golden Chows of all shapes and sizes began to invade my dreams; ultimately they consumed the better part of my analysis with Freud.

Toward the completion of my analysis, which took longer than expected, Freud's interpretation of my associations hinged on a repressed scene of *coitus á tergo*. But in an inspired twist he speculated that this recovered 'memory' didn't involve my parents at all, but my baby-sitters Jones and Kann. To this speculative end, he even deduced that Jones once played a sordid game of 'doggy-love' with Kann in an attempt to overcome his own case of caninophilia. With characteristic indiscretion, Freud assured me in this respect that his hypothesis was entirely confirmed by a colleague, Sándor Ferenczi, who had analysed Jones years earlier. In any case, Freud proceeded to demonstrate that my fear of dogs masked a repressed homosexual attachment to Jones, who had always played the role of substitute father in my life; as Freud emphasized, Jones was my spiritual 'God father'. And there was more. Since Jones was merely a representative of psychoanalysis, Freud reasoned that my phobia was indirectly tied to the 'grand-father' of all analysts: namely, to Freud himself. With a hearty laugh, he closed my analysis with the suggestion that I appeared doomed from birth to play 'puppy-love' with the father of psychoanalysis. Freud enjoyed playing with this canine metaphor – at least when he wasn't playing with Jofi – ultimately bidding me farewell with the assurance that I was destined 'to bite the hand that feeds you'. Wagging my tale, so to speak, I nodded in protest, gratefully shook the Professor's hand, and set off to conquer the neurotic world.

Caught in the grip of this family romance, it is really no wonder that psychoanalysis has left me speechless. For although I always suspected the hypnotic grounds of my tie to Freud and analysis, even this realization was preempted by Freud's interpretation: I was just being an ungrateful dog! To be certain, Freud's ability to checkmate an opponent was the essence of his creative genius. But it was also the crux of his political savvy: for how could one manoeuvre, let alone escape, when both rebellion and submission formed the knot he called psychoanalysis?

And yet, in a way, I did break the sorcerer's spell to step outside the bind that is discipleship. For Jones had not only infected me with his fear of dogs, but with his intense love of skating. As he once confided to me in the 1950s, skating was always his best means of escape from Freud and analysis. 'Why did you think,' he added with a wry smile, 'I recommended skating as your best education?' With retrospect, I probably should have guessed that his passionate attachment to figure skating betrayed a heretical streak, that 'Grapevines' inoculated him in some small way from the peculiar circumlocutions of psychoanalysis.

To celebrate my forty-fourth birthday, Jones sent me a copy of his newly revised skating book, along with the following inscription: 'Who said you can't teach an old dog new tricks!' Two months later my oldest son brought home a stray dog. To my wife's great surprise, I decided to keep him – provided, however, that we name him Ernest. While I can't say that little Ernie, any more than psycho-analysis, didn't rattle me at times, I at least learnt how and when to ignore them both! For sometimes, and I suppose this is the moral, a dog is just a dog – even when its tail has repeatedly wagged the tale of my life as a psychoanalyst.

PART III

Cultural Studies in Psychoanalysis:
Analysts at Play, Working

Like many professional activities, especially those involving intellectual labour, psychoanalysis is a kind of work that is hard to leave at the office. So it is no surprise that analysts often import psychoanalytic ideas into activities that have little or nothing to do with analysis – at least on the surface. As such, they are instances of 'wild' analysis. Freud himself can be credited with many such wild analyses, which would include his works of applied psychoanalysis – for example, his interpretations of long-dead figures like da Vinci and Dostoevski, and his co-authored psychopathography of Woodrow Wilson – and even his late application of analysis to cultural and philosophical questions. For these 'analyses', if that is indeed the right word, were in some respects the intellectual expression of Freud's own personal interests. That Freud gave vent to such interests, and thus made them 'legitimate' activities for his followers, doesn't make them any less wild.

On the other hand, Freud also recognized that such activities threatened to undermine the gravity of psychoanalysis as a theory and practice. And so, for example, Freud was not very keen about a follower's 'psychoanalysis of chess' – the sort of work that, in the public realm, might bring analysis into disrepute. As Freud is often credited with saying, sometimes a cigar is just a cigar. Similarly, sometimes a game of chess is just that – a game of chess.

In the following two chapters I explore two footnotes in the history of psychoanalysis. In the first, I examine (with my colleague, Gary Genosko) the largely forgotten book that Jones wrote and then rewrote, *The Elements of Figure Skating*. Our contention is that Jones's rather dry book is a perfect expression of his humourless transference to Freud's theories. The second essay briefly explores the impact of dogs in the theory, practice and institutionalization of psychoanalysis during Freud's lifetime. My basic claim is that we need to attend to these extra-professional attachments as a way of understanding the rich, human dimensions of what came to be understood, especially in North America, as a cold and detached theory and practice; that is to say, as an objectively true piece of scientific business. Freud and his followers creatively manipulated not just the theories to the events of their lives, but their lives to the theories. In this respect the marginal detail, such as an extra-professional attachment to psychoanalysis, can be a perfect way to illuminate the essential character of psychoanalysis as a *lifestyle*. Or, if you prefer, as a bad habit.

10 Psychoanalysis on Thin Ice: Jones and Figure Skating

Call my style infirm and its figures faint,
All the critics say, and more blame yet,
And not an angry word you get.
Robert Browning, *Time's Revenges*
                    (Ernest Jones, Epigram to
                    The Elements of Figure Skating)

In 1931, the well-known British psychoanalyst Ernest Jones published a short, pocket-sized book entitled *The Elements of Figure Skating*.[297] In 1952, after the 'success that attended the first edition',[298] Jones produced a revised and enlarged second edition, which he dedicated 'To My Partner, Katherine'. More than twice the length of the first, the second edition provides detailed descriptions and illustrations far beyond the 'Eights' and 'Threes' of the first edition.[299] For example, he added substantial analyses of such skating figures as Loops, Combination Steps, Mohawks/Choctaws, Grape Vines, expanded a section on Ice Dancing, wrote an Appendix on the 'History of Skating', and compiled a new subject–author index. Directed primarily at the beginner by a self-professed beginner, Jones's *Elements* has not, however, fared well in the figure-skating literature concerned with technique. It is rarely mentioned in contemporary books on the subject. Moreover, the two editions of the *Elements* have received just as little attention from historians of psychoanalysis. In both fields it remains Jones's forgotten or 'lost' text.

In what follows we are concerned with figure skating only insofar as it contributes to our understanding of Jones's *Elements* as a psychological text. To this particular end, we have in the first section briefly outlined some of the (at times anecdotal) literature around Jones and skating. In the second section, however, we adopt a textual approach with the goal of unearthing Jones's psychological insights into skating, and offer what we believe is the first thorough analytic reading ever advanced of the book. It is our hope that this chapter will encourage more psychoanalytically oriented readers to reconsider not just the suggestive relationship between Jones's passions for skating and psychoanalysis, but other instances of odd pairings in the history of psychoanalysis.

1.

When the *Elements* is referred to in figure-skating circles, such as in Lynn Copley-Graves's *Figure Skating History*, it is for its historical insights. For instance, Copley-Graves attributes to the first edition the observation that 'the name "mohawk" for this turn [the outside forward combined with the outside backwards, or "spread-eagle" position] was derived from a cut-like step used by the Mohawk Indians in their war dances'.[300] Actually, there is no mention of this piece of sporting ethnography in the first edition. Jones mentions the 'so-called Mohawk step' only twice, and on neither occasion does he refer to its origin in the colonial practices of the British Empire in the late nineteenth century, a time in which Mohawk warriors were displayed as living museum pieces before paying audiences in London. It was only in the second edition that Jones noted that 'the term Mohawk is derived from a step used by the New York State tribe of that name in their War Dance'.[301] Taken together with Copley-Graves's misspelling of 'Earnest' Jones, this misquote is symptomatic of the inattentiveness of the skating literature as it concerns Jones.

Another Jones – Robert – wrote in 1772 what is widely recognized to have been the first textbook on figure skating, descriptively entitled *A Treatise on Skating: Founded on certain Principles deduced from many Years Experience By Which That noble Exercise is now reduced to an Art, and may be taught and learned by a regular Method, with both Ease and Safety.* 'How times have changed,' Ernest Jones muses, 'since that Golden Age of Innocence.'[302] In fact, the existence of this early treatise was not lost on Jones. In the Preface to the second edition Jones suggests that 'since it was a Captain Jones who wrote the first book on the elements of Figure Skating, just two hundred years ago, it would perhaps seem appropriate if a Captain Jones – such happens to be my military title – should write the last one'.[303] However, Jones's authoritarian zeal and 'military manner'[304] is inspired less by his own military experiences[305] than by his loyal adherence (albeit with 'useful' modifications) to his friend's 'already classical' textbook, 'Captain' T. D. Richardson's *Modern Figure Skating.*[306] Despite Jones's characteristic immodesty, as one might guess, his book was not the last word on skating technique.

As noted, Jones's skating book has received only passing consideration in the psychoanalytic literature. In his biography of Jones, Vincent Brome expends little energy on his passion for figure skating – what he merely refers to as one of Jones's 'concessions to the frailties of relaxation'.[307] According to Paul Roazen, though, what Brome calls a concession Helene Deutsch considered a sign of independence and strength: 'In later years, though she had a personal distaste for the analyst Ernest Jones, Freud's official biographer, she admired him for his breadth in having written a book about skating.'[308] Later Roazen adds that Deutsch 'admired him because his interests were less narrow than the local Viennese she dealt with'.[309] It turns out that Deutsch was also a skater whose childhood winters were spent on the frozen San river near her birthplace in the town of Przemysl, Poland.

Unfortunately, Jones does not mention his lifelong passion for figure skating in his autobiography *Free Associations*, probably because his last years were consumed with the monumental task of writing Freud's biography.[310] Jones's son Mervyn was, though, able to correct this oversight in an appended Epilogue to the autobiography. In it Mervyn writes:

> First among these [hobbies] was skating. He practiced hard at rinks in London and on winter holidays in Switzerland, and was no mean performer.
>
> Characteristically, he found that there was no satisfactory book for people who wanted to take up figure skating, and wrote one. He was delighted when some one who knew him as a psychoanalyst remarked: 'There's a good book on skating by a man of your name.'[311]

More than anyone, Mervyn Jones has written on his father's hobby. In his own autobiography, *Chances*, Mervyn notes that he shares his father's hobbies, although it seems his skills paled against those of his able father. While completing a form for inclusion in Britain's *Who's Who*, Mervyn faced the item 'recreations':

> After some pondering, I put: 'chess and skating'. It didn't strike me until afterwards that my father had put exactly the same. But he had studied the theory of chess, played over the games of the masters, solved chess problems, and was engaged at any given time in a number of correspondence games. Still more impressively, he had taken his silver as a skater, served as a judge, and written a book called the *Elements of Figure Skating*. (It gave him great pleasure when someone who knew him as a psycho-analyst said: 'D'you know, the best book about skating is by a man with your name.') I could never do more than play chess with friends of my own modest standard, and make an ungraceful dab at the easiest skating figures. Without my father's instruction, I shouldn't have got that far.[312]

The elder Jones seems to have been familiar with the London rinks. In the *Elements* he appended a section on 'The Rinks of Britain', detailing their hours of operation, fees, clubs, etc. The chart lists six rinks in London. According to Mervyn, Jones skated at The Ice Club, Grosvenor Road, the second largest of the six rinks: 'I remember from the 1920's and 1930's that he was a member of the skating club in the Grosvenor House Hotel (it ceased to exist in 1939) and skated on Sunday mornings when it was closed to the public and only open to members.'[313] Years later, Mervyn and his own children frequented the rink in Streatham.

Ernest and his wife Katherine Jones (née Jokl[314]) often vacationed at Sils Maria in the Upper Engadine near St Moritz, Switzerland. Although this popular village was known for its skiing – a sport which neither made their own – the lake provided ample opportunity for practising outdoor figures. In fact, the area was the centre of activity for figure skating during the 1880s.[315] Jones's attention to Grape Vines in the second edition was based in part on his outdoor skating on lakes, since the Vines were 'useful for country skaters in the open where the ice cannot have the evenness of that in rinks'.[316] However, in what is vintage Jones, he also admits that his motivation to describe the so-called 'obsolescent Grape Vines' was based on the fact that 'no adequate account of them exists. To describe them in detail has been held to be impossible, a challenge which I found hard to resist.'[317] Later on he adds: 'To teach, or even adequately to describe, Grape Vines either verbally or in print is held to be impossible, there being nothing to it but sheer imitation. . . . [B]ut the very difficulty of a task spurs one to attempt it, which must be my excuse for exceeding a little the province proper of this book.'[318]

As we have shown, there are several variations on the often repeated anecdote illustrating Jones's gratification that his apparent namesake was acknowledged by one of his psychoanalytic colleagues to have written a book on figure skating. This was not an ordinary book: according to Jones, it was first of all 'a good book', and later 'the best book'. Jones also refers to it as 'the last one' on figure skating. As Mervyn put it, his father 'always wanted to do things well or not at all'.[319] Jones's penchant for self-aggrandizement, a matter often raised by critics of *Free Associations*, is much in evidence in the *Elements*. Still, although he did consider himself to be, at least rhetorically, a 'beginner', he did win a silver medal at his home rink, served as judge of applicants for the Third Class Test, and even gave short demonstrations on technique.[320] According to Mervyn, he also invented the phrase 'life-saving stop' when attempting Threes, which appears in the *Elements* as 'emphatic' or 'life-saving stamp'.[321] 'You are not supposed to do this,' Mervyn adds, 'but it's hard to resist.'

Among Jones's tiny date-books[322] – many of which were originally presented to him as Christmas presents by his son Mervyn – those for the years 1930 and 1931 reveal the intensification of his passion for skating while preparing the first edition of the *Elements*. From his entries, it is clear that he skated regularly on Sunday evenings, practised waltzing steps in particular, and met occasionally with Captain Richardson. But these entries are often no more than a record of his failure on a given outing. On 14 December 1930 he remarked 'First waltz to change of edge'; on the 23rd, 'skated in morning and afternoon, but 3 falls, so didn't go in evening'. And thus, on Christmas Eve's day, it is perhaps not surprising to find the words, 'woke with stiff neck'. A bad fall onto his left knee on 25 January 1931 at a private rink resulted in x-rays of his finger and knee on the 29th. But Jones was on his feet again on the 31st: 'tried skating again but fell again (wearing guard) on the same spot'. These setbacks did not prevent him from taking Joan and Evelyn Riviere and his wife Katherine to the rink on 15 February. And the following Sunday (the 22nd), Jones was on the ice at Golder's Green (London) in the evening. He notes the presence of skating starlet Vivi-Anne Hulten, about whom we will have more to say momentarily. Having become a rink-rat of sorts, Jones was back on the blades for two more hours on the morning of the 23rd, and again on the 24th, but only for an hour on the 25th.

Jones skated at the Golder's Green and Streatham rinks in London during March, sometimes on the same day, and on the 14th he took in a hockey game, witnessing England defeat Switzerland in Brighton. On 2 April he announced: 'started skating book'. At first glance, he seems to have finished the *Elements* on 21 April. On the other hand, the 13th and 14th are also marked 'finished skating book', although they have been subsequently crossed out. Jones then indicates that the dates on these pages should be antedated one week, which seems to mean that the 13th must indeed be the correct date of its completion. If so, then Jones wrote the *Elements* in a period of some twelve days! But even if he took from the 2nd to the 21st, this was no mean feat in itself.

With his text finished, Jones was on the ice again on 19 April and 3 May. He attended another hockey match on the 14th, and commented on the soft ice during a late afternoon skate on the 16th. During May Jones was worried about Katherine's thyroid operation (which took place on 12 May; on 22 May, the day she came home from the hospital, Jones scribbled: 'K. comes home!!!!'). He skated throughout June complaining of his 'bad hips', and took a test on the 29th, scoring nineteen marks. He did not mention that this was a failing mark. In the autumn (September) he was again skating regularly, and 'started sexuality lectures at the institute' by 23 October. Given his heavy professional schedule and need for practice time, he postponed his second skating test – originally scheduled for 3 December – taking it instead on the 17th. On this date he notes: 'Failed test . . . 19 1/2 marks.' His heavy practice schedule and his passionate involvement in the sport did not in the end result in a successful test on his second try. The test in question was the National Skating Association Test (Third Class or Bronze).[323] In order to pass, one must receive at least twenty points out of a possible thirty-six. Jones was, then, very close to passing this test. Despite his failure at the hands of the skating judges, 23 December brought the good news that his *Elements* had appeared in print. But in December 1931, Jones had not mastered figure skating enough to pass the Third Class Test. This did not, of course, disqualify him from later judging this test. Moreover, while he may have won a silver medal at his home rink, it is not at all clear for what feat this medal was awarded.

The skating club at the Grosvenor rink provided Jones with a number of contacts outside his psychoanalytic circles. Jones, for instance, skated and was friends with Sir Stanley Unwin, who we might suppose encouraged Jones to prepare the second edition of the *Elements* for his publishing firm of Allen & Unwin. Jones's personal contact with the stars of the international skating world included, according to Mervyn, Sonja Henie, Norwegian and World Champion, and star of ice-dancing films. However, Henie's auto-biography *Wings on My Feet* makes no mention of Jones. Notably, it is not a photograph of Henie that adorns the frontispiece of the *Elements*; it is rather an 'ornament', as Jones puts it, of Miss Vivi-Anne Hulten, Lady Champion of Sweden, which appears. Incidentally, this is the only photograph in the text. It may also have been fateful that Jones skated with Sir Samuel Hoare, Home Secretary under Prime Minister Neville Chamberlain (1937–40). For according to Mervyn: 'On a few occasions he [Jones] talked to Hoare at the club about visas for German and Austrian analysts who wanted to come to Britain and, congratulating Hoare on his skating (Hoare was a vain man) persuaded him to grant the visas.'[324] Jones, who was instrumental in getting a number of analysts out of occupied Germany and Austria, including of course the Freuds, writes: 'The Home Secretary at that time was Sir Samuel Hoare (now Lord Templewood), whom I knew slightly through belonging to the same private skating club; that was why I referred to him in my letters to Vienna, which had to be disguised, as "my skating friend".'[325] Although Jones also procured the support of some others, including Sir William Bragg, a famous physicist and President of the influential Royal Society, it is a little disturbing to think that the lives of so many people may have rested on his fortuitous relation-ship with a 'skating friend'!

Unfortunately, the letter Jones refers to above is missing from the published Freud–Jones correspondence, perhaps misplaced after he used it for the Freud biography; or it may eventually appear as a letter from Jones to Anna Freud, who sometimes acted as inter-mediary between the two men. In any case, it is certainly strange that there is no mention of skating in the entire correspondence – a fact which indicates either Jones's general reluctance to discuss his hobby, or the limited scope of their friendship. It may be that Jones was wary that Freud would regard his work on figure skating with scorn; as another regrettable instance of wild analysis. Freud certainly wasn't always very pleased with the way his disciples applied psychoanalysis. Apparently, Freud once responded to a paper on chess and psychoanalysis by saying: 'This is the kind of paper that will bring psychoanalysis into disrepute. You cannot reduce everything to the Oedipus Complex. Stop!'[326]

We can, moreover, only wonder why Jones's *Elements* is missing from the otherwise extensive bibliography of his work provided in the Freud–Jones correspondence. On the other hand, this would not be the first 'complete' bibliography of Jones to overlook the *Elements*. This is regrettable, since, as Jones puts it, the skating 'revolution' of the London Skating Club, 'like most revolutions, brought both good and evil with it. It was of the kind that lends itself to interesting psychological reflections.'[327] Considering these rather grand sentiments, not to mention Jones's pivotal role in the history of psychoanalysis, it is curious that it has taken so long for someone to pay *The Elements of Figure Skating* the kind of attention it demands.

2.

Despite the fact that the *Elements* is essentially a textbook of skating technique, it deserves a small but noteworthy place in the history of the psychoanalytic movement. Written only one year after his presentation of 'The Problem of Paul Morphy: A Contribution to the Psychology of Chess' to the British Psycho-Analytical Society (on 19 November 1930),[328] Jones opens the book with the following remark: 'This book is addressed by a beginner to beginners, and the distinctive feature of it is its psychological approach to their problems in studying Figure Skating.'[329] Although Mervyn is understandably uncertain about the relationship between skating and psychoanalysis, preferring instead the traditional one between chess and psychoanalysis, he does admit that some psychological interest lies with his father's consideration of 'the fears or anxieties which hamper learners in skating. He noted that beginners can't believe you have to skate on the edge of the blade and expect to fall over . . . – so they do fall over.'[330]

Indeed, according to Jones this meta-discourse on skating was taken as a kind of *analysis* of the problems faced by beginners. 'Analysis' is precisely the term he placed in italics to provide a sense of how the instructor must treat and respond to the fears and frustrations of every beginner's work on the elemental figures.[331] This approach makes the book psychoanalytically interesting even though, at least from the point of view of those learning to skate, it does not make it any less frustrating. For the beginner, in fact, the enlarged second edition must be especially frustrating, since it is not just a simple manual of technique, but is often a theoretical, thickly described, jargon-heavy account of skating technique. It is certainly hard to imagine any beginner, even those more intellectually inclined like Jones, bothering to read through this book from beginning to end. That the book contains sixteen chapters in addition to the opening Preface and closing 'Appendix' probably explains why it has been so consistently overlooked. Jones might have heeded his own good advice when, in a chapter entitled 'On the Art of Teaching Figure Skating', he writes:

> One of the main difficulties a beginner has is what appears to him the endless number of matters he has to attend to simultaneously. Now psychologists tell us that there are definite limits to the number of thoughts to which the mind can attend in a moment of time, and that these limits are still further reduced when the subject is in a state of bewilderment, apprehension and uncertainty. Therefore the instructor has again to restrain his eagerness to impart information on the dozens of points that call for it . . . [332]

On the other hand, it is precisely the more bookish aspects of Jones's *Elements* that are, from our perspective as historians, the richest in psychological material.

Jones opens this particular chapter with some anecdotal bio-graphical information, imparts to us his 'debt' to former skating instructors, and even lists his 'qualifications' for embarking on a psychology of skating. On this last point Jones writes:

> Having taken lessons from some twenty instructors on various rinks in England and Switzerland I have noticed that they too have their problems, and the wish has occurred to me to repay a little of what I owe them by offering a few hints in linking up their problems with those of the beginner . . . As to my own qualifications to say anything on such a matter I may mention that my professional work includes the training of students to find out and understand the psychological difficulties of other people, a position which may as here be regarded somewhat as that of a *liaison* officer.[333]

It needs to be emphasized that this self-appointed 'position', that of 'liaison officer', is only one metaphor among others that links Jones's text to what we could call an *erotics of skating*. Italicized only in the first edition, 'liaison' operates throughout as a 'binding' force, of which there are two recognized sorts. The first is 'sexual' and refers to an illicit relationship, while the second is 'military' and refers to the role of the Liaison Officer, someone who maintains contact between different commands.[334] Even leaving aside the wealth of biographical material with which we might convincingly link Jones to sexual and military motifs throughout his life and work, it is possible to locate these themes through a close reading of the *Elements* alone. For as we will see, even the most cursory reading of the Introduction to this book reveals the persistent and thematic coupling of pleasure and power, danger and control, in Jones's thought.

Briefly, Jones argues that pleasure and enjoyment are tied to 'con-fidence', and that confidence is made possible 'by appreciating two things – rhythm and poise'.[335] By these he means 'co-ordination amongst parts' and 'balance and security'. In turn, he argues that these two function properly by means of 'control', which serves what is essentially a synthetic function:

> It is important to understand what is meant by this mysterious word 'control' . . . They [muscles] must neither be relaxed to flabbiness . . . nor must they be contracted in a cramped fashion . . . They must be neither lax nor tight, but somewhat taut and therefore 'alive' . . . It is this exact degree of tone that constitutes 'control' . . . [and] which generates the pleasurable sensations promised at the beginning of the chapter.[336]

By no means, then, is sexuality and power foreshadowed only in the military titles of 'Captains' Jones (Robert and Ernest) and Richardson, but in the almost hermeneutical thematic which links together such explosive words as conquer, pleasure, power, rhythm, poise, danger, control, confidence, security, mastery and so on, in the *Elements*.

For these reasons Peter Gay is on the right track when, in a brief footnote in *Freud: A Life For Our Time*, he draws Jones's *Elements* into an analytic fold through an undeveloped notion of the erotics of skating. This is notable, if only because Gay is alone in his observation that the *Elements* 'exhibits Jones's irrepressible erotic impulses'.[337] It is worth citing the passage that Gay mentions, which appears on the very first page of Jones's Introduction to the second edition:

> All art, however refined, disguised and elaborated its technique, takes its ultimate source in love for the human body and the desire to command it. In the Art of Figure Skating this ultimate source is directly and immediately recognized; hence the purity and simplicity of its aims. It achieves beauty only when the difficult technique of acquiring control over every fibre of the body is attained, so that free rein can be given to the inspired impulse of movement. [. . .] There comes a genius whose sense of beauty and grace pours itself wholly into the ecstasy of motion.

Now place this vehicle at his command, and we shall witness one of the supreme triumphs of humanity. [338]

From this rich passage it is sufficiently clear that Jones considered skating a privileged activity, one that culminates in nothing short of what he calls an 'ecstasy of motion'. Consequently, Gay is right when he adds (in a personal communication) that 'the book dwells with evident enjoyment on the pleasure that graceful motion and exhilarating, effortless-seeming gliding can provide'; or again, that the *Elements* 'does suggest a certain erotic pleasure in the making of loops and tracing of the designs'.[339]

As we are perhaps beginning to appreciate, it is almost impossible to downplay the role that control (as defined by Jones) plays in the *Elements*. In practical terms, it consists in the mastery of all the 'simple edges'[340] – for it is a 'tremendous truth', Jones suggests, 'that the moving skater is safe and secure only when he is on the edge'.[341] On the other hand, being on the edge always seems a little dangerous to the beginner, which leads Jones to admit, rather dramatically, that: 'When one has already risked one's bodily integrity by venturing on skates, it certainly does seem uncalled for to take away the last hope of safety by trying to ride on a razor-blade edge.'[342] Ultimately, though, the significance of control manifests itself in what must be called a *metapsychology* of figure skating. For instance, Jones elaborates on what he calls 'the one great principle of Figure Skating, namely, *Economy of Effort*': '*the highest ideal in Figure Skating is to control one's poise and rhythm as to need the minimum of effort to execute the figure*'.[343] In keeping with the dated scientific rhetoric, Jones suggests that the Economy of Effort is comprised of 'four subordinate, but important' principles.[344] In the course of his rather pedantic discussion of the third of these principles – that being '*The direction along a curve is controlled by the interplay of two systems of bodily twist*' – Jones introduces the following:

two great systems, which for the sake of convenience may be called the primary and secondary systems; the function of the former is to impel a curving or revolving movement, that of the latter to resist or control it. Now try to realize that these two structures twining round each other, and for this purpose think of an analogy that appeals to you; two twining stems of ivy or honeysuckle, two coiled wires of an electric flex, twisted sticks of barley sugar, or – to ascend in dignity – the intertwining components of a Byzantine column.[345]

With these 'two great systems of Twist and Counter-Twist',[346] which he likens in both editions 'to two springs coiled round each other',[347] control is broken down into its metapsychological essentials. As such, Jones's book simply begs to be read against psychoanalysis and the scientific rhetoric with which Freud thought and wrote. At the same time, it is apparent that we have glimpsed an unappreciated part of Jones's somewhat fantastical and idealized identification of skating with psychoanalysis; what we are calling his intense transference onto psychoanalytic theory.

Consequently, we should probably be more attentive to the role that skating might have played in Jones's life and work. It is, for example, imminently possible to re-interpret the loop which often accompanied his signature in letters – $\mathcal{P}$ – not only as his private symbol for 'Science' and his sister Sybil, as he suggests in his self-analysis, but as an expression of a deeply felt erotics of skating.[348] Upon examination, this loop belies its insouciance in closing in on itself, suggesting the more meticulously cut enclosing loops of the Grape Vines whose illustration Jones took great care in rendering. Yet the signature, like the skating figure, is inscribed in a single stroke, just as the left skate alone describes the forward enclosing loop of a Double Vine. In any case, that Jones's use of this symbol precedes his encounter with psychoanalysis only demonstrates the extent to which skating and psychoanalysis informed or, as it were, eventually twined around each other in his thought.

Jones's appeal to the analytic categories of primary and secondary systems is not restricted to only one passage in the *Elements*. In an attempt to repay his 'debt' to his many instructors,

Jones writes: 'What I imagine to be the most useful hint to offer I have reserved for last. It is the value of distinguishing between the primary and secondary faults.'[349] He argues that the instructors must not mistake 'secondary faults' for 'primary' ones; that, in other words, the instructor (and beginner) locate the root problem in technique and not be fooled by everything else which issues from that problem. It is here, in fact, that Jones introduces the loaded word 'analysis':

> The instructor has seized on the obvious, just because it was the most obvious thing wrong. But he has omitted the most essential part of his task in helping the beginner, namely to conduct a precise *analysis* of what has happened. This, it is true, is often not very easy . . . But it is what most reveals the genius of the real teacher, what makes his work much more interesting, and what is the greatest help to the beginner. It changes a grinding occupation into a source of mutual interest.[350]

The parallel here with the primary and secondary psychical agencies or processes first articulated by Freud in 1900, and with it the interpretive credo that 'if we were to restrict ourselves to considering what the second agency contributes to dreams, we could never arrive at an understanding of them',[351] is striking. Like dreaming, skating has a 'secret meaning' which may be revealed through a certain kind of *psycho*analysis. And like the analyst, Jones is interested to move skating instruction from the secondary to the primary, the manifest to the latent, from what is, at last, a 'grinding occupation' to a mutually interested *depth* psychology.

Jones is, in fact, not at all deaf to the relationship between skating and dreaming. Once again, the relation hinges on the theme of pleasure acquired by 'exercising control over every fibre of the body'. At the beginning of the Introduction Jones writes:

> The aim of Figure Skating is so to train the sense of rhythmic poise as to enable the would-be skater to enjoy a particular pleas-

urable experience. The nature of the promised pleasure, already contemplated in imagination, is the exhilarating sensation of gliding without effort or resistance while one feels all the while under one's sure control . . . It combines and surpasses the joys of flying and dancing; only in a certain type of dream do we ever else attain a higher degree of the same experience of exultantly skimming the earth.[352]

The type of dream Jones has in mind is discussed by Freud in several passages of *The Interpretation of Dreams*. After rejecting the interpretation of dreams of flying based upon somatic stimuli (on the grounds that such dreams would occur more frequently if they were simply provoked by 'the rising and sinking of the lobes of the lungs'), Freud instead pursues the 'special motives' behind them, namely, primary motives.

Freud twice refers to 'childish romping' as the pleasurable experience reproduced in dreams of flying. The connection between genital arousal and flight appears, for instance, in 'A Staircase Dream'. The general lesson of this dream is that although flying is a typical dream event, its interpretation must not be wooden; attention must be paid to the particular features of the dreamer's childhood experiences. Moreover, the reproduction of the pleasurable feelings of 'romping' when it takes the form of flying often excludes the fact that the child was, in a sense, once taken flying in the arms of an adult. Freud suggests that such pleasurable impressions may provoke sexual feelings which are in turn transformed into feelings of anxiety. Of particular interest here is the idea that flying fulfils a wish for the perfect execution of a motor skill such as climbing stairs. What is absent from dreams of flying, then, is how (i.e., the means of support) the pleasure was procured. With regard to skating, instruction and practise give way, like the supportive arms of a parent, to dreams of ice capades. Yet even more than dreams of flying, one may imagine that dreams of escapades over the frozen earth unite power and pleasure in the masterfully executed figures of skating.

It seems to us, then, that we can no longer avoid the force with which Jones qua 'liaison officer' brings about the binding power of not just sexuality and power – which in itself is striking enough – but of hobby and science, skating and analysis. It thus becomes possible, recalling our Greek, to speak of Jones's project as a kind of dreamlike *psuche*-analysis; '*psuche*' standing for the 'cold breath which informs [the] "psyche"' of psychoanalysis.[353] For it is, after all, the cold breath of psychoanalysis which best informs the spirit of Jones on ice.

While control and mastery remain for Jones the ideal horizon of the *Elements*, he is nonetheless aware that very few of us will ever become absolute masters of skating. Thus he points out that 'there is such a thing as an *art of falling*'.[354] In what must seem a curious suggestion, Jones further recommends that 'it is worth learning how to fall skilfully, as exponents of ju-jutsu or of hunting well know. The place to learn is in your bedroom, with an ample supply of cushions and eiderdowns.' Later in that same paragraph he adds: 'to learn to slither is really the art of falling on ice'.[355]

Jones also lets the beginner know what he considers the aesthetic qualities of a skater:

> The two qualities – apart from physical appearance – of chief importance are a sense of life and a sense of rhythm. First consider the former. A stiff, over-careful skater . . . makes a lifeless impression. It is largely a psychological problem, one with which an inspiring instructor is sometimes able to cope. Similarly, the matter of rhythm is really one of personality – . . . but, alas! those ungifted can do little but admire the gifted.[356]

Poor skating can also reflect for Jones a lack of 'good taste'. 'Deplorable attitudes of mind,' Jones writes, 'will of course be reflected in the style of skating.'

For Jones, the burden of learning how to skate sits mostly on the shoulders of the beginner and not the instructor. In a similar sense, the burden of psychoanalysis lies with the analysand; as a reader of the unconscious the analyst must guide the analysand to self-discovery, a guidance particular to every analysis. This connection, again, is not entirely fortuitous since there is a striking relation between the instruction of figure skating and the transmission of psychoanalysis throughout the book. First, consider at some length what Jones says at the end of the Introduction:

> I desire to point out here that the amount of benefit the pupil receives when being taught skating depends much more upon himself than on the instructor. There are two reasons for this, both of which are due to the sense of insecurity . . . that must accompany the first stages. In such a situation, according to certain interesting psychological laws, any instruction – however helpfully intended – is very apt to be received as if it were the adverse criticism or even blame. When the pupil receives it this way . . . he will find it difficult to respond in the ideal way depicted in the passage from Browning which I have chosen as the motto for this book [see the epigraph of this essay]. He should watch for the first signs of resentment on his part, since this would only lead – without his intending – to a defiant stupidity and would thus diminish the value of the help being offered to him. The second reason, probably also derived from the same source, is that self-criticism, or even simple self-observation, appears to be far harder to achieve with Figure Skating than with any other exercise. In short, if a pupil wants to learn he has to be willing to learn from someone else: any passion he has for self-teaching had better be kept within bounds until he attains the exalted heights of Free Skating.[357]

But while skating roughly coincides with the tenets of psychoanalysis, Jones appears to leave psychology behind at a crucial point in his approach to instruction. As usual, the critical passage deals with the attainment of control and mastery. Jones writes: 'One famous skater – let him be nameless – has pronounced that only after acquiring a complete mastery of all the school figures . . . does one begin to get an idea of what skating really is.'[358] Against this view, Jones argues that with 'a few months of serious practice' – later in the first edition he says 'a good six months'[359] – 'one begins to taste the joys that lie ahead and, through appreciative understanding, to enter in the imagination into the experiences of the master skaters who are generous in giving us exhibitions of their skill'.[360] It is worth noting, in passing, that in the second edition the master's 'skill' has now become an 'accomplishment', an alteration that possibly reflects Jones's assessment of psychoanalysis after Freud's death.[361]

In what immediately follows, Jones elaborates upon the beginner's psychological problems, but recommends what must be seen as a drastic 'remedy' beyond or outside psychology proper. Again, the passage is worth citing in full:

> Now the main obstacle to progress along the felicitous path we have set out may be described in one word – Fear . . . [I]t is the enemy of confidence, which is always the indispensable condition of enjoyment. It is an attitude of mind which nowadays can be remedied by psychological 'treatment', *but we are concerned here with only one remedy – exact knowledge* . . . To provide enough knowledge to give the beginner confidence is, I repeat, the object of this book, and he will attain it if he faithfully follows the instructions given.[362]

Similarly, in the Preface Jones claims that unless the beginner 'is absolutely clear about what he is attempting, and the exact position in which every part of his body is to be, unless, in short, he *knows* – he wavers, is uncertain and insecure, and cannot achieve the necessary confidence'.[363] And again, later in the book, Jones writes: 'Psychologically, however, he [the skater] has to capture a combination of apparently letting go of the situation and at the same time an imperceptible but none the less complete control of it.'[364] We should also recall here that Jones adopts a similar tone in his analytic essay on the chess master Paul Morphy. 'Careful consideration of the whole of Morphy's play yields,' Jones writes, 'the indubitable conclusion that the outstanding characteristic he exhibited in it was an almost unbelievable supreme *confidence*. He knew, as if it was a simple fact of nature, that he was bound to win, and he acted quietly on this knowledge.'[365]

What makes these passages extraordinary is the fact that Jones clearly equates mastery and control, and hence pleasure, with a 'supreme confidence' that culminates in 'exact knowledge'. Finally, in other words, it is masterful knowledge and not depth analysis which Jones demands as the 'one remedy' to the beginner's prob-lematic fear of skating.[366] Jones thus advocates a position beyond psychological 'treatment' (a word he puts in scare quotes), a position equal to what Jacques Lacan accurately calls a 'completed discourse, the embodiment of absolute knowledge, [which] is the instrument of power, the sceptre and the property of those who know'.[367] At stake here, of course, is the mysterious transition from beginner to instructor in both skating and psychoanalysis. For how does one become a skater/analyst? How does one teach the Grape Vines that are psychoanalysis? Or as Lacan once asked, 'How can what psycho-analysis teaches us be taught?'[368] By turning to 'exact knowledge', Jones – in a way anticipating Lacan – finally initiates the passage into the position of 'the subject who knows', what we could with some license call the *skating passe*; a position not entirely reducible to either practice of skating or analysis, yet somehow essential to both. If so, it would appear that when it is a question of instruction and transmission one must always be excused, as Jones put it, 'for exceeding a little the province proper' of skating and analysis.[369]

Awestruck by the 'supreme triumphs of humanity' embodied in the 'ecstasy of motion' reserved for 'genius',[370] it is not surprising that Jones in turn affirms the special privilege of the master. He writes:

Now, just as great poets, painters and musicians may develop a style that is in opposition to the rules taught by the schools, so may a great skater perform his figures in ways that would be forbidden to a beginner. But for him to do so is not the same as for a beginner to do so. There is all the difference in the world

between a genius transcending the accepted rules, passing beyond
them or creating new ones, and a beginner refusing to go through
the preliminary discipline of the rules . . .[371]

Clearly, this passage tells us something about the roles of mastery
and discipleship in the transmission of psychoanalysis. First of all,
the passage reads like the standard apology for the master's exceptional position as founder of a movement, something we have heard
before in the history of psychoanalysis.[372] As Julius Tandler put it in
a private memorandum the very year that the *Elements* first
appeared: 'He [Freud] is a person who is only accountable to his
own law, who lives according to its direction and cannot subordinate
himself to rules. He is incapable of adapting to a mould because of
his proportions.'[373] Second, the 'difference' between master and
beginner risks being fetishized by Jones to the point where, for
instance, he can accept Freud's notion that 'the simplest way of
learning psychoanalysis was to believe that all he [Freud] wrote was
true and then, after understanding it, one could criticize it any way
one wished . . .'[374] The great risk, of course, is that it 'might prove
difficult . . . to emerge from that initial state of belief'.[375] For finally,
if we take this difficulty seriously, we must ask along with Adam
Phillips a few fundamental questions of psychoanalysis, such as:
'Who in psychoanalysis is in a position to speak and to be believed?
Who has privileged access to the depths, the deepest depths? Or, to
put it another way: who's in charge . . . ?'[376]

Without going much further, it is sufficiently clear that Jones
viewed his function and position in the worlds of skating and psychoanalysis in similar ways. As an analyst and 'diplomat' of the
international psychoanalytic movement, Jones was a protective and
faithful interpreter of Freud's work. As a skater and 'liaison officer'
of the skating world he was an attentive and respectful promulgator
of Captain Richardson's descriptions of the figures and 'system of
sixteen edges' found in *Modern Figure Skating*. As we have seen,
Jones relied heavily on this book, describing it as 'already classical'
and modifying it only 'with consent'. This was high praise indeed

for a book published in 1930, only one year before his own first edition of the *Elements* appeared. But like Jones's book, Richardson's *Modern Figure Skating* has long since gone out-of-print.

3.

In conclusion, we have tried to demonstrate that Jones's lost text, his *Elements of Figure Skating*, deserves to be considered amongst his psychological texts. The book is not just unique in its psychological approach to the problems of skating; more than this, it is a fascinating expression of Jones's professional approach to an extra-professional passion. Unlike Freud, whose hobbies found their way into his theoretical writings in diverse ways during his career, Jones's hobby of figure skating worked itself out in well defined, if humourless, formulations into which flowed his professional preoccupations. Thus while figure skating may not have held for Jones the evocative power, both personal and theoretical, that classical archaeology held for Freud, his hobby nonetheless gave expression to important themes in his life and work. With this in mind, we argue that Jones's service in the cause of figure skating tapped the enormous reserve of energy he expended on psychoanalysis. Without a doubt, psychoanalysis and figure skating are the two great systems twined around the intriguing figure of Ernest Jones.

11 Psychoanalysis, Doggie Style

From Anna O., through the famous case studies, to the succession of chows that Freud owned, dogs have played an interesting but mostly neglected role in the history of psychoanalysis. Actually, dogs already play a small role in Freud's life during pre-psychoanalytic times. Recall that Freud conducted research in Salomon Stricker's experimental pathology laboratory on the salivary glands of dogs in August 1878, even as he signed his letters to his friend Eduard Silberstein 'Your Cipion', the name of a talking dog in Cervantes's *Novelas Ejemplares*. By 1880 Freud continued in this spirit, signing letters thus: 'Your Cipion, dog under examination' and 'Your faithful Cipion, dog at the hospital of Seville'.[377] Of course, Freud may have identified the 'dog within' in these playful letters, but he typically reserved for himself the role of Cervantes's *smart* dog, 'the critical, pedagogic, and clever Cipion'.[378] And, of course, this is only right, since the young Freud was indeed a precocious puppy.

In the following I explore Freud's late love of dogs, briefly outlining its impact on his professional activity, psychoanalysis. It is true that, quite unlike Ernest Jones's analytically overdetermined pastime, figure skating (Chapter 10), Freud's love of dogs was never simply filtered through the sieve of analysis. Even so, it is not hard to pick up the scent of dogs in psychoanalysis – in Freud's life, theory and practice – and to that extent provide a modestly divergent portrait of the great man and his Cause.

Doggie Scraps: Theories

As we know from anecdotal and biographical sources, Freud eventually came to feel that dogs lacked the sort of ambivalence that made relations among people so frustrating, if not potentially treacherous. For this reason, it is probably no accident that his chows appeared on the psychoanalytic scene – in the waiting room, behind the couch, in his correspondence, and so on – even as his pessimism about human nature grew. This was the era of Freud's late, brooding, 'cultural' or 'social' works; works that are, just the same, anti-cultural and anti-social to the bone. It is certainly tempting to see in Freud's turn toward dogs a simultaneously turn away from those he considered 'unworthy' of psychoanalysis: the angry mob or, better yet, the howling pack as described in his group psychology.

Freud of course felt that the mob could not be expected to sublimate their animal instincts in socially productive ways. As he argues in *The Future of an Illusion*, while sublimation propels the elite to engage the fields of science and art, the majority would have to rely on the old standbys, namely, superstition and religion. Either way, one had to tame the animal within. As Freud put it during a private meeting of colleagues, an unnamed world-famous surgeon began his career with an auspicious act of brutality: cutting, in a drunken humour, the tails of every loose dog he could find.[379] For Freud, sadism definitely had its uses.

Unlike the almost magical process of sublimation, which shapes and refines instinct along socially productive lines, repression puts instinct in a hole and buries it – but never quite deep enough to avoid stumbling over it on occasion. In a speculative footnote in *Civilization and Its Discontents*, Freud contends that the origin of repression is tied to the overcoming of smell as our dominant sense. Apparently an upright posture makes smelling-out friend, foe and sexual partner a job better suited to our sense of sight. And here is where Freud finds an explanation for a puzzling piece of modern, although perfectly retrograde, human psychology: 'in spite of all man's developmental advances, he scarcely finds *his own* excreta repulsive, but only that of other people's'.[380] Of course, Freud recognizes that dogs share this peculiarity with human beings, especially with their youngest (i.e., most primitive) members. Like the least social of human beings, children, dogs never abhor a foul smell, nor do they deny their 'sexual functions'.

As always, though, Freud seems to both admonish and admire such asocial behaviour. Certainly in easy-going, *gemütlich* Vienna, one would find such dog-like behaviour among people just more fodder for low humour, often of the scatological variety. But among psychoanalysts, humour, human foibles and dog-like behaviours were also fodder for insight into our primitive condition. At least on a theoretical level, asocial characters were not only admirable, but even commendable. It is partly in this respect that Freud came to admire and respect his own dogs. As he wrote when Jofi first arrived, 'She is a charming creature, so interesting, in her feminine characteristics too, wild, impulsive, gentle, intelligent and yet not so dependent as dogs often are. One cannot help feeling respect for animals like this.'[381] Like a child, Jofi 'the lioness'[382] promised Freud a glimpse into our archaic past. That the trained and thoroughly socialized child-dog could ever provide such hope is, of course, problematic to the extreme. But psychoanalysis always plays with puppies while it speaks of wolves.

Discipleship: A Man and His Dogs

> Have you ever seen a dog falling upon a marrow-bone? He is, as Plato says, the most philosophical beast in the world.
>
> (Rabelais, *Gargantua*)

As pack-leader of his often unruly horde of parricidal brothers, many have argued that Freud demanded the sort of obedience from his followers better suited for his dogs. For not only did Freud – 'The old dog', as he himself once put it[383] – 'muzzle' his Viennese colleagues who needed to be kept 'like dogs on a leash'.[384] He is also reported to have complained[385] that some of his followers would 'take a bone from the table, and chew it independently in the corner. But it is my bone!'[386] A similar comment is recorded by the analyst Richard Sterba, this time with direct reference to a particularly naughty follower: 'Adler took a bone out of psychoanalysis and now he sits over it in a corner and growls.'[387] Given all the dog-talk, it is perhaps not surprising that Carl Jung would finally remark that Freud produced 'either slavish sons or impudent puppies'.[388]

Even though innate human aggressiveness became the cornerstone of Freud's late works, the civilized, self-controlled, discontented Freud drifted away from an active role as leader of the Cause. Increasingly, Freud worked his influence, his animal magnetism, at a safe distance. No doubt he tired of the in-fighting among the competing sons and puppies, especially as he did battle with cancer in the 1920s and 1930s. During this period Freud tried to explain why it is that man is a wolf to man, '*homo homini lupus*'.[389] In this respect, relations with his own obedient dogs and would-be philosophers were arguably a replacement for active relations with his sometimes defiant followers. As Roazen puts it, 'Freud's attachment to dogs was a substitute for his old relationships with people, as he found it increasingly difficult to start out anew.'[390]

Moreover, dogs fit the bill in a way that no other animal (or human) could. According to the poet and analysand Hilda Doolittle, Freud never liked cats or monkeys. Of them Freud is recorded as saying: 'We have not the satisfaction of their being like us, nor the satisfaction of their being enemies.'[391] Presumably dogs promised both these satisfactions: once wild and dangerous creatures, they had been tamed (that is, repressed) by society over the centuries. Such, perhaps, is the shared group psychology of man and dog, where the repression of instinct leads to inevitable conflicts which require, in the end, the firm hand of a Master or Leader. In this regard the institutionalization of the training analysis in the 1920s, which is to say the Word of Freud, was nothing more than house training for disobedient, or potentially disobedient, dogs.

Unlike his most devoted followers, however, Freud was free to put analysis aside whenever it suited him. An example is recounted by Ernst Simmel. During a walk, Freud and Simmel encountered a chained-up police dog. Ignoring Simmel's warnings, Freud unchained the dog and received sloppy kisses for his kindness. 'If you had been chained up all your life,' Freud told Simmel, 'you'd be vicious too.'[392] Of course, human psychology was never, for the psychoanalyst in Freud, reducible to such a social (that is, humane) explanation. So it would seem that Freud was willing to extend to dogs the kind of practical considerations that he was unwilling to extend to his fellow man – especially in theory.

Puppy Love

Whatever one makes of these myriad tales, it is certainly true that the presence of dogs within Freud's office after 1928 complicated the transference. It cannot be surprising to learn that the appearance of Anna's walking companion, an Alsatian named Wolf (ca. 1925), and Freud's chows, Lun Yug, Jumbo, Jofi (a.k.a. Jo-fi or Yofi) and Lün, would have unnerved some analysands. For instance, American psychiatrist Roy Grinker reports that he waited at the front door of Bergasse 19 for the first time 'while dogs barked and growled' from within.[393] Other analysands were regularly met by Jofi at the door or in the hallway. In fact, according to Freud's son, Martin Freud, 'Our dogs had the freedom of the flat and met everyone who came, being quite selective, even judicious, in the receptions they offered.'[394] Another American psychiatrist, Joseph Wortis, recalled the scene as follows: 'The dog and I were both admitted at the same time [to Freud's office].'[395] One can only wonder how many analysands were brave enough to make Smiley Blanton's request: namely, that Wolf be removed during his sessions in 1929.[396]

That the dog was a 'wild card' in the analysis is undeniable.[397] One rather humorous instance of this is described by Wortis: 'At this point [in the analysis] Freud's big chow was heard scratching on the door, and Freud rose, as he had before, to let the dog in. She settled on the carpet and began licking her private parts. Freud did not approve of this behaviour, and tried to make her stop. "It's just like psychoanalysis," he said.'[398] In an earlier report of this same incident, Wortis quotes Freud as saying: 'She [Jofi] always behaves psychoanalytically.'[399] Apparently the jocular Freud had the habit of telling patients that his chows were 'psychoanalytic dogs'.[400]

However humorous one finds the presence of dogs in Freud's late practice, it is clear that they provided an easy vehicle for the resistances of either analyst or analysand. Thus Doolittle reports how 'I was annoyed at the end of my session as Yofi would wander about and I felt the Professor was more interested in Yofi than in my story.'[401] However, it may have been that Jofi simply had a better sense than Doolittle of what a fifty-minute hour felt like. As Martin Freud writes: 'He [Freud] always claimed, and we must accept his word since there were never any witnesses during analytical treatment, that he never had to look at his watch to decide when the hour's treatment should end. When Jofi got up and yawned, the time was up; she was never late in announcing the end of a session, although father did admit that she was capable of an error of perhaps a minute, at the expense of the patient.'[402]

Naturally, apologists for Freud have tried to downplay the presence of dogs in his office, claiming that they 'stayed quietly . . . sitting soberly' during analytic sessions[403]; or again, that the 'dog would sit quietly at the foot of the couch during the analytic hour'.[404] But it is evident that dogs were a noticeable and disturbing, if not well-known part, of Freud's later practice. Who wouldn't notice the smell of dogs in Freud's office or, worse, their 'rhythmical panting' during sessions?[405] As for how just well-known a part of Freud's clinical practice dogs were, one need only recall the successful hoax that Odette Pannetier, a French journalist, played on Freud in 1936 in order to get a rare interview with him: she pretended to suffer from a dog phobia.[406]

It is abundantly clear that by indulging his love for dogs Freud disregarded his precious council concerning proper analytic technique, namely, the idea that analysts should strive for neutrality while freely attending to the patient's unconscious. Of course, dogs were just one part of Freud's general disregard for his own rules, which after all were only offered as rough guidelines or, more accurately, as pretty window-dressings for troublesome interlopers – especially those of a critical bent looking to make trouble for psychoanalysis. In reality Freud's office was anything but neutral, reflecting his personality in multiple ways, from his antiquities on display and his incessant cigar smoking to his dogs. As Gary Genosko puts it, 'the dog was always there in the communicational channel. There is nothing neutral about the presence of a dog; puppy love puts one's [evenly suspended] attention off balance.'[407]

It is worth recalling that Freud does refer to dogs in the context of his recommendations concerning analytic technique.[408] Freud insists that analysts must avoid gratifying the sexual advances of the patient on pain of confusing the illusory love found in analysis with (the potential for) real love outside. The analyst 'must not stage the scene of a dog-race in which the prize was to be a garland of sausages but which some humorist spoilt by throwing a single sausage on the track'.[409] In effect, the psychoanalyst must not permit himself to go into heat and offer the patient his sausage-penis; instead the responsible analyst must encourage the patient to leave the analytical dog-house.

Of course, the transference helped keep the Cause viable among those happy to love Freud, those who had indeed accepted the sausage of psychoanalysis rather than get on with their lives. And dogs played their part in this love affair. After an initial encounter, dogs became objects through which Freud and his followers could maintain friendly ties. During her analysis proper, Doolittle and Freud would often chat about the dogs:

> We talked again of Yofi [the golden 'lioness']. I asked of Yofi's father. Yofi is to be a mother. He told me that Yofi's first husband was a black chow and Yofi had one black baby, 'as black as the devil'. It died when it was three-quarters of a year old. Now the father is lion-gold and the Professor hopes that Yofi's children will survive, this time.[410]

The subtext of racial purity makes these discussions interesting, and not a little disturbing. But it also undermines the idea that dogs were an incidental, extra-analytic, hobby of Freud's. The presence of dogs in analysis, like the recounting of a dream, inevitably provided an opportunity to discuss whatever came to mind – such as the inheritance of racial characteristics. A similar conclusion can be drawn from a letter Freud sent to Doolittle after the analysis was completed. Speaking of 'much commotion in the dog-state', Freud states: 'Wulf [sic] had to be shipped off to Kagran, because both ladies were in heat, and the fierce antagonism between Yofi and Lün, which is rooted in the nature of women, resulted in good, gentle Lün's being bitten by Yofi.'[411] Lün was eventually shipped back to Dorothy Burlingham, where she remained until Jofi's death in January 1937. But the main point here is Freud's throw-away line that the jealousy between female dogs is 'rooted in the nature of *women*' – as contentious and offensive a statement as any of Freud's. (Perhaps Freud was thinking of the three 'bitches' in his life: Martha, Minna and Anna.)

With some others, though, the dogs would simply get in the way of any meaningful relationship to the father of psychoanalysis. Sandor Rado reports that, during his last visit with Freud in 1932, 'about 90 percent of his [Freud's] affection went to the dog and the rest to me'.[412] Obviously dogs were a diversion that Freud didn't hesitate to use. Moreover, dogs were thought capable of sniffing out undesirable characters, and thus problematizing their relationship to the master. Such natural 'insight' was an especially useful talent since Freud himself is often considered to have been a notoriously poor *Mennschenkenner*, a judge of men. As Martin Freud later recalled, if Jofi didn't like a visitor, 'there was at once a strong suspicion that there was something wrong with that caller's character. Contemplating Jofi's selective qualities at this distance of years, I am bound to admit that her judgement was most reliable.'[413]

Apparently Anna's Wolf passed just such a verdict on Freud's devoted follower, Ernest Jones. As Jones claims in his unfinished memoir, Wolf 'flew at me and tore a piece of my thigh',[414] adding:

'Freud, who was present, sagely remarked on how dogs instinctively recognise those who dislike them or are afraid of them, and at once treat them like enemies.' But Jones, rather characteristically, didn't suspect Freud's actual feelings. In a letter of 13 September 1927 to Max Eitingon, Freud wrote the following: 'I had to punish him [Wolf] for that, but did so reluctantly, for he – Jones – deserved it.'[415]

So what became of puppy love in the history of psychoanalysis? First of all, other analysts didn't hesitate to introduce 'psychoanalytic dogs' to their practice, from Karen Horney to Kurt Eissler. And the extra-professional attachment to dogs would continue to pop up here and there in the literature, as when Lacan would talk to his dog Justine, concluding aloud to a student that 'the only difference between her and you is that you went to university'.[416] As for the transference, few have felt obliged to confront its animal dimensions – in particular the affective dimension. As Lacan put it, 'Keep going in that direction and I dare say the last word in the transference will be a reciprocal sniffing.'[417] But that's the sad truth of it. The dog with the best nose wins.

Doggie Heaven

If dogs provided a common medium through which Freud could communicate with a follower, this was nowhere more true than in the case of his relationship with long-time supporter and friend Marie Bonaparte, the Princess George of Greece. In fact, it was Bonaparte who gave Freud his first chow, Lun-Yug, the sister of the more famous Jofi. As Martin Freud put it: 'Under father's guidance, the Princess made psychoanalysis one of her main interests in life; under the influence of the Princess, Sigmund Freud became a commonplace dog-lover.'[418]

In the mid 1930s, Bonaparte prepared a little book about her chow named Topsy, what her biographer calls 'a curious and touching hymn to life and love'.[419] Originally published in 1937 as *Topsy, chow-chow au poil d'or*, the book was later translated into

German by Freud and Anna in 1939 (publishing it that year in Amsterdam), while the English translation by Bonaparte's daughter Princess Eugénie appeared in 1940. That Freud expressed such interest in the book points again to his own extra-analytic love of dogs. But the translation was also a show of gratitude for Bonaparte who was a close friend and, along with Ernest Jones, was able to help secure Freud's escape from the Nazis.

During the winter of 1935, Bonaparte noticed a tumour on Topsy's lip, which upon inspection proved to be lymphosarcoma. Having already donated generously to the Curie Institute, Bonaparte took the extraordinary step of having Topsy treated with X-rays.[420] The investment paid off, since Topsy in fact recovered. The resulting book, *Topsy: The Story of a Golden-Haired Dog*, is thus a story of premature mourning for a dog sick with cancer of the mouth. As such, the book begs to be read against the fact that Freud also suffered from cancer of the jaw at this time (from 1923 until his death in 1939), and also that Bonaparte's own father Prince Roland had already died of cancer in 1924. The book also reflects the social conditions that were making life more difficult in France and elsewhere[421]; consequently, for both Bonaparte and Freud, dogs provided some 'Respite From Things Human' – the title of a chapter late in the book. To these ends, Bonaparte explores her ambivalent relationship to Topsy and the spectre of death which binds them together as 'sisters'. Yet, insofar as Topsy is ignorant of death, the dog exemplifies for Bonaparte the good sense, even 'wisdom', that escapes the philosopher's grasp: sometimes it is best not to anticipate the future or be haunted by the memory of one's past. A dog growls over a bone, not as a philosopher contemplating existence, but as a simple animal savouring the moment. Still, Bonaparte hardly gives up on Topsy, and recounts her treatment with the 'Magical Rays' of radiation therapy. When Topsy recovers, Bonaparte regains some of her distance to the dog, but notes that death and mourning were, of course, only deferred. As Freud liked to say in a misquote of Shakespeare, 'everyone owes nature a death and must expect to pay that debt'.[422] Even so, the recovered Topsy becomes for Bonaparte a 'magical dog', a 'Talisman of life' which promises protection from this inevitable horizon.[423]

As it happened, Freud received the manuscript for *Topsy* not long before Jofi died from two ovarian cysts. So the book may have helped with Freud's grieving, although the return of Lün, who had been boarding with Dorothy Burlingham for four years, was the best medicine. Having read the manuscript, Freud wrote Bonaparte the following letter on 6 December 1937:

> Your card from Athens and the manuscript of the Topsy book have just arrived. I love it; it is so movingly real and true. It is, of course, not an analytic work, but the analyst's search for truth and knowledge can be perceived behind this creation. It really gives the real reasons for the remarkable fact that one can love an animal like Topsy (or my Jo-fi) so deeply: affection without any ambivalence, the simplicity of life free from the conflicts of civilization that are so hard to endure, the beauty of existence complete in itself. And in spite of the remoteness in the organic development there is nevertheless a feeling of close relationship, of undeniably belonging together. Often when I stroke Jo-fi I find myself humming a melody which, unmusical though I am, I can recognize as the (Octavio) aria from Don Juan:

> *A bond of friendship*
> *binds us both, etc.*

The Absolute Master

Thanks to numerous operations on his jaw between 1924 and 1939, Freud's death from cancer had been postponed for years. But they had taken their toll. After one operation in late 1936, Freud suffered badly, a locked jaw making it difficult to eat or drink without great pain. 'I carry on with my analyses,' Freud wrote, 'by changing a hot water bottle every half hour to hold to my cheek.'[424] And then he added, 'I wish you could have seen what sympathy Jo-fi shows me in my suffering, just as if she understood everything.'

When his dog, Bellet-Bonne, licked the ailing Voltaire, the philosopher is reported to have remarked that it was 'Life kissing Death' – a sentiment Freud and Bonaparte would have appreciated. But in the end Freud didn't share Voltaire's good luck, being abandoned by his dog Lün. The story is rather sad. According to Freud's personal physician, Max Schur, cancer had caused a secondary infection. As a consequence, 'the skin over [Freud's] cheekbone became gangrenous, eventually creating a hole and open communication between the oral cavity and the outside'.[425] And so Lün – who was a recent addition to the family; one who had been stuck in quarantine for six months, according to British law – kept his distance. 'The chow to which Freud was so attached,' Schur writes, 'could not tolerate the smell, and could not be prodded into coming near him. When brought into the room the dog crouched in the farthest corner. Freud knew what this meant, and looked at his pet with a tragic and knowing sadness.'[426] Like the youngest, asocial child, Freud knew that his dog – 'the dearest friend of father's later years'[427] – could never tell a lie. The master was dying.

When he first suspected his cancer in 1924, Freud intimated to his physician, Felix Deutsch, that he would prefer to make a quick, sensible end to it all. In turn Deutsch kept the bad news from him, a fact that greatly angered Freud. Yet the ailing Freud strikes a heroic, or at least stoical, figure. Despite his growing pessimism about people, and despite his own thoughts concerning suicide, Freud battled his disease until almost the very end. 'It's nothing but torture,' Freud finally told Schur in September 1939, 'and it makes no sense any more.'[428] Schur mercifully helped put an end to his pain; with a total of three morphine injections over two days, Freud slipped into a coma and died at 3 a.m. on 23 September 1939.

On the one hand, Freud's death by cancer seems an embodiment of his death drive theory: it did its work almost silently from the inside. As Freud put it to Lou Andreas-Salome, and not long after he first learned about the cancer, 'A crust of indifference is slowly creeping up around me; a fact I state without complaining. It is a natural development, a way of beginning to grow inorganic. The "detachment of old age", I think it is called.'[429] In short, the interruption called life was winding down. On the other hand, Freud's death by cancer is nearly a cosmic mockery of Freud – the father of the 'talking cure' who, after operations for a prosthesis of the lower jaw, could only with pain and difficulty speak to his family and patients. If Freud finally adopted a silent posture behind the couch, it didn't come easily.

Freud only late in life became a dog-lover. And then, according to his maid, Paula, he would begin every day stroking his dog's head, and then that of the 'Baboon of Thoth', a marble baboon that was considered a 'god of intellectual pursuits' for the cult Thoth.[430] Obviously the clever Cipion recognized himself in this special baboon. Indeed, Freud always expected greatness from himself. And so he paid his debt to nature, to biological necessity, by first of all becoming what he was – the master of psychoanalysis, the leader of a world-wide Cause – and then, secondly, by becoming what he was driven to be according to the dictates of biology: dead. In both pursuits Freud proved how attractive it can be to believe so completely in one's self, one's delusion, one's mission. This is not a criticism – or, rather, it is not just a criticism. For one cannot help but admire someone willing and able to pay a debt to nature in full. Sometimes one cannot help but admire a dogmatist his dogmatism.

PART IV

Interview

12 *Psychoanalysis, Parasites and the 'Culture of Banality'*

by Antonio Greco

Antonio Greco: How do psychoanalytic studies compare with academic work done in other fields?

Todd Dufresne: Very poorly. Frankly, in very few fields is the level of scholarship so slipshod. The blame for this problem can be traced to the fact that Freud and his close followers established psychoanalysis outside the university system by creating their own training institutes. For the goal of these institutes was less research and intellectual activity than the protection and transmission of doctrine from generation to generation. It was politics and religiosity, rather than ideas, that gave birth to institutional psychoanalysis in the 1920s.

Of course, this situation explains why analysts and their patients generally make for such lousy intellectuals, but it doesn't explain why intellectuals themselves have produced so many lousy books on psychoanalysis. It really is depressing to see how many bad books have been stamped, and will continue to be stamped, with the library code BF 173.

AG: So the academics are not much better than the publishing analysts and their patients?

TD: Although there are exceptions, of course, the field is overrun by advocates who have lost sight of anything resembling intellectual standards. In this respect, blind loyalty to psychoanalysis can often be correlated with the number of years someone has spent on the couch. Obviously it is hard to conclude, after significant emotional and financial investment, that psychoanalysis is groundless and, therefore, a waste of time. However, corruption comes in many forms and really can't be reduced to money and time spent. In my line of work I am more disturbed by the corruption that accompanies the intellectual investment in psychoanalysis. Certainly you don't need to have been analysed for years to become a zealous advocate on behalf of Freud and psychoanalysis. All you need to have done, depending on the size of your ego, is deliver a lecture or publish a book review, article, chapter, book or books, to become incapable of backing out of the enterprise. One goes public with one's ego and becomes incapable of retracting false beliefs.

AG: But surely these problems are found elsewhere in the university.

TD: You're right, of course. By definition, commentary in every field is parasitical and unavoidably requires a body of literature, a host, in which to set up shop. As such it's easy to see how intellectuals discipline and order themselves. For without the host, the parasite dies; the insights of post-structuralism notwithstanding, 'secondary' activities exist because we are willing to accept, at least contingently, that some other activities are primary. For this reason parasitical intellectuals often establish cosy and conservative attitudes toward their host subject. In some cases, the intellectual even becomes an advocate on behalf of his or her field. And while this advocacy may or may not be justified given the social or political context, such advocacy has very little to do with scholarship.

But while this problem of corruption is present in all intellectual activity, it is rampant in Freud studies. To begin with, the central roles of fantasy and transference in psychoanalytic theory and practice seem to rationalize in advance the contamination of objectivity – and make it a routine cost of doing business. Thus do psychoanalysts laugh at the philosopher's naive belief in reality, since for them reality is merely a stage upon which we enact our subjective desires and fantasies. What is 'true' for a Lacanian, for example, is quite simply this subjective appreciation of reality. So objectivity, including the problems of representation and correspondence, is left conveniently at the door of the analyst's office. Knowledge becomes a matter of conveying one's desire to another.

AG: What about the competing desires of the critics?

TD: Unfortunately, too many critics are willing to play by the rules of this self-serving game, gullibly accepting the idea that their judgements can be – or should be – subject to the same belittling discourse that is applied to patients. Consequently, a critic might in advance tone down his or her language; sprinkle flattery over a particularly damning conclusion; and make sure to promote Freud's genius at certain points in his or her argument. In short, the infected critic will police his or her conclusions in order to avoid the obvious charges of resistance, Oedipal-inspired parricide, negative transference, and so on. Other critics, typically those of a postmodernist bent, will accept that his or her subject position is 'always already' entangled in Freudian discourse. And so the ideal of objectivity is abandoned even before the critique has begun.

AG: How would you situate your own thought *vis-a-vis* that of Freud critic Frederick Crews?

TD: That's a difficult question. I certainly agree with his critical assessment of Freud and psychoanalysis, and have the greatest respect for what he has done for Freud criticism. Moreover, I generally endorse his stand on rationality, which he ties explicitly to the ideals of democracy. In a recent interview,[432] Crews basically told me that he wants to protect democratic principles from the kind of intellectual thuggery and hypocrisy that inevitably snuggles up to grand interpretive schemes like psychoanalysis. Unlike Crews, though, I have a measured affection for many of the thugs and con-artists he finds morally and intellectually repulsive. For example, I am merely *amused* by the colossal absurdities of Freudo-Marxism. I also find the works of explicitly anti-democratic thinkers attractive, which, after all, includes among their ranks recognizably great figures like Socrates and Nietzsche. My impish playfulness reflects a part of postmodernism that Crews rejects – the part he views, I would guess, as irrational and socially irresponsible. So, to put a fine point on it, while we are both happy gadflies attacking the established truths of psychoanalysis, my style or mood is quite different from his.

At the same time, and despite my retrograde attraction to some aspects of post-structuralism and Continental philosophy, the analytic rebel in me finds Crews's faith in reason and social justice attractive. I also recognize that the indulgence of radical elements within democracy is itself a luxury afforded by democracy. But for me the ideal of democracy is strengthened by a certain amount of what Nietzsche once called 'illiberality to the point of malice'.

AG: What about Crews's adamant belief in science and empiricism?

TD: Obviously, I agree that science and empiricism are essential mediums for acquiring a certain kind of knowledge about things. I like bridges that don't fall down and toilets that flush. But I approach these achievements much the same way I do democracy. That is, I embrace the anti-scientific thinkers as an essential and interesting part of the process. And so I am in principle favourably disposed to the epistemological anarchism of Feyerabend, the undecidability of Derrida and Lyotard and, from both sides of the Atlantic, the sorts of nominalism found in Foucault and Goodman. Also, I am often less interested in truth and reality than in truth-effects and discourse. From this orientation follows my interest in historicizing the discourse of psychoanalysis.

I must also say, though, that I am not an expert in the philosophy of science and reserve the right to change my mind! Who knows – Crews may yet convince me to abandon my few remaining delusions. The important thing to remember is that Crews and I agree that Freud's theories are *not* what he claimed they were, namely, empirically based truths. Given Freud's own assumptions, we can easily agree that he was a rotten scientist.

AG: Some say that critics of Freud go too far, and are merely advocates and polemicists for the opposing camp.

TD: It is true that I am in another camp than many, perhaps even the majority, of Freud scholars. But I would say that this is true for a very simple reason: they happen to be mostly wrong, while we are mostly right!

AG: I know you are joking, but doesn't this sort of statement prove the point that you aren't free from the corrupting effect of polemicizing?

TD: Look, I'm a big fan of clear and distinct, cool and restrained argumentation. But there is a time and a place for polemics. This reminds me of an amusing remark that Ferenczi once made to Freud. Let me read this passage from a letter of March 9, 1911: 'As for polemicizing against opponents, I am entirely of your opinion. This kind of polemic is also boring and painful to me. And yet I also want to force myself to do it in the future.'[433] So when is it a good time and place for polemics? Precisely after one has made a clear and distinct argument. The right to make a polemical remark has to be earned in order to be respected.

AG: But don't you deplore the polemics of your opponents?

TD: Yes and no. I respect anyone willing to argue a case with passion and wit. It is to Freud's credit as an artist that he was such a great writer and a clever polemicist on behalf of his beliefs. But the artist was fundamentally mistaken about many things; or, to put it more accurately, Freud's artistry always came before the facts. Clearly Freud's admirable passion and wit is not always supported by rigorous argumentation. On the contrary, he was a romantic thinker who used reason to rationalize his mistaken, sometimes laughably mistaken, beliefs – from his meta-biological fantasies to his psycho-analytic portraits of historical figures.

The same point holds for current debates in the field. I am happy to argue about Freud with anyone, provided the humour isn't too malicious and the arguments aren't merely *ad hominem*. But I have no patience whatsoever with my colleagues who spin the facts to suit their arguments, and who resort to name-calling to smear an opponent. As one of the original petitioners of the Library of Congress Freud exhibit, I can appreciate what it is like to be the victim of misinformation, lies and hate. As a group we were called fascists, ayatollahs, censors and so on. Of course this verdict is ironic since our advocacy was on behalf of openness and fairness. Moreover we share no political agenda in common and – let's be honest – don't necessarily know, like or even respect one another. So these are the facts. But a certain brand of polemicist doesn't care one whit about facts. I am afraid that well-reasoned, clear and distinct ideas are in too little evidence in Freud studies. Consequently, the polemics are often undisciplined and personal, even among fellow-travellers.

AG: Aren't 'clear and distinct ideas', a staple of Anglo-American philosophy, unsuited to someone influenced by post-structuralism?

TD: I have had that observation thrown in my face a number of times – typically, and I think tellingly, by angry graduate students with nothing to lose but time. Well, nowadays I take that observation as a compliment, backhanded or otherwise. Why? Quite simply because I now see much of post-structuralism as a handmaiden of psychoanalysis. And since I think psychoanalysis has been a terrible mistake, I cannot approve of another theoretical movement that advances this mistaken agenda. Of course, I didn't recognize this complicity as a problem at first – and to be honest I wasn't willing to recognize it. You need to have ears to hear such things, especially when you are young and trying to earn some interest on your hard-won intellectual investments.

AG: You are still young!

TD: But hopefully less foolish. At one point in my graduate education I realized that it was just too easy to go along and ape the mind-set and, above all, the styles of various post-structuralists. So what began for me as an exciting project on the edge of traditional thinking quickly became dull and conventional. Nowadays I tend to think that clear and distinct ideas, no matter how boring they can be, are often the most radical way of proceeding. Of course, we have all been trained over the last thirty years or so to think that well-considered arguments and cold, hard truths are inherently violent, misogynistic, patriarchal, logocentric and so on. But again, this view, once adopted to criticize dominant ideologies, has become just another ideology. Worst of all, it has lent its intellectual authority and institutional prestige to the abuses of identity politics. But is it really acceptable that deviations from the party line result in a litany of abusive name-calling and blacklisting? Does our thinking have to be so policed and banal? Dare I say it, so 'fascistic' – to throw it back at these critics? For me, this culture of banality, grown on the back of post-structuralist critiques of essentialism, has nothing to do with decent scholarship and everything to do with advocacy. I've certainly had enough of it.

AG: But can't we thank post-structuralism for challenging old pre-conceptions inherited from a father-knows-best philosophy?

TD: Sure we can. Post-structuralism began with a radical impulse to dismantle and reassess the philosophical tradition, beginning with a critique of the modernist subject inherited from Descartes. Scholars like Derrida and Foucault taught us how to read old texts differently, and we owe them a substantial debt. I certainly do, in any case. But to keep churning out this stuff twenty-five years later has become a bore and, as it has become more acceptable within the university, merely another kind of convention. We do these thinkers a disservice when we ignore their own radical impulses – but so do they when they establish themselves, or are established by others, as the latest in a line of gurus and prophets. We need fresh air to breath, and I recommend using their theoretical sophistication against them.

AG: In *Tales* you turn the proliferation of opinion about Freud's death drive theory to critical advantage. But what does this proliferation of opinion teach us about Freud's critics?

TD: I tried to make the heterogeneity of opinion about Freud's death drive theory work on a few levels, one being a pointed criticism of the arbitrary nature of criticism in the history of psychoanalysis. In this respect the apparent dissensus about the fundamentals of psychoanalysis is a scandal. For this dissensus implies that for over one hundred years smart people haven't been able to derive any conclusions about Freud's so-called discoveries – that the verdict is still out. But that's untrue! Informed critics know very well that Freud fabricated his findings and was motivated by factors other than science and objectivity.

So why do so few people know, or care to know, about these sometimes stunning facts? In no small measure, and as you were just hinting, the pundits and critics themselves are to blame. In *Tales* I tried to expose the irreconcilable absurdity of Freud commentary over the last hundred years, from Reich and Marcuse to Lacan and Derrida. It's obviously not the case that these people are ignorant. It is rather the case that these critics, like Freud before them, are motivated by special interests; for example, by Marxist, structuralist, or post-structuralist interests. And because their works are dogmatically blind to intractable problems in Freud's work, including basic facts, they have the effect of blinding nearly everyone who reads them. We love to be dazzled, even by the spectacle of crushed glass.

AG: But what is a 'basic fact', and who is in a position to know one when he or she sees one? Isn't this where the post-modernist appreciation of Freud comes in?

TD: That's a lot of questions to answer all at once! First of all, yes, the 'posties' – post-modernists and post-structuralists – have generally embraced the idea that history is just a kind of fiction. I am sympathetic to this idea and am willing to entertain it up to a point. I have written about fiction and history in psychoanalysis precisely because, given the pre-eminent role of fantasy in the field, one has a tough time distinguishing between fact and fiction, history and case study. I think this is an interesting and amusing state of affairs, and have even written a short story that is meant as a send-up of the kind of historical work that we all read. But I attempt this work in an ironical spirit, believing that there are indeed facts – even if psychoanalysis has made it seem near impossible for us to know them. This, then, is a problem for psychoanalysis – but not really for me.

Naturally, though, I do worry about being too cavalier about facts in history. Is it really the case that the opinion of, say, a Holocaust denier is equal to another who believes that three million Jews, rather than six million, were killed in concentration camps? One says it didn't happen at all, while another questions the interpretation of facts. I reject the idea that truth is relative at the level of basic facts, and to this extent echo something Borch-Jacobsen once said[434]: namely, any relativist who ignores the facts risks becoming a dogmatist. And he's right. So when posties say, for example, that the fabricated foundations of psychoanalysis don't matter – primarily, they claim, because psychoanalysis is only interested in fantasy – they are being absurd dogmatists.

But this response is still not very satisfactory, since it doesn't address your first two questions: namely, what is a basic fact, and how can we purport to know one? I would suggest, loosely following the historian R. G. Collingwood, that there are two kinds of history: one that barely deserves the name as it was once practised long ago;

and modern history. The first is what Collingwood rightly calls 'scissor and paste' history, and is more or less concerned with recording dates, names and events: for example, on the ides of March Caesar crossed the Rubicon. The second is interpretive history, and is concerned with the interpretation of dates, names and events: for example, on the ides of March Caesar crossed the Rubicon because he was a megalomaniac, or because he wanted to defeat his enemies, or because he was a compulsive bed-wetter, and so on.

How does this distinction between basic and interpretive history help us? Well, because the majority of Freud scholarship is so obviously an *interpretive history*. The posties know this better than anyone, and are absolutely right to conclude that such interpretation, like analysis, is interminable. We can engage in debate about motives forever. However, there is a fundamental problem here in the case of psychoanalysis. Why? Because all historical interpretation, even the freewheeling interpretive history of post-modernists, is based on the 'scissor and paste' history of mere dates, names and events. And this is where the posties drop the ball. For almost all of the best critiques of Freud made over the last thirty years – the kind I associate with the creation of Critical Freud Studies – have begun by examining basic facts about dates, names and events.

What these critics have found is that the history of Freud interpretation is the history of misinterpretation of a fundamental kind. Namely, it is interpretation of 'facts' or 'events' that *never happened*. For example, they have found that Freud, during the period of 'discovery' and subsequent abandonment of the Seduction Theory, exaggerated his results and, when necessary, simply made them up.

AG: He said he crossed the Rubicon when he didn't?

TD: Worse. Not only didn't he cross the Rubicon, to extend the analogy, but it turns out in this case that the Rubicon itself doesn't exist! It's all a myth. And so, while the posties inevitably berate Cioffi, Crews and others for their naive belief in facts, they have simply fallen into the rabbit hole that Freud dug for them. For his part, Borch-Jacobsen replies that it is really these nay-sayers who are being naive. I would only repeat my suspicion that our gullible colleagues have risked their egos on baseless interpretations that they are now incapable of retracting.

Of course, the stakes are now very high. For if the critics are right, then the majority of Freud interpretation is utterly worthless. And it is worthless in at least two ways: as history and as interpretation. At best, these groundless interpretations are a kind of literary garbage – works of unwitting fiction along the lines of Medieval discussions of angels.[435] Sure these works tell us a lot about the beliefs of a certain period, in this case the twentieth century, but they don't work the way the authors intended them. For me, they are cautionary tales – what Lacan would call 'poubellications', or published trash.

AG: If empiricism is just a theory, isn't a 'basic fact' just an interpretation among others?

TD: That is true and a little bit clever, but a degree of certainty is all I am after. I'm not saying that we can't get our basic facts wrong, which we obviously do. It is rather that we must be willing to revise our interpretations on the basis of the basic facts we do have. I don't blame Freud scholars for making a mess of everything with their erroneous interpretations. Freud misled everyone, beginning with himself and his closest followers. Psychoanalysis is a con-game, after all. That said, short of sticking our heads in the sand, we must confront the basic facts and rewrite the history of psychoanalysis anew.

AG: Unlike what you call the best critics of recent years, you have leapt head-first into the 'interpretive garbage'. Is this a significant shift in emphasis?

TD: I think so. The best critics, such as Cioffi, Sulloway and Borch-Jacobsen, have pretty much milked the scissor and paste history of psychoanalysis. I mean, I'm sure that there are many more things to discover about the fabricated origins of psychoanalysis, but the foundation for an alternative history has now been laid. That's what we should do now, and what I have attempted. And, you're right, unlike most of my colleagues, I am fascinated and amused and disgusted by the interpretive garbage, something I say explicitly in the Preface to *Tales*.

AG: And so the game of interpretation begins again!

TD: Yes, I'm afraid it does. But interpretation is a potentially valuable part of scholarship, so I'm not worried.

AG: Do you consider *Tales* to be a 'true' history of the death drive?

TD: There is more to say about Freud's late theories, including the death drive theory, but I think my contribution rings true. We can always argue about the bits and pieces. But it's plausible interpretive work because it's not blatantly false work. To begin with, I recognize facts that some others don't recognize at all – such as Freud's essential biologism.

AG: Isn't there a danger that, having destroyed the accepted inter-pretations of psychoanalysis, you have also destroyed your own position as a critic? Aren't you the worst kind of parasite, namely, a parricide?

TD: On the one hand, you're right. I understand why people are uncomfortable with this sort of activity. To them, a virulent kind of criticism destroys everything, leaving nothing. To carry on your metaphor, such criticism is considered a virus that kills its own hosts – which seems inherently stupid and self-defeating. I, however, see things quite differently. First of all, it is time we flipped the metaphor of host and parasite on its head. For as I suggest in *Tales*, it is psychoanalysis that has lived off its critics – not the other way around. It is Freud, not the university, that has benefited the most from this relationship. And so the claim that critics are 'killing' Freud is merely a melodramatic way of saying that some of us cannot believe in the claims of psychoanalysis and are willing to demonstrate why to anyone willing to read our arguments. Having said that, the truth is that I still enjoy reading Freud and am happy to teach his work to my students. At last Freud has been transformed into a proper object of historical and intellectual interest; a figure suitable for examination in the university.

AG: Freud studies have finally come of age?

TD: Freud scholars, in any case. The lost cause of psychoanalysis, so infused with a non-intellectual and even anti-intellectual bias, dominated by partisan interests, and characterized by a stunning degree of ill-will and prickish behaviour, has finally made way for a new cause – actually an old one – that of rigorous, informed scholarship. That's why the death of this era should inspire a few years of celebration. We've certainly earned it.

PART V

Coda

13 Crisis, Death and the
Futures of Psychoanalysis

> Looking back, then, over the patch-work of my life's labours, I
> can say that I have made many beginnings and thrown out many
> suggestions. Something will come of them in the future.
>
> (Sigmund Freud, *An Autobiographical Study*)

Psychoanalysis has been a notable part of Western culture, from its
highest to lowest expressions, for over 100 years now. So it's no
wonder the many producers and consumers of this culture have
been left confused by its precipitous decline. Of course, confusion
about Freud's legacy has always been a staple of the history of psychoanalysis, if not the actual condition of its acceptance across a
heterogeneous landscape.[436]

The current confusion about what constitutes Freud's essential
legacy is just the latest crisis in a long history of crises. No one, not
even Freud's closest followers, has ever convincingly separated the
good ideas from the bad. Instead, they accept certain ideas on a
hunch, intuition or misunderstanding – and run with them. The
story of this 'impossible profession', as Freud put it in 1937, is
simply the story of an impossible consensus among its participants.
Otherwise put, it is the history of schisms, where anyone with a
modicum of ambition, talent and self-respect has broken off from
one schism to found another.

An impulse to crisis, which has been undeniably constructive in
its self-destruction, came to its surreal climax with Jacques Lacan.
Unable to find acceptance with established psychoanalysis, Lacan

started his own analytic movement, and then another, and then another. Why surreal? Because members of the first, second, and third groups could all claim in good faith that they were authentically 'Lacanian', and could on that basis disdain all the rest. This apparently singular situation in France was, however, only the absurd repetition of what was always already the case: Freud would gather supporters, then excommunicate them; would help establish someone's credentials, then would take them away.[437] In response, dissenters such as Alfred Adler, Otto Rank and Wilhelm Reich would lay claim to some part of psychoanalysis, repackage it, and then carry on with their activities: writing speculative works of psychology, gathering and instructing students, and treating patients. The more they drifted from Freud the more perfectly Freudian they became: that is to say, creative and wild.

Consider a thumbnail sketch of the history of the psychoanalytic movement. In the early days of psychoanalysis, Freud meets with an uneven group of supporters every Wednesday. They discuss psychoanalytic ideas, but the group disappoints and probably bores Freud, too. Freud drifts from this group when he gathers the support of more worthy supporters, such as Carl Jung. Not long thereafter, however, members of the new group also disappoint Freud, and some go off on their own. Ultimately, even stalwart supporters like Sándor Ferenczi earn the disapproval and anger of an increasingly intolerant Freud. Meanwhile, in the USA there arises a new culture of psychoanalysis, which Freud dislikes, narrowly grounded in medicine. Yet the main thinkers of psychoanalysis in America will be transplanted Europeans, especially those fleeing Nazi Germany. 'Neo-Freudian' or 'culturalist' critics such as Karen Horney, Erich Fromm and Harry Stack Sullivan voice their opposition to Freud's biologically derived pessimism, and reorient the theory and practice toward social and environmental concerns. Other analysts, beginning with Heinz Hartmann, Rudolph Lowenstein and Ernst Kris, push psychoanalysis even further in the direction of adaptation to environment, and found 'ego psychology'. Others in the New World continue to push psychoanalysis in directions suggested by a host of other thinkers, including a group of core dissident analysts such as Adler (superiority), Jung (collective unconscious), Rank (birth trauma) and Reich (orgone energy). Erik Erikson and others take up the task of 'applied psychoanalysis' that Freud attempts in his most speculative moments; still others push psychoanalysis into new contexts, such as psychosomatic medicine (e.g., Franz Alexander), personality studies (e.g., Abram Kardiner, Ruth Benedict), and criminology. Meanwhile, psychiatrists embrace psychoanalysis, with many leading figures training and practising in both fields. Out of this melting pot of competing ideas and applications arises numerous new psychological movements, eventually dubbed self-psychology, relational psychology and interpersonal psychoanalysis. Psychoanalysis also flourishes in artistic communities, from the surrealists to the Beat poets. The British are an important part of this story, where major battles rage over the instinct/society, biology/psychology tension that is evident in Freud's own work (it all depends on which work, from which time, you consult). The theory of 'object relations' gains new adherents, originally centred on Melanie Klein's biologically grounded speculations about child development. Freud, ever a protective papa, rejects Klein's theory in support of the less Freudian, less imaginative, but nonetheless dutiful daughter, Anna. This stance rightly confuses partisans of Freud's late metapsychology. Finally, after years of xenophobic resistance to Freud, the French graft psychoanalysis onto their own past and current preoccupations: the glorious history of French philosophy, especially the philosophy of the rational subject as first formulated by René Descartes, and the fashionable investigations in surrealism, cybernetics and structuralism. Lacan becomes the pre-eminent psychoanalytic thinker, actually a guru, that makes psychoanalysis speak French. And, finally, Jacques Derrida and other French post-structuralists use psychoanalysis to advance their own Nietzsche-inspired theories about the unstable Cartesian subject, and this material is in turn exported to the English-speaking world. In transplanted form, 'postie' discourses influence everything from fashion and architecture to feminism and literary criticism. Invariably the Western world learns to speak or mimic a kind of Parisian French, and to this extent the 'Freudian' revolution is complete. Now we can all enjoy our own object *petit a.*

Partisans of psychoanalysis everywhere can trace their own commitments to some version of psychoanalysis, or to one of its seminal figures, briefly sketched above. Most contradict each other. Most, in fact, are expressly designed as criticisms of one or more other modes of psychoanalysis. And all of them, perhaps with the exception of the post-structuralists – and not even then – think they own the true and/or best Freud; that their version of psychoanalysis is the best one; that the others are, by and large, idiotic or, at least, woefully misguided. And all of this, in a nutshell, is why the history of psychoanalysis is the history of crises and schisms.

This is also why one finds sprinkled throughout the psychoanalytic literature countless warnings about the multiple directions of psychoanalysis and, inevitably, about its uncertain future. These warnings are nicely framed snapshots of the many crises in psychoanalysis and, taken singly, capture the concern of a given author in the face of a perceived problem that threatens to undermine his or her own worldview (a.k.a. his or her own schism). As such, the countless discussions about the 'future of psychoanalysis' are models par excellence of psychoanalysis in general, where any given crisis reveals itself as the most perfect mode of transmission in psychoanalysis; where the 'crisis of psychoanalysis' *is* psychoanalysis; where, finally, every new crisis signifies the essential (non-) identity of a heterogeneous psychoanalysis.

One would never guess this from Marylou Lionells. Consider her recent piece of science fiction, which opens a collection devoted to *The Death of Psychoanalysis: Murder? Suicide? Or Rumor Greatly Exaggerated?*: 'As we move into the next century, I imagine a psychoanalysis no longer dominated by the internal rivalries . . . The future of psychoanalysis will include more heterogeneity along with greater tolerance and respect for divergent views and methods.'[438] Lionells misses the point. The critical culture and dissension she regrets is a vital aspect of the crisis-induced (non-)identity of psychoanalysis, where all attacks *on* psychoanalysis, internal or external, partisan or otherwise, do all the heavy lifting *of* psychoanalysis. It's not just that one generation's *enfant terrible* is invariably the next generation's honoured speaker – an appropriation that reflects less the growing sophistication of psychoanalysts than it does their own over-inflated, and dated, sense of rebellion. It is rather that, in the case of psychoanalysis, the traditional parasite/host, critic/artist dichotomy has been completely undone, if not reversed; where critics don't so much live off the creative and scientific efforts of the psychoanalysts, as provide fundamental direction, form and meaning to these activities. And so, if the crisis best captures the conflicted essence of psychoanalysis, it is the critic who best expresses or realizes that essence.[439] Critics are the 'infusorians' that Freud first described in 1895 and then again in 1920, the 'enemy' agents that attack the delicate organism (in this case, psychoanalysis), but for that very reason make it tougher, hidebound, ever more highly developed. Consequently, even the most nasty, vociferous critic has been an essential and entirely complicit part of this reality check that makes all psychoanalytic life possible. And, sure enough, from the beginning psychoanalysis has cunningly appropriated such resistance, both inside and outside, making much (everything, actually) out of 'resistance' to the cause. Obviously this is a very useful strategy for world domination where, as Lacan nicely put it, psychoanalysis does nothing but produce psychoanalysts.

Probably the most prevalent kind of 'future of psychoanalysis' has been written by critical infusorians on the inside, namely, by those people immediately invested in the practice of psychoanalysis. Freud himself is an obvious example of this kind of partisan future, not least of all because he was always attuned to considerations of his own future.[440] As the old Freud is reported to have once said, 'What will they do with my theory after my death? Will it still resemble my basic thoughts?'[441] So Freud did his best to determine the life of psychoanalysis after his own death. He expunged his files of compromising details, such as original case notes[442] and letters, carefully rewrote old texts to update and also bury the inconvenient past, deftly spread a trail of dissimulation in scores of private letters, and carefully wrote fantastically partial, sometimes baldly inaccurate, histories and overviews of his own thought and movement. In these efforts Freud waged battle with himself, often because he changed his mind or realized a colossal blunder, and waged battle with his enemies – perceived and real. Actually, it was the *perception* of enemies that helped to create them, for we know that Freud's version of his lone heroic battle against the 'enemies of psychoanalysis', repeated *ad nauseam* by his eager followers, is fictitious. Despite Freud's so-called time of 'splendid isolation', commentators certainly did take note of Freud's earliest efforts and, in thoughtful reviews, provide gentle criticisms. He was not ignored. On the other hand, Freud's contemporaries hardly recognized him as the enemy of Victorian morality that we find portrayed in his own retrospective accounts. He just wasn't that important in the eyes of his contemporaries.

So, yes, Freud was indeed a man fifty or even seventy years ahead of his time, not as someone who 'discovered' the truths of psychology, but as someone who wittingly or not pioneered twentieth-century marketing. Obviously he never fully understood this campaign, where his wizened image would become the centrepiece, along with other fetish objects of Freudiana – the cigar, the accent, the antiquities, the couch. But what Freud lacked in bankable charisma and media savvy, such as that utilized by Adolf Hitler, he made up for with Old World charm and the appearance of authenticity. Moreover, Freud did exhibit an unusual degree of media savvy throughout his career, where letter-writing campaigns and historical overviews did the work of propagating *die Sache*, the Cause. Add to his own impressive efforts the spin control of his closest followers, christened the 'secret committee', and you get a pretty clear picture of media manipulation. The upshot: naive consumers of this era were unprepared for the elaborate confidence game called psychoanalysis, rigged on the back of a political organization, fronted by the vaunted rhetoric of science and liberation, and fuelled by capitalist desire.

Another, albeit extreme, example of a partisan future of psycho-analysis can be found in Kurt Eissler's *Medical Orthodoxy and The Future of Psychoanalysis* of 1965. Eissler perfectly recognizes that the success of psychoanalysis 'may be its undoing', and bemoans a situation where all the partial renderings of Freud's original vision leave us with 'a heap of nonsense'.[443] He adds: 'Its eclectic side is rather apparent. The modern psychoanalyst is supposedly bound to acknowledge the warrantability of every last claim and approach that sprouts in the ill-defined area of psychoanalysis.'[444] Eissler will have nothing of this, and his future is precisely one in which the aberrant forms of psychoanalysis have ceded to the only one worthy of the name – namely, the psychoanalysis associated with the genius of Freud. This conclusion follows naturally enough from his high opinion of Freud's achievement: 'Right now, if the truth is to be faced, one must admit that there is very little chance that the student of the human psyche, by applying the psychoanalytic technique, could make an essential advance beyond Freud's work. The pain of acknowledging this may be severe . . .'[445] Eissler, at least, suffered this severe pain. As for the rest, they were apparently incapable of under-standing just how 'obnoxious' were their efforts to improve on the Master's plan.[446]

The key to understanding Eissler's kind of partisan future is simply this: there isn't any. Or rather, there shouldn't be any. Instead he envisions the future of psychoanalysis as the mummification of its glorious past. Like a religious zealot, Eissler condemns anything less as a form of heresy. The obvious problem with Eissler's pickled future is that, despite his admirable erudition, the past he knows and accepts is entirely determined by the past that Freud gave him. And that past is in many ways demonstrably false. Entirely blinded by the legend of Freud, with which he is so completely identified, Eissler is ironically, perhaps tragically, the least Freudian analyst to have lived. Now *that's* painful.

Another prevalent species of 'future of psychoanalysis' is the critical-but-optimistic future; one that turns on this 'but', since the criticism is intended mostly as a warning to its readers and not as a dire prophesy about the end of psychoanalysis. Take the example of Erich Fromm's *The Crisis of Psychoanalysis*, published in 1970. The book opens with an essay on this latest crisis, which for Fromm has to do with the direction of organized psychoanalysis, especially ego psychology. 'The ego-psychological school,' Fromm reports, 'constitutes a retreat from the essence of psychoanalysis.'[447]

Here as elsewhere, Fromm is a competent and often insightful thinker. He understands that psychoanalysis in the West filled a void for liberals in an increasingly secularized society; that, in short, it 'offered a substitute for religion, politics, and philosophy'.[448] The problem for Fromm is that as progressive-minded liberalism became ever more conservative in the twentieth century, the role of psychoanalysis became less and less clear.[449] He also traces this crisis to the poor practices of some analysts.[450] But as a Marxist, Fromm keeps his eye on the enemy: ego psychologists who align psychoanalysis to this new conservatism and court 'adaptation and respectability'.[451] In effect, Fromm accuses organized psychoanalysis of having become bourgeois. Thus he intimates that it will earn the contempt of those who demand 'honesty' in their psychology, based on Freud's insights about the unconscious, including student radicals protesting 'against the sham and fraudulency of bourgeois society, expressed in its ideas as well as in many of its actions and in its language'.[452] For Fromm, indeed, the crisis of psychoanalysis is reflected in the 1960s counter-culture protest against institutional hypocrisy and, more generally, against consumerism. His message is simple enough: if it goes down the road of ego psychology, psychoanalysis will no longer be the choice of progressive-minded people. But this need not be its fate, hence his closing optimism. 'In spite of some disquieting symptoms,' Fromm reassures, 'psychoanalysis is far from dead. But its death can be predicted, *unless* it changes its direction. This is what is meant here by "the crisis of psychoanalysis".'[453]

For good measure, the Freudo-Marxist Fromm also throws in an attack on his Freudo-Marxist nemesis, Herbert Marcuse, who never found Fromm radical enough. In fact, the philosopher Marcuse had already accused the analyst Fromm of flirting with the conservatism he actually decries.[454] Naturally, then, Fromm does the same to Marcuse in this essay, condemning his 'anti-Freudian' and 'anti-Marxian' ideas.[455] The not-so-subtle subtext of Fromm's essay on 'The Crisis of Psychoanalysis' is in fact this battle with a fellow-traveller. Consequently, it is fair to add that the 'crisis' Fromm experiences most fully in 1970 is the lingering sting of a civil war that goes back to the late 1950s.[456] The ego psychologists may be bad for psychoanalysis, indeed bad for society, but not as personally wounding as a natural ally plunging a knife in your back.

There are, of course, futures of psychoanalysis that are neither partisan nor critical. Rather, they are ambivalent. A good example is Thomas Mann's 1936 lecture, 'Freud and the Future', written to celebrate Freud's eightieth birthday. The lecture, which he delivered numerous times and read to Freud himself, is a fascinatingly ambivalent tribute, not only because Mann relates and even appropriates psychoanalysis to his own creative work, but because he goes on at length about Freud's actual debt to literature, philosophy and myth. Apparently, Freud enjoyed the lecture.[457] But the ambivalence of Mann's tribute is notable because it reflects the average educated view of Freud and psychoanalysis in the twentieth century. Here is Mann's conclusion about Freud and the future: as a 'revolutionary' vehicle of humanism, psychoanalysis represents the hope that people in the future will be 'free from fear and hate, and ripe for peace'.[458] These are beautiful, if unoffensive sentiments. Of course, they are far more beautiful, unoffensive and optimistic than anything Freud himself actually said or wrote; just think of *Civilization and Its Discontents* written six years earlier. But that is the point: psychoanalysis has proliferated precisely because smart, well-meaning thinkers like Mann have refused to take Freud at his word; in this case appropriating him to a humanistic belief that psychoanalysis is a kind of literature, philosophy and mythology that teaches noble truths to a modern world.

Between the cautiously hopeful, doubtful and ambivalent futures of psychoanalysis, one is able to weave a faithful story about the rise and dominance of psychoanalysis in Western culture. One defends, one attacks and one equivocates – but as we are beginning to see, they all spread Freudiana across the cultural landscape. Yet, to parse McLuhan, the future isn't what it used to be. What has changed? What is the future of psychoanalysis today? What should we make about all the talk, yet again, about death and crisis in psychoanalysis?

*   *   *

Ah, yes: there is nothing like a crisis, or the threat of death, to sharpen the mind and make one feel more fully alive. In 1915, Freud explicitly associates this piece of folk psychology with his own reflections on the psychology of war. As he put it, 'Life is impoverished, it loses in interest, when the highest stake in the game of living, life itself, may not be risked.'[459] Debate among pro- and anti-Freudians is sometimes framed in these satisfying, melodramatic terms, casting its participants as combatants, its experiences as heroic battles. After all, one's livelihood and entire worldview may be at stake. And so partisans of psychoanalysis quite naturally mobilize all defences to the cause of preservation, while critics do just the opposite. Meanwhile the ambivalent majority is confirmed in their ambivalence.

I am happy to announce that the warring symbiosis has finally come to an end – or has very nearly so. For not even the most cunning spin doctors of psychoanalysis can save this patient. Nor can even the most vicious, truculent critic shock psychoanalysis back to life. Nothing anyone can say, pro or con or somewhere in between, can transform this death into an unpleasant rumour greatly exaggerated. At first glance, it appears the ambivalent majority has weighed in with the 'Freud bashers'. This is an illusion. The truth is rather more prosaic: typical ambivalence has ceded to typical indifference. People just don't care about psychoanalysis like they used to, and consequently have less at stake in its future.

It bears repeating that this whimpering end was written into the original programme, into all programmes if you believe Freud, where the psychoanalytic organism was always destined to choke on its own contradictions and exhaust itself. And, sure enough, all that's left from 100 years of crisis-induced schisms are the waste-products of all the accumulated effort, to wit, death and crap. We are therefore close to a privileged moment in the history of psycho-analysis, since we finally have, as Freud put it in 1927, the necessary distance from which to judge the present.[460] How so? Because the presence of psychoanalysis, including its many imagined futures, has finally become a matter of retrospection, of the past, and can now be readily assessed. With this in mind, let's briefly consider the limited and futureless future of three fields influenced by psycho-analysis: psychotherapy, intellectual activity and culture.

1. As a psychotherapy, psychoanalysis has no future. Most middle-class patients, for decades squeezed by economic pressures, have already abandoned the couch. As a result analysts nowadays have to be flexible if they want patients, which means abandoning classic psychoanalysis. Sandor Rado predicted this in the mid-1960s, rightly concluding that 'the heydays of analysis are over'.[461] Other shorter therapies will continue to find more popularity with patients, including those that reject altogether the dredging up of problematic memories. And why not? These therapies are at least as efficacious as psychoanalysis. At the same time market share has shifted in favour of psycho-pharmacology, which has proven to be an irresistible alternative to psychoanalysis. Given time and money restrictions, it will certainly continue to flourish and overshadow lengthy psychotherapies, most especially psychoanalysis.

In short, consumers have outgrown psychoanalysis. It is unlikely that the future of psychotherapy will see a return to full-blown psy-choanalysis, although there is no doubt that some practices – such as the use of a couch and free association – will continue to be used in some limited form. But even this will fade. Having been emptied of their theoretical justification, such practices already feel nostalgic; and nostalgic, they are open to parody and contempt. I suspect fewer and fewer psychotherapists will want to be associated with these signs, not of wisdom, knowledge and prestige, but of failure.

2. As an intellectual activity, psychoanalysis has a limited future. After all, to what intellectual activity will psychoanalysis attach itself? Not high theory. The death of psychoanalysis already precipitated the 'decline of theory', since each cause hitched a ride on the other. Consequently, there's no point looking to delirious theorists, at least in the near future, for help resuscitating psychoanalysis. This is a good thing. Although not many of us want a return to the good old days BD (before-Derrida) it's clear that we don't need more psychoanalytically inspired theory making on the French model. In this respect, Patrick Kavanaugh has missed the boat. He readily concedes that traditional psychoanalysis is suffering a profound crisis, but believes a new era of postmodern psychoanalysis will transform and save it.[462] I disagree. The once-dangerous paths of postmodernism, full of resistance and experimentation, have mostly been charted; as such they are often as stimulating and dangerous as a strip mall. And so, given the decline of theory in the death of psychoanalysis, the future of theorizing psychoanalysis will rather be, I submit, a future devoted to historicing the claims of psychoanalysis. That's not nothing, of course, but psychoanalysis will never again find a theoretical culture as fertile as it did with most postie theory.

As for 'applied psychoanalysis', a pastime that was once a staple of the humanities and social science literature, fewer and fewer intellectuals even bother today. It is increasingly impossible to play along with these interpretations, which were from the beginning laughable. And so, for example, psychoanalytic literary criticism has come and gone. It has become just another critical movement for bewildered undergraduate students in English to ponder. The situation is similar among historians and their students: on the whole, they no longer feel obliged to consider psychoanalysis, not even in the context of an obligatory historiography course. Of course, historians are among the least fanciful of social scientists. The same cannot be said of journalists writing about history. For them, I'm afraid, psychoanalysis will continue to influence the speculative tone of their arguments. The rule in this regard is simple enough: the less material they have (for whatever reason), the more pressed they are to make it up. This tendency won't fade quickly in a society hooked on tabloid exposes about the dark recesses of human behaviour. Luckily, though, consumers in the West hardly believe this stuff anymore, and so this form of intellectual activity has degenerated into a form of mass entertainment (see number 3).

Two academic fields, however, have maintained fairly strong ties to the theory and application of psychoanalysis: film studies and post-colonial studies. Suffice to say that both fields are long overdue sites for critical engagement – and we can expect passionate debates among partisans and critics in the very near future. The outcome? The critics will win and possibly gloat. The partisans will sulk and call them rude names.

3. As a culture, psychoanalysis has a limited future. Psychoanalysis was always more popular among an educated lay public than among scientists, a situation that originally favoured the interest of intellectuals in the humanities and social sciences. But with human and social scientists finally in retreat as it concerns psychoanalysis, popular culture and entertainment is about all that psychoanalysis has left. Psychoanalysis will continue to have a future in this regard, at least insofar as culture brokers – script-writers, comedians, novelists, editors, visual artists, publishers, journalists, etc. – continue to mine the couch for insight, and thus in some way echo and promote the old claims of psychoanalytic thought. True, most of this work is grossly uninformed. And true, most of this work is lightweight fare. (Recent automobile advertisement: 'Freud asked, (thick German accent) "Vat does viman vant?" The answer: Zero percent financing.') But it means that psychoanalysis will continue to have currency in popular culture. This is not entirely regrettable, since a certain amount of cultural literacy concerning psychoanalysis is still worthwhile given the vast amount of twentieth-century works influenced by that code. Barring that, knowing a thing or two about psychoanalysis is at least good for generating easy laughs.

And this is as it should be. Psychoanalysis has always been a long-running joke, possibly the longest in history. That some don't find its decline very funny is not surprising, first, because they lack a sense of humour, second, are unequipped intellectually and/or culturally to appreciate the 'black humour' of others, and third, may even consider themselves the brunt of the joke. I propose a classic end-run around this glum band of sourpusses: not everyone is supposed to laugh, for not everyone is invited to celebrate the futureless future of psychoanalysis. My advice: these detractors with ears too small to hear should buy themselves earplugs. As for those of us willing to laugh at our own culture and at ourselves, who are culturally literate enough to read the cues, and know enough to make our future intellectual and cultural investments elsewhere – well, we must be forgiven for laughing at the laughable. Psychoanalysis is indeed dead, and it is to be expected that at least some of us will enjoy our *Schadenfreude* at the dawning of the twenty-first century.

Did I mention that some of us will gloat? That, too, will pass.

Notes

1. See Crews, 1995.
2. The cure is reading. An example: In a melancholy 1998 *New Yorker* article about his six-year analysis, journalist Adam Gopnik admits that, having read Crews on Freud, he finally sat down and read Freud 'for the first time'. The result? He was 'struck at once by the absurdity of the arguments as arguments', and felt himself 'in the presence of a kind of showman'. In Gopnik, 1998: 118.
3. In Wortis, 1954: 49.
4. Freud and Breuer, 1893–5: 17.
5. Carnegie, 1944: 190.
6. Freud and Breuer, 1893–5: 8.
7. Ibid., 222.
8. Stevenson, 1886: 123.
9. Jones, 1953: 223.
10. Throughout what follows I refer to Breuer's case *report*, actually a long referral note of 22 pages, and Breuer's case *study*, the first referring to the 1882 report, the second to the published study of 1895. The report, and the follow-up report, have been published in Hirschmüller (1978). Hirschmüller tells us that Breuer's report is unusually long – about 'ten or twenty times longer than usual for the period' (129).
11. Ellenberger, 1972: 272.
12. See Hirschmüller, 1978: 98, 132; Merskey, 1992: 192–3; and Webster, 1995.
13. Crabtree, 1993: 252–7.
14. For details see Hansen, 1991.
15. See also Hirschmüller, 1978: 92; and Shorter, 1992: 151–3.
16. Ellenberger, 1970: 168.
17. See Hirschmüller, 1978.
18. Ibid., 99–101.

19. Freud and Breuer, 1893–5: 218.
20. In Hirschmüller, 1978: 277.
21. Freud and Breuer, 1893–5:11; see also Hirschmüller, 1978: 219.
22. Freud and Breuer, 1893–5: 13.
23. Ibid., 12; see also 215. Freud also proposed in the *Studies* that hysteria can result from defence, which was to play an important part in psychoanalytic theory. Breuer wasn't entirely convinced by this idea, which he qualified as applicable only in 'idiosyncratic' cases of hysteria (235–6). Moreover, he argues that defence still requires the existence of a hypnoid state if there is to occur a '*genuine* splitting of the mind' (my emphasis).
24. See Ellenberger, 1970: 484; Macmillan, 1997: 14. Jacob was also the uncle of Martha Bernays, Freud's wife in 1886.
25. Borch-Jacobsen, 1996: 50.
26. Aristotle: I449.
27. Freud and Breuer, 1893–5: 25.
28. See Crabtree, 1993.
29. Freud and Breuer, 1893–5: 4; 15.
30. Borch-Jacobsen, 1996: 67.
31. Figure cited in Borch-Jacobsen, 1996: 43.
32. See Hirschmüller, 1978: 129.
33. Ellenberger, 1970: 484.
34. Shorter, 1992: 134–50.
35. Ibid., 150–5.
36. Freud and Breuer, 1893–5: 24.
37. Ibid., 46; see also 13.
38. Ibid., 227.
39. See Borch-Jacobsen, 1996: 83–4; and Shorter, 1997.
40. In this respect he connects 'love' to this state, as Freud himself does many years later. How does sick-nursing cause hypnoid states? By an excess of quiet, attentive concentration on the patient. In short, one is *entranced* by the patient.
41. Shorter, 1997: 27.
42. Freud and Breuer, 1893–5: 27.
43. In Hirschmüller, 1978: 285.
44. Freud and Breuer, 1893–5: 27.
45. Hirschmüller, 1978: 103.
46. In Hirschmüller, 1978: 280. Hirschmüller informs us that Breuer diagnosed Pappenheim's cough as hysterical on the strength of descriptions already made by Charles Lasegue (ca. 1854) and others about this particular manifestation (ibid., 108–9).

47. Ellenberger, 1972: 271.
48. Strümpell, 1896: 161; also in Kiell, 1988: 74.
49. Freud and Breuer, 1893–5: 46; see also Hirschmüller, 1978: 295.
50. Freud and Breuer, 1893–5: 46.
51. Borch-Jacobsen, 1996: 87–9; and also Dufresne, 1997a.
52. Freud and Breuer, 1893–5: 228; cf. 46.
53. Borch-Jacobsen, 1996: 87.
54. Freud and Breuer, 1893–5: 21 (the very first paragraph, his emphasis).
55. Ibid., 21; 43; 36–7; 43. Some of these assurances can be found in the case report: 'I take her to be absolutely truthful, although falsehoods do occur occasionally during her illness. At any rate, it is always best to accept her word, or to seem to do so, for nothing is so contemptible to her mind than lying. It is only ever possible to influence her by appealing to her good qualities.' (in Hirschmüller, 1978: 277).
56. Ibid., 43.
57. Ibid., 7.
58. Ibid., 46. My emphasis.
59. Macmillan, 1997: 40.
60. Shorter, 1992: 174.
61. Freud and Breuer, 1893–5: 217.
62. Ibid., 12.
63. Ibid., 23.
64. Borch-Jacobsen, 1996: 80.
65. See, for example, Freud's discussion of splitting in his book of 1938, 'An Outline of Psycho-Analysis': 202.
66. See Webster, 1995: 96–102. Legend has it that Freud mentioned the case of Bertha Pappenheim to Charcot, who found it unremarkable. See Freud, 1925: 19–20; Jones, 1953: 226.
67. Freud, 1960: 86.
68. On this matter see Ellenberger, 1970: 485–6; Macmillan, 1997 [1991]: 45–7; Borch-Jacobsen, 1996b.
69. Freud and Breuer, 1893–5: 101.
70. Freud, 1888: 79.
71. Freud, 1896: 86.
72. Bleuler, 1896: 525; also in Kiell, 1988: 72–4.
73. Clarke, 1896: 414; also in Kiell, 1988: 75–82. Cf. Borch-Jacobsen, 1996c.
74. Borch-Jacobsen, 1996: 84.
75. Shorter, 1997: 33.
76. Goethe, 1801: 118.

77. Shorter, 1992: 196.
78. Freud and Breuer, 1893–5: 7.
79. Borch-Jacobsen, 1996: 49–61.
80. Ibid., 60.
81. Ibid., 54–5.
82. The Bellevue Sanitarium in Kreuzlingen, near Constanz, which was founded by Ludwig Binswanger and operated, after 1880, by his son Robert.
83. Pappenheim was admitted to the sanatorium another three times between 1883 and 1887, and on each occasion was diagnosed with hysteria. In Hirschmüller, 1978: 115; Borch-Jacobsen, 1996: 24.
84. In Hirschmüller, 1978: 291.
85. Ibid., 116.
86. Ibid., 116.
87. See Jones, 1953: 224–5.
88. Gay, 1988: 69.
89. Ellenberger, 1972: 272.
90. See Borch-Jacobsen, 1996: 32.
91. Freud and Breuer, 1893–5: 246–7.
92. Hirschmüller, 1978: 131.
93. See Freud, 1914: 12; 1925: 26; 1960: 266.
94. Borch-Jacobsen, 1996: 48.
95. Hirschmüller, 1978: 131.
96. See Freud, 1925: 21.
97. Borch-Jacobsen, 1996: 28.
98. Webster, 1995: 134–5.
99. Cited in Borch-Jacobsen, 1996: 27.
100. Freud and Breuer, 1893–5: 49.
101. Borch-Jacobsen,1996a.
102. See Crews, 1995; 1997.
103. Freud and Breuer, 1893–5: 250.
104. Ibid., 6; 221.
105. Freud, 1900: 600. His emphasis.
106. Among others, Bonanno *et al.* (1995) find that 'emotional avoidance' among bereaving individuals is an effective coping strategy, contrary to traditional assumptions about repression that begin with Freud. Consequently, we must rethink the clinical impulse to encourage catharsis or abreaction about a traumatic event. Although Bonanno *et al.* do not spell it out, this also means that historians have to rethink just how much damage this old therapeutic paradigm has caused patients.

107. Cf. Shorter, 1992: 193–6.
108. See, for example, the discussion in Clarke, 1894: 130–1, under heading of *'Hysteria a Disease of Representation'*.
109. In Shorter, 1992: 196.
110. Freud and Breuer, 1893–5: 58.
111. Ibid., note 2.
112. Ibid., 260–7.
113. Breuer merely pastes another footnote to Benedikt in his text of 1895, citing only Benedikt's book of 1894. See Ibid., 287.
114. Ibid., 261.
115. Ibid., 260.
116. In Shorter, 1992: 240.
117. Freud and Breuer, 1893–5: 261.
118. Ibid., 308.
119. Ibid.
120. Ibid., 309.
121. Ibid., 312 and 321.
122. Ibid., 321.
123. Ibid., 165–6.
124. Ibid., 333.
125. Cf. Havelock, 1963.
126. In Dufresne, 1996.
127. Jones, 1957: 46.
128. For example, critics of the Library of Congress Freud exhibit have been characterized as parricides, puritans, inquisitors, right-wing extremists, anti-Semites, Nazis, ayatollahs and politically correct (read ugly) Americans. For an overview, see Crews's 'Introduction' (1998: xvii–xxxi). Peter Swales has deposited over 300 pages of documents concerning this controversy in the Library of Congress.
129. Crews, 1998: ix.
130. Ibid., xxviii.
131. Borch-Jacobsen in Ibid., 45–53.
132. Freud, 1888: 79. Freud would repeat this claim elsewhere, for example, in an 'Appendix' of 1896.
133. Crews, 1998: 47.
134. Freud and Fliess, 1985: 224.
135. See Swales 1989, 1989a; and Crews 1997.
136. Freud and Fliess, 1985: 227.
137. Ibid., 184.

138. See Freud,1974.
139. Swales in Crews, 1998: 31–2.
140. Cioffi, 1998: 200.
141. Ibid., 42.
142. Ibid., 117; 136.
143. Crews, 1998: xxvii.
144. See Cioffi, 1998: 200; 247.
145. Ibid., 206, 244.
146. In Borch-Jacobsen in Crews, 1998: 46; cf. Cioffi, 1998: 203.
147. Cioffi, 1998: 204; cf. Borch-Jacobsen in Crews, 1998: 52.
148. Roustang in Crews, 1998: 248–59.
149. Esterson in Crews, 1998: 150; Borch-Jacobsen in Crews, 1998: 52.
150. Grünbaum in Crews, 1998: 78–84.
151. Timpanaro in Crews, 1998: 105.
152. Ibid., 97–105.
153. Ibid., 101.
154. Esterson in Crews, 1998: 149–61.
155. Sulloway in Crews, 1998: 175–85.
156. Fish in Crews, 1998: 199.
157. Crews, 1998: 215.
158. In Edmund in Crews, 1998: 265.
159. Ibid., 267.
160. Cioffi, 1998: 36. See his recent discussion, and clarification, of this matter. In Dufresne, 2002: 11–12.
161. Thereafter collected in Crews, 1995.
162. In Wortis, 1954: 57.
163. On 17 September 1992, at the invitation of Dr René Major. A round-table followed with W. Granoff, P. Guyomar, R. Major and E. Roudinesco.
164. Freud-Zweig, 1970: 127; trans. modified, with reference to Freud, 1960: 430.
165. Sachs, 1945: 108.
166. Freud, 1916–17: 18.
167. Freud and Fliess, 1985: 264.
168. Roustang, 1983: 37.
169. Nietzsche, 1989: 6.
170. Forrester, 1990: 253.
171. On this see Hacking, 1988: 442.
172. Freud, 1916–17: 18.
173. Roazen, 1969: xiv.

174. Marcus, 1984: 213.
175. Cf. Vichyn, 1993: 134–8.
176. In print Anna Freud refers to Roazen in particular as 'a malicious American author', referring to his *Brother Animal*. In a private letter she dramatically suggests that Roazen 'is a menace whatever he writes'. See Roazen, 1993: 201.
177. Freud, 1940: 159.
178. In Szasz, 1976: 119.
179. Freud and Fliess, 1985: 447.
180. Borch-Jacobsen, 1993: 46–7.
181. Freud, 1940: 178.
182. Borch-Jacobsen, 1988: 150; cf. 1993: 58–9.
183. Roustang, 1983: 38.
184. In Jones, 1959: 204.
185. In Dufresne, 1995.
186. Borch-Jacobsen, 1993: 59.
187. Cf. Roazen, 1975: 354.
188. Schneiderman, 1983: 86.
189. Borch-Jacobsen, 1991: 166.
190. Kardiner, 1977: 17.
191. Borch-Jacobsen, 1993: 57.
192. See Lacan, 1966: 591.
193. Derrida, 1980: 510.
194. Freud, 1900: xxiii–xxiv.
195. Roazen, 1975: 87.
196. Freud, 1911: 79.
197. Roazen, 1969: 47.
198. Fromm, 1959: 47.
199. Roustang, 1982: 34.
200. Nietzsche, 1974: 260.
201. Freud, 1930: 81.
202. Grosskurth, 1991: 53.
203. Roazen, 1975: 86.
204. Derrida, 1992: 238. His emphasis.
205. See Freud, 1916–17: 42, 60.
206. In Szasz, 1976: 24.
207. Freud and Fliess, 1985: 281.
208. Freud, 1937: 248.
209. Gay, 1988: 97.

210. Ceiman, 1992.
211. Jay, 1993: 167.
212. In Schneiderman, 1983: 91.
213. Derrida, 1980: 305.
214. See, for example, Rieff, 1959: 71.
215. Lacan, 1988: 21.
216. In Wortis, 1954: 11–12.
217. Freud and Fliess, 1985: 279.
218. Marcus, 1984: 12.
219. Roazen, 1991: 213–14; 1992: 11–12.
220. Freud, 1914: 43.
221. In Roazen, 1975: 323.
222. Jones, 1955: 69.
223. See Jones, 1955: 153–4; Paskauskas, 1985; Grosskurth, 1991.
224. In Grossman, 1965: 102.
225. In Roazen, 1975: 124. *Quod licet Jovi, non licet bovi.*
226. Roustang, 1983: 62.
227. Doolittle, 1974: 119.
228. In Reik, 1956: 6.
229. In Ferenczi, 1988: 93.
230. In Sachs, 1945: 105.
231. In Roazen, 1991: 329.
232. In Weizsaecker, 1957: 62.
233. Fromm, 1959: 37.
234. Roazen, 1992: 10; cf. Weiss, 1991: 127.
235. Roazen, 1975: 439.
236. In Freud, 1992: 284.
237. Foucault, 1973: 387.
238. In a letter to Paul Schilder, 1935, cited in Gay, 1988: 97.
239. In Wortis, 1954: 17. *Ich habe doch die Psychoanalyse entdeckt. Das kann man mir doch verzeihen.*
240. One can argue that Foucault's subject is not 'liquidated' either, as Derrida does, but that is not my concern here. See Derrida, 1991: 96–119.
241. Freud, 1969: 48.
242. Szasz, 1976: 35; cf. Fromm, 1959: 67; Deutsch, 1973: 170–9.
243. Roustang, 1982: 7.
244. In Roazen, 1975: 303.
245. Freud and Jung, 1974: 534–5.
246. In Roazen, 1969: 163.

247. Genosko, 1993: 629; see also Part III, Chapter 11 of this book.
248. In Jones, 1955: 71.
249. Freud, 1914: 39.
250. In Natenberg, 1955: 189.
251. Freud, 1930: 111.
252. Freud, 1901: 149; cf. Jones, 1953: 188–9.
253. In Reik, 1954: 513. It is probably no accident that Freud said this to Riek, the lay analyst accused of quackery in Vienna. For according to Kardiner (1977), Reik was once jokingly referred to within Freud's inner circle as 'the imitation Freud' (84).
254. Borch-Jacobsen, 1993: 267.
255. Nietzsche, 1954: 190.
256. Derrida, 1994: 12.
257. Derrida, 1974: 6.
258. On this issue see Bennington and Derrida, 1993.
259. Derrida, 1972: 43.
260. Gasché, 1987: 19.
261. Derrida, 1995: 84.
262. Derrida, 1995: 17.
263. Freud, 1930: 91–2.
264. Derrida, 1995: 10.
265. Ibid., 67.
266. Ibid., 34.
267. Ibid., 29.
268. Ibid., 59.
269. Ibid., 40.
270. This is an important question that other scholars have long pondered, including, among many others, literary critic Harold Bloom. In his book *Ruin the Sacred Truths* (1987), Bloom not only discusses one of Yerushalmi's books on Freud and Judaism, but makes a point of rejecting the French reading of Freud's dualism in this regard (151). Bloom essentially argues that the difference between Hegelian and Freudian versions of negation, *Verneinung*, 'is evaded by the French Freudians' – by whom he means 'Lacan, Deleuze, Laplanche, even Derrida'. He believes this emphasis on the dialectical tradition – which defines the stakes of the French game – 'invalidates' their interpretations of the dualistic Freud, who was in this respect, as Yerushalmi suggests, much closer to traditional Jewish beliefs about negation, dualism, memory, and so on.
271. Derrida, 1995: 76.

272. Ibid., 77.
273. Ibid., 25.
274. Ibid., 97.
275. Ibid., 50.
276. Ibid., 89.
277. Kermode, 1987: 109.
278. Derrida, 1988: 31, note 1.
279. Derrida, 1995: 87.
280. Note that Yerushalmi was also invited to the Freud Museum conference/fundraiser, the text of which is now available in the *Journal of European Psychoanalysis* (1996–7). In his lecture he speaks about the politics of the archive.
281. In Dufresne, 1996.
282. Derrida, 1995: 4.
283. See Harari's discussion of the events surrounding this open letter in Chapter 11 of his book *Las Dispaciones de lo Inconciente* (1996).
284. Leader and Groves, 1995.
285. Lacan, 1990: 3.
286. In Roazen, 1995: 22.
287. See Jones, 1957: 103.
288. Ibid., 114; cf. Gay, 1988: 453–5.
289. In Schur, 1972: 343.
290. In Wortis, 1954: 164.
291. In Gay, 1988: 160.
292. Jones, 1957: 389.
293. Bougnoux, 1997: 92–3.
294. Lacan, 1990: 3.
295. A not dissimilar situation arose in the Lacanian journal *Scilicet*. In it all articles were published anonymously – except those written by Lacan.
296. For more details, see Roudinesco, 1990: 689–92 and Weber, 1990: 21–7.
297. Wherever possible, we have provided references to both original editions and have noted slight changes to text.
298. Jones 1952: 7.
299. The 1931 and 1952 editions are 142 and 312 pages respectively.
300. Copley-Graves, 1992: 10.
301. Jones, 1952: 208.
302. Ibid., 94.
303. Ibid., 7.
304. See Roazen, 1975: 342.

305. In the First World War Jones served in the Royal Medical Army Corps on the home-front, having been deemed unfit for active service, but where he advanced the cause of psychoanalysis through his seminal work on war trauma. In the Second World War he was a Medical Officer of the Home Guard, a largely titular post given in his advanced age. Cf. Vincent Brome, 1983: 102–3; 200.

306. According to Mervyn Jones, his father was 'friendly with a man named Richardson who was high-up in the National Skating Association . . . and was also a movie entrepreneur' (M. Jones to Dufresne, personal communication, 1 December 1992). The man in question was in fact the author of *Modern Figure Skating* (London: Methuen & Co., 1930). Mervyn may have confused this Richardson with the British film director Tony Richardson.

307. Brome, 1983: 141.

308. Roazen, 1985: 5.

309. Ibid., 254.

310. We should probably not exaggerate Jones's personal sacrifice in this regard, for the official biography was also his opportunity to guarantee his own role and depiction of that history. Roazen for one puts it this way: 'Ernest Jones had been seeking this job for years. [. . .] History gets written by accident. Jones lived the longest of those six men, and as a survivor had the last word' (1975: 9–10).

311. M. Jones, 1990: 262.

312. M. Jones, 1987: 9.

313. M. Jones to Dufresne.

314. On one of the last pages of the second edition Jones briefly describes and illustrates a 'free skating' figure of that name, 'The Jokl Step' (1952: 305, 307).

315. Cf. Barbara Schrodt, 1988: 763.

316. Jones, 1952: 8.

317. Ibid., 8.

318. Ibid., 218.

319. M. Jones to Dufresne.

320. Ibid., 130, 276. Cf. also the Appendix A; M. Jones to Dufresne.

321. Jones, 1931: 80, 88; 1952: 145, 149.

322. These materials are available for consultation in the Jones Archive, Diaries 1909–52, at the British Psycho-Analytical Society in London.

323. Details of the National Association Tests are found in a skating book by another Captain, S. Duff-Taylor (1937). The contents of this Captain's book were drawn from Hon. Neville Lytton's 1930 collection of articles on winter sports.

324. M. Jones to Dufresne.

325. Jones, 1957: 222.

326. In Kardiner, 1957: 50. For a slightly different version of the same anecdote, see Kardiner, 1977: 85–6. According to this latter text, Freud was responding to a paper delivered by 'Jokel'. However, this is likely a stenographic error, and the name should read [Ludwig] Jekels.

327. Jones, 1952: 279–80.

328. Jones mentioned his forthcoming work on the psychoanalysis of chess in a letter to Freud on 26 August 1930, and dutifully reported on having read it to the Society in a letter of 20 November. See also Freud–Jones, 1993: 676, 679.

329. Jones, 1931: 5; 1952: 7.

330. M. Jones to Dufresne.

331. Jones, 1931: 134; 1952: 276.

332. Ibid, 132; ibid., 274–5.

333. Ibid., 130; ibid, 273.

334. Jones, who thought of himself as a 'diplomat', played the role of 'liaison officer' in the psychoanalytic movement. In the 'Ernest Jones Centenary', Arcangelo R. T. D'Amore thus writes: 'It was propitious that Jones settled in Canada from 1908 to 1913, but did not choose to settle permanently in North America. Psychoanalysis has been fortunate to have had Ernest Jones mediating between the Europeans and the Americans during its formative years' (60). In this light consider what Jones (1952) writes about Jackson Haines, whom he calls the 'Father of Figure Skating': 'both English and Americans made invaluable contributions to sheer technique . . . The world waited for a genius to give life to the new possibilities thus provided, to create out of them a true art. He came, and, appropriately enough, from Canada the land whose mission it seems to be to draw together the divided halves of the Anglo-Saxon race' (284). It is likely that Jones identified with Haines, since both did their part in the establishment of movements, and both had connections to Canada. Or, at least, so Jones thought; actually, Haines was an American.

335. Jones, 1931: 13; Jones, 1952: 17.

336. Ibid., 14–15; ibid., 17–18.

337. Gay, 1988: 183.

338. Jones, 1952: 15.

339. Gay to Dufresne, personal communication, 4 January 1993.

340. Jones, 1931: 32; Jones, 1952: 48.

341. Jones, 1931: 41.

342. Jones, 1931: 20; 1952: 22.
343. Jones, 1952: 32–3. His emphasis.
344. Ibid., 34.
345. Jones, 1931: 49–50; 1952: 37.
346. Jones, 1952: 72.
347. Jones, 1931: 52; 1952: 38.
348. To Freud from Toronto on 12 February 1910, Jones writes: 'From about the age of 12 until almost the present I had the obsession never to write anything, a letter, address an envelope, school task, etc., without under-signing it thus. I always interpreted it to myself as standing for Science, which I greatly idealized. I know now [from self-analysis] that it stands for Sybil, the name of my younger sister' (Freud-Jones, 1993: 44). According to the editor of the correspondence, Andrew Paskauskas, 'the symbol appears in his student "Notebook" of 1896–1897, and in all of the letters – to Freud and to others – written during the Toronto period.' See Paskauskas, 1985: 241. Due, it seems, to some error, the letters with the looping symbol are not in fact indicated in the published correspondence (see 'List of Correspondence').
349. Jones, 1931: 133; 1952: 275.
350. Ibid., 134; ibid., 276.
351. Freud, 1900: 146.
352. Jones, 1932: 11; 1952: 15–16.
353. Ulmer, 1985: 138; cf. Roback, 1954.
354. Jones, 1952: 18. His emphasis.
355. Ibid., 19.
356. Ibid., 47.
357. Jones, 1931: 28–9; 1952: 28–9.
358. Ibid., 12; ibid., 16.
359. Jones, 1931: 127, 129.
360. Jones, 1931: 12–13; 1952: 16.
361. Also consider in this light the fact that it is only in the second edition that Jones refers to the 'International Skating Union', the 'National Skating Association' and the 'German Skating Association'.
362. Jones, 1931: 13; 1952: 17. Our emphasis.
363. Jones, 1931: 5; 1952: 8. His emphasis.
364. Ibid., 79–80; ibid., 145.
365. Jones, 1974: 176.
366. It is interesting to note that turn of the century discourse on the object of therapeutic treatment repeats precisely this sort of language. This is especially true of the work done on war trauma, which adopts the same sort of military

metaphors and notions of intellectual mastery that Jones adopts here.
367. Lacan, 1953–4: 71.
368. Lacan, 1966: 439.
369. Jones, 1952: 8.
370. Ibid., 15.
371. Ibid., 32.
372. Since the first edition appeared in 1931, five years after Klein relocated to London, perhaps this passage and some others also help rationalize her work, her position as a new analyst, and the controversy she provoked. Jones thought highly of Klein, and had her analyse his children in 1926.
373. In Freud, 1992: 284.
374. Jones, 1959: 204.
375. Roazen, 1975: 354. See also Roustang, 1982; 1983.
376. Phillips, 1993: 10.
377. Freud and Silberstein, 1990: 178–9.
378. Boehlich, 1990: xv.
379. In Roazen, 1968: 68.
380. Freud, 1930: 100, note.
381. Freud and Andreas-Salome, 1972: 188; Clark, 1980: 483–4.
382. Doolittle, 1974: 117.
383. Freud and Ferenczi, 1993: 150.
384. Ibid., 205; 227.
385. 'Frequently', according to Roazen.
386. In Roazen, 1990: 163.
387. Sterba, 1982: 119.
388. Freud and Jung, 1974: 534.
389. Freud, 1930: 111.
390. Roazen, 1975: 499.
391. Doolittle, 1974: 172.
392. In Clark, 1980: 483.
393. Grinker, 1940: 851.
394. M. Freud, 1958: 191.
395. Wortis, 1954: 32.
396. Blanton, 1971: 70–1.
397. Genosko, 1994: 8.
398. Wortis, 1954: 76.
399. Wortis, 1940: 845.
400. In Freeman and Strean, 1981: 90.
401. Doolittle, 1974: 162.

402. M. Freud, 1958: 190–1.
403. Ruitenbeek, 1973: 19.
404. Gay, 1989: 540.
405. Genosko, 1994: 6.
406. See Ellenberger, 1970: 461.
407. Genosko, 1994: 11.
408. Ibid., 8–11.
409. Freud, 1915: 169.
410. Doolittle, 1974: 166.
411. Doolittle, 1974: 191.
412. In Roazen and Swerdloff, 1995.
413. M. Freud, 1958: 192.
414. Jones, 1959: 41.
415. In Freud, 1992: 206; Genosko, 1994: 3.
416. Lacan, 1990: 117.
417. Lacan, 1977: 57; Borch-Jacobsen, 1997: 226.
418. M. Freud, 1958: 203.
419. Bertin, 1982: 192.
420. Ibid., 192.
421. Genosko, 1994.
422. Freud, 1915: 289.
423. Bonaparte, 1937: 75; 162–4. In addition to this rather compelling, if senti-
     mental, love story, the book is potentially interesting from a semiotic
     perspective. For instance, throughout the book Bonaparte repeats sentences,
     phrases and words – a sort of repetition compulsion – in what seems an
     attempt to master her fear of death. In this sense, the writing itself (as mastery
     of repetition) becomes the very detour through which life expresses itself for
     Bonaparte. Other commentators have prepared more food for semiotic
     thoughts. See Genosko's Introduction, 1994.
424. In Jones, 1957: 210.
425. Schur, 1972: 527.
426. Ibid., 526.
427. M. Freud, 1958: 190.
428. In Schur, 1972: 529.
429. Freud and Andreas-Salome, 1972: 154.
430. See Gamwell, 1989: 27; and 56–7.
431. Typically, interviews with academics are highly processed objects. This
     interview is no exception. It actually began as a long informal chat over two
     days in November 1999 during a visit to Toronto. The present version, while

faithful to the spirit and scope of the discussion, was edited for clarity and economy by Greco and then by me.

432. Dufresne, 1999.
433. Freud and Ferenczi, 1993: 258.
434. See Dufresne, 1998.
435. Cioffi makes a similar remark in Dufresne, 2002: 12.
436. Sonu Shamdasani (2002) develops this idea in 'Psychoanalysis Inc.', although in the service of another point: namely, that the importance of psychoanalysis in the twentieth century owes more to institutional politics than to any other factor. I agree with this thesis, but would insist that, just the same, it doesn't mean that psychoanalytic culture hasn't in fact played a significant role in Western culture. So bullish statements about its significance are often true, even though they were made possible by the politics of the movement (see Dufresne, 2000: 182). I think this usually non-controversial claim gets lost in Shamdasani's otherwise very convincing argument.
437. See Roustang, 1982; 1983.
438. Lionells, 1999: 22.
439. See *Tales*, Dufresne, 2000, for a discussion of the death drive and criticism.
440. See Mannoni, 1968: 166, who opens his 'Afterword: The Future of a Disillusion' with this well-noted characteristic of Freud.
441. In Choisy, 1955: 294.
442. Unfortunately for Freud, notes survived for the Rat Man.
443. Eissler, 1965: 2.
444. Ibid., 4.
445. Ibid., 7.
446. Ibid., 8.
447. Fromm, 1970: 28.
448. Ibid., 2. See also Fromm's excellent *Sigmund Freud's Mission*.
449. Ibid., 13.
450. Ibid., 4.
451. Ibid., 28.
452. Ibid., 5 note 1.
453. Ibid., 28.
454. This is a game of one-upmanship (or downmanship, depending on your perspective) that characterizes most disagreements among Marxists. And, actually, it is pretty standard fare among theorists generally.
455. Fromm, 1970: 20.
456. Having already devoted a page to Marcuse in this essay, Fromm declares that

'I shall restrict myself to a few remarks' (ibid., 16), and then spends over four pages attacking Marcuse's thought.

457. See Jones, 1957: 205. It would be more characteristic of Freud to have appreciated Mann's gesture, and perhaps his style, but not the message. He never liked being reminded of his predecessors.

458. Mann, 1936: 74–5.

459. Freud, 1915: 290.

460. Freud, 1927: 5.

461. Rado in Roazen and Swerdloff, 1995: 141.

462. Kavanaugh, 1999.

Acknowledgements

Many people have generously given their time on parts of what follows here, some of which I delivered at conferences, or published in part or whole. A version of Chapter One, Section I, was delivered at the Psychoanalytic Thought Program of the University of Toronto on 27 January 1998; and to the Thunder Bay Bioethics Interest Group of Lakehead University on 18 November 1998. The second chapter was presented at the Histories of Theory Conference at the University of Western Ontario on 17 April 1998; and again at the Research in Progress Seminar of the Archives on the History of Canadian Psychiatry and the Museum of Mental Health Services in Toronto on 12 June 1998. An early version of Chapter One, Section II, was delivered at the Strategies of Critique conference at York University on 2 April 1993. And, finally, a version of Chapter Three of this section was presented at The Psychoanalytic Thought Program of the University of Toronto on 6 February 1997. Many thanks to everyone involved, especially those who issued invitations: Guy Allen, Cyril Greenland, and Tilottama Rajan.

Parts of this book have appeared, in different versions, elsewhere. Chapter Four, Section II, appeared in *Returns of the 'French Freud': Freud, Lacan, and Beyond*, ed. T. Dufresne (New York and London: Routledge, 1997): 117–31. Chapter Ten, Section III, appeared in *The Semiotic Review of Books*, September 2000: 2–4. Chapter Five, Section II, appeared in French at *Scansions*, trans. S. Schauder, Numéro spécial, Décembre, no. 6/7: 5. Chapter Nine, Section II, appeared in *Freud Under Analysis: History, Theory, Practice*, ed.

T. Dufresne (Northvale, N.J.: Jason Aronson, 1997). A version of Chapter Ten, Section III, appeared in *The International Journal of Psychoanalysis*, 76: 123–33. Family has been a source of strength, and I am happy to issue a global thanks. Many thanks also to my friends and colleagues who encouraged me in the past and/or helped improve my efforts without, it is true, being responsible for my work, let alone my blunders. They include Mikkel Borch-Jacobsen, Clara Sacchetti and Fred Crews, who have been among my first readers, and Paul Antze, Rodolphe Gasché, Jim Dicenso, Theo Theoharis, Howard Adelman, Tom Kemple, Edward Shorter, Paul Roazen, Andrej Zaslove and Tony Greco. To my friends and colleagues in Thunder Bay, I am grateful for your support and encouragement. I would also like to acknowledge student researchers I have had during the last few years, Peter Munoz and Kezia Picard. Special notice to Gary Genosko, who long ago inspired my interest in Freud's 'precious objects', including essays here on Jones and skating, and on Freud and dogs. He kindly encouraged the reprint of our essay on Jones and figure skating, which appears here in a revised form. This essay benefited from the goodwill of two people, with whom I corresponded briefly, and am pleased to recognize: Mervyn Jones and Peter Gay.

Killing Freud was developed during a period of research generously funded by the Social Science and Humanities Research Council (SSHRC) of Canada, which I gratefully acknowledge. Since 1998, Lakehead University (LU) has also provided course-release and financial support. In this regard, I am pleased to acknowledge the efforts of LU's Research Office, especially Andrew Hacquoil. Other staff at LU have been helpful, including Freda Brown in Philosophy and Nancy Pazianos at Interlibrary Loans. Finally, this book would not have found a home without the wise and generous council of Tristan Palmer at Continuum. Thanks. Cheers to everyone.

Bibliography

Aristotle (1947). 'Rhetoric and Poetry', *Introduction to Aristotle*, ed. Richard McKeon, New York: Modern Library.

Benedikt, Moritz (1894). *Hypnotismus und Suggestion: Eine klinisch-psychologische Studie*, Vienna: M. Brietenstein.

Bennington, Geoffrey and Jacques Derrida (1993). *Jacques Derrida*, trans. G. Bennington, Chicago: University of Chicago Press.

Bernays, Jacob (1880). *Zwei Abhandlungen über die Aristotelische Theorie des Drama*, Berlin: Wilhelm Hertz.

Bertin, Celia (1982). *Marie Bonaparte: A Life*, New Haven: Yale University Press.

Blanton, Smiley (1971). *Diary of my Analysis With Sigmund Freud*, New York: Hawthorn Books.

Bleuler, Eugen (1896). [review of Breuer and Freud], *Münchener medizinische Wochenschrift*, 43: 524–5.

Bloom, Harold (1987). *Ruin the Sacred Truths*, Cambridge, MA: Harvard University Press.

Boehlich, Walter (1990). 'Introduction', in *The Letters of Sigmund Freud and Eduard Silberstein, 1871–1881*, ed. W. Boehlich, trans. A. J. Pomerans, Cambridge, MA: The Belknap Press of Harvard University Press.

Bonanno, George et al. (1995). 'When Avoiding Unpleasant Emotions Might Not Be Such a Bad Thing: Verbal-Autonomic Response Dissociation and Midlife Conjugal Bereavement', *Journal of Personality and Social Psychology*, vol. 69, 5: 975–89.

Bonaparte, Marie (1937). *Topsy: The Story of a Golden-Haired Dog*, New Brunswick, NJ: Transaction Press, 1994.

Borch-Jacobsen, Mikkel (1988). *The Freudian Subject*, trans. Catherine Porter, Stanford: Stanford University Press.

— (1991). *Lacan: The Absolute Master*, trans. Douglas Brick, Stanford: Stanford University Press.

— (1993). *The Emotional Tie: Psychoanalysis, Mimesis, and Affect*, trans. Douglas Brick and others, Stanford: Stanford University Press.

— (1996a). *Remembering Anna O.: A Century of Mystification*, New York: Routledge.

— (1996b). [untitled lecture]. Institute for Contemporary Arts, 5 December.

— (1996c). 'Neurotica: Freud and the Seduction Theory', *October* 76: 15–43.

— (1997). 'Basta Cosi!: Mikkel Borch-Jacobsen on Psychoanalysis and Philosophy', in *Returns of the 'French Freud'*, ed. T. Dufresne, New York: Routledge: 209–27.

Bougnoux, Daniel (1997). 'Lacan, Sure – And Then What?', in *Returns of the 'French Freud': Freud, Lacan, and Beyond,* ed. T. Dufresne, New York: Routledge.

Brome, Vincent (1983). *Freud's Alter Ego*, New York: Norton.

Carnegie, Dale (1944). *How to Stop Worrying and Start Living*, New York: Simon and Schuster.

Ceiman, Alberto S. (1992). 'A Foundation for Psychoanalysis: Lacan, Reader of Freud', presented at The American Academy of Psychoanalysis, Cancun, Mexico (4 December).

Choisy, Maryse (1955) 'Memories of My Visits With Freud', in *Freud as We Knew Him*, ed. Hendrick M. Ruitenbeek, Detroit: Wayne State University Press.

Cioffi, Frank (1998). *Freud and The Question of Pseudoscience*, Chicago: Open Court.

Clarke, John Michell (1896a). [review of Breuer and Freud], *Brain: A Journal of Neurology*, 19: 401–14.

— (1896b). [review of Gilles de Tourette], *Brain: A Journal of Neurology*, vol. XIX: 415–31.

Collingwood, R. G. (1956). *The Idea of History*, London: Oxford University Press.

Copley-Graves, Lynn (1992). *Figure Skating History: The Evolution of Dance on Ice*, Columbus: Platoro Press.

Crabtree, Adam (1993). *From Freud to Mesmer: Magnetic Healing and the Roots of Psychological Health*, New York: Yale University Press.

Crews, Frederick (1995). *The Memory Wars: Freud's Legacy in Dispute*, New York: New York Review.

— (1997). 'The Legacy of Salem: Demonology for an Age of Science', *Skeptic*, vol. 5, no. 1: 36–44.

— ed., (1998). *Unauthorized Freud: Doubters Confront a Legend*, New York: Viking.

D'Amore, Arcangelo R. T. (1979). 'Ernest Jones: Founder of the American Psychoanalytic Association', *The International Journal of Psychoanalysis*.

Derrida, Jacques (1972). *Positions*, trans. Alan Bass (1981), Chicago: University of Chicago Press.

— (1974). *Glas*, trans. John P. Leavey, Jr., and Richard Rand (1986), Lincoln: University of Nebraska Press.

— (1980). 'To Speculate – On "Freud"', in *The Post Card: From Socrates to Freud and Beyond*, trans. Alan Bass (1987), Chicago: University of Chicago Press.

— (1988). 'My Chances/Mes Chances: A Rendezvous with Some Epicurean Stereophanies', in *Taking Chances: Derrida, Psychoanalysis, and Literature*, ed. Joseph H. Smith and William Kerrigan, Baltimore: Johns Hopkins University Press.

— (1991). 'Eating Well, or the Calculation of the Subject: An Interview With Jacques Derrida', in *Who Comes After the Subject?*, ed. Eduardo Cadava et al., New York: Routledge.

— (1992). 'The Law of Genre', in *Acts of Literature*, ed. Derek Attridge, New York: Routledge.

— (1994). [interview], in *Deconstruction and the Visual Art*, ed. Brunette and Wills, Cambridge: Cambridge University Press.

— (1995). *Archive Fever: A Freudian Impression*, trans. Eric Prenowitz (1996), Chicago: University of Chicago Press.

Deutsch, Helene (1973). 'Freud and His Pupils: A Footnote to the History of the Psychoanalytic Movement', in *Freud as We Knew Him*, ed. Hendrick M. Ruitenbeek, Detroit: Wayne State University Press.

Doolittle, Hilda (1974). *Tribute to Freud*, New York: A New Directions Book.

Duff-Taylor, S. (1937). *Skating*, London: Seely, Service & Co.

Dufresne, Todd (1994). 'Joseph Wortis: notorischer Anti-Psychoanalytiker', *Werkblatt*, 34: 90–118; also as 'An Interview With Joseph Wortis', *The Psychoanalytic Review*, 83(3), 1996: 455–75.

— (1996). Interview with David Bakan (19 July), unpublished.

— (1998). 'Analysing Freud: An Interview With Mikkel Borch-Jacobsen', *can*, vol. 1, no. 1: 9–12; also available in French trans. as 'Retour à Delboeuf', *Ethnopsi*. (October 2001).

— (1999). 'The Making of a Freud Skeptic: An Interview With Frederick Crews', *Skeptic*, vol. 7, no. 3: 42–9.

— (2000). *Tales From the Freudian Crypt: The Death Drive in Text and Context*, Stanford: Stanford University Press.

— (2002). 'Facticity, Freud, & Territorial Markings: An Interview With Frank Cioffi and Allen Esterson', *The Semiotic Review of Books*, Special Issue, 13.1 (Fall).

Eissler, Kurt R. (1965). *Medical Orthodoxy and the Future of Psychoanalysis*, New York: International Universities Press.

Ellenberger, Henri (1970). *The Discovery of the Unconscious: The History and Evolution of Dynamic Psychiatry*, New York: Basic Books.

— (1972). 'The Story of "Anna O.": A Critical Review With New Data', in *Beyond the Unconscious*, intro. and ed. Mark S. Micale (1993), Princeton: Princeton University Press.

Ferenczi, Sándor (1988). *The Clinical Diary of Sándor Ferenczi*, ed. Judith Dupont, Cambridge, MA: Harvard University Press.

Forrester, John (1990). *The Seductions of Psychoanalysis: Freud, Lacan, Derrida*, Cambridge: Cambridge University Press.

Foucault, Michel (1973). *The Order of Things: An Archaeology of the Human Sciences*, trans. Alan Sheridan, New York: Vintage.

Freeman, Lucy and Herbert Strean (1981). *Freud and Women*, New York: Frederick Ungar.

Freud, Martin (1958). *Sigmund Freud – Man and Father*, New York: Vanguard Press.

Freud, Sigmund and Josef Breuer (1893–5). *Studies on Hysteria, Standard Edition of the Complete Psychological Works of Sigmund Freud* (SE), ed. James Strachey, London: Hogarth Press, 1953–74, vol. 2.

Freud, Sigmund (1888). 'Preface to the Translation of Bernheim's *Suggestion*', *Standard Edition of the Complete Psychological Works of Sigmund Freud* (SE), ed. James Strachey, London: Hogarth Press, 1953–74, vol. 1: 71–85.

— (1892). 'Sketches for the "Preliminary Communication" of 1893', SE 1: 145–54.

— (1896). 'Appendix', SE 1: 86–7.

— (1900). *The Interpretation of Dreams*, SE 4, 5.

— (1901). *The Psychopathology of Everyday Life*, SE 6.

— (1911). 'Psychoanalytic Notes on an Autobiographical Account of a Case of Paranoia', SE 12: 1–82.

— (1914). 'On the History of the Psychoanalytic Movement', SE 14: 7–66.

— (1915). 'Thoughts for the Times on War and Death', SE 14: 273–300.

— (1916–17). *Introductory Lectures in Psychoanalysis*, SE 15, 16.

— (1920). *Beyond the Pleasure Principle*, SE 18: 7–64.

— (1925). *An Autobiographical Study*, SE 20: 1–74.

— (1930). *Civilization and Its Discontents*, SE 21: 64–145.

— (1937). 'Analysis Terminable and Interminable', SE 23: 211–53.

— (1940). *An Outline of Psychoanalysis*, SE 23: 141–207.

— (1960). *Letters of Sigmund Freud*, ed. Ernst Freud, trans. Tania and James Stern, New York: Basic Books.

— (1974). *Cocaine Papers*, notes by Anna Freud, ed. Robert Byck, New York: Stonehill.

— (1992). *The Diary of Sigmund Freud*, ed., trans., and intro. Michael Molnar, New York: Scribner's.

Freud, Sigmund and Sándor Ferenczi (1993). *The Correspondence of Sigmund Freud and Sándor Ferenczi, Volume 1, 1908–1914*, ed. E. Brabant et. al., trans. P. T. Hoffer, Cambridge, MA: Harvard University Press.

Freud, Sigmund and Wilhelm Fliess (1985). *The Complete Letters of Sigmund Freud to Wilhelm Fliess, 1887–1904*, ed. Jeffrey M. Masson, Cambridge, MA: Harvard University Press.

Freud, Sigmund and Ernest Jones (1993). *The Complete Correspondence of Sigmund Freud and Ernest Jones, 1909–1939*, ed. R. Andrew Paskauskas, intro. Riccardo Steiner, London: Belknap Press.

Freud, Sigmund and Carl Jung (1974). *The Freud/Jung Letters: The Correspondence Between Sigmund Freud and C. G. Jung,* ed. William McGuire, trans. Ralph Manheim and R. F. C. Hull, Cambridge, MA: Harvard University Press.

Freud, Sigmund and Lou Andreas-Salome (1972). *Sigmund Freud and Lou Andreas-Salome Letters*, trans. William and Elaine Robson-Scott, London: Hogarth Press.

Freud, Sigmund and Eduard Silberstein (1990). *The Letters of Sigmund Freud and Eduard Silberstein, 1871–1881*, ed. W. Boehlich, trans. A. J. Pomerans, Cambridge, MA: The Belknap Press of Harvard University Press.

Freud, Sigmund and Arnold Zweig (1970). *The Letters of Sigmund Freud and Arnold Zweig*, ed. Ernst Freud, trans. William and Elaine Robson-Scott, London: Hogarth Press.

Fromm, Erich (1959). *Sigmund Freud's Mission: An Analysis of His Personality and Influence*, New York: Grove Press.

— (1970). *The Crisis of Psychoanalysis*, New York: Holt, Rinehart, Winston.

Gamwell, Lynn (1989). 'The Origins of Freud's Antiquities Collection', in *Sigmund Freud and Art*, intro. P. Gay, New York: Harry N. Abrams: 21–32.

Gasché, Rodolphe (1987). 'Infrastructures and Systematicity', in *Deconstruction and Philosophy: The Texts of Jacques Derrida*, ed. John Sallis, Chicago: University of Chicago Press.

Gay, Peter (1988). *Freud: A Life for Our Times,* New York: Norton.

Genosko, Gary (1993). 'Freud's Bestiary: How Does Psychoanalysis Treat Animals?' *Psychoanalytic Review,* 80(4): 603–32.

— (1994). 'Introduction,' *Topsy*, New Brunswick, NJ: Transaction Press.

Goethe, J. W. von (1801). *Faust, Part One*, trans. Philip Wayne, New York: Penguin, 1987.

Gopnik, Adam (1998). 'Man Goes to See a Doctor', *The New Yorker* (August 24 and 31): 113–21.

Grinker, Roy (1940). 'Reminiscences of a Personal Contact With Freud', *American Journal of Orthopsychiatry*, 10: 850–4.

Grosskurth, Phyllis (1991). *The Secret Ring: Freud's Inner Circle and the Politics of Psychoanalysis*, Reading, MA: Addison-Wesley.

Grossman, Carl and Sylvia (1965). *The Wild Analyst: The Life and Work of George Groddeck*, New York: George Braziller.

Hacking, Ian (1988). 'Telepathy: Origins of Randomization in Experimental Design', *ISIS*, 79: 427–51.

Hansen, Uffe (1991). *Hypnotisøren Carl Hansen og Sigmund Freud*, Copenhagen: Akademisk Forlag.

Hirschmüller, Albrecht (1978). *The Life and Work of Josef Breuer*, New York: New York University Press, 1989.

Jay, Martin (1993). *Force Fields: Between Intellectual History and Cultural Debate*, New York: Routledge.

Jones, Ernest (1931). *The Elements of Figure Skating*, London: Methuen.

— (1952). *The Elements of Figure Skating*, revised and enlarged, London: George Allen & Unwin.

— (1953). *The Life and Work of Sigmund Freud, Volume 1: The Formative Years, 1856–1900*, New York: Basic Books.

— (1955). *The Life and Work of Sigmund Freud, Volume 2: The Years of Maturity, 1901–1919*, New York: Basic Books.

— (1957). *The Life and Work Of Sigmund Freud, Volume 3: The Last Phase, 1919–1939*, New York: Basic Books.

— (1959). *Free Associations: Memories of a Psycho-Analyst*, New York: Basic Books.

— (1974). 'The Problem of Paul Morphy: A Contribution to the Psychology of Chess', in *Psycho-Myth, Psycho-History: Essays in Applied Psychoanalysis*, New York: Hillstone.

Jones, Mervyn (1987). *Chances: An Autobiography*, London: Verso.

— (1990). 'Epilogue', in *Free Associations: Memories of a Psycho-Analyst*, ed., Ernest Jones, London: Transaction Press.

Kardiner, Abram (1957). 'Freud: The Man I Knew, The Scientist, and His Influence', in *Freud and the 20th Century*, ed. Benjamin Nelson, New York: Meridian Books.

— (1977). *My Analysis With Freud: Reminiscences*, New York: Norton.

Kavanaugh, Patrick B. (1999). 'Is Psychoanalysis in Crisis?', in *The Deaths of Psychoanalysis: Murder? Suicide? Or Rumor Greatly Exaggerated?*, ed. R. M. Prince, Northvale, NJ: Jason Aronson.

Kermode, Frank (1987). 'Frank Kermode [interview],' in *Criticism in Society*, ed. Imre Salusinszky, New York: Methuen.

Kiell, Norman (1988). *Freud Without Hindsight: Reviews of His Work*, Madison: International Universities Press.

Lacan, Jacques (1966). *Ecrit*, Paris: Seuil.

— (1988). *The Seminar, Book I: Freud's Papers on Technique, 1953–1954*, trans. with notes John Forrester, Cambridge: Cambridge University Press.

— (1990). *Television*, trans. Denis Hollier et. al., ed. Joan Copjec, New York: Norton.

Leader, Darian and Judy Groves (1995). *Lacan For Beginners*, Cambridge: Icon Books.

Lionells, Marylou (1999). 'Thanatos is Alive and Well and Living in Psychoanalysis', in *The Death of Psychoanalysis: Murder? Suicide? Or Rumor Greatly Exaggerated?*, ed. R. M. Prince, Northvale, NJ: Jason Aronson.

Macmillan, Malcolm (1997). *Freud Evaluated: The Completed Arc*, 2nd edition, Cambridge, MA: The MIT Press.

Mann, Thomas (1936). 'Freud and the Future', in *Freud: Modern Judgements*, ed. F. Cioffi (1973), London: Macmillan.

Mannoni, O. (1968). *Freud*, trans. R. Bruce (1971), New York: Pantheon.

Marcus, Steven (1984). *Freud and the Culture of Psychoanalysis: Studies in the Transition from Victorian Humanism to Modernity*, New York: Norton.

Merskey, Harold (1992). 'Anna O. Had a Severe Depressive Illness', *British Journal of Psychiatry*, 161: 185–94.

Nietzsche, Friedrich (1954). *The Portable Nietzsche*, ed. and trans. Walter Kaufmann, New York: Penguin.

— (1974). *The Gay Science*, trans. Walter Kaufmann, New York: Vintage.

— (1989). *Beyond Good and Evil*, trans. Walter Kaufmann, New York: Vintage.

Paskauskas, R. Andrew (1985). 'Ernest Jones: A Critical Study of His Scientific Development', unpublished PhD Dissertation, Institute for the History and Philosophy of Science and Technology, University of Toronto.

Phillips, Adam (1993). 'The Unimportance of Being Ernest', in *The London Review of Books*, 15/15 (August 5): 9–10.

Reiff, Phillip (1959). *Freud: The Mind of a Moralist*, London: Gollancz.

Reik, Theodore (1954). *Listening With the Third Ear: The Inner Experience of a Psychoanalyst*, New York: Farrar, Strauss and Cudahy.

— (1956). *The Search Within: The Inner Experiences of a Psychoanalyst*, New York: Farrar, Strauss and Cudahy.

Richardson, T. D. (1930). *Modern Figure Skating*, London: Methuen.

Roazen, Paul (1968). *Freud: Political and Social Thought*, New York: Knopf.

— (1969). *Brother Animal: The Story of Freud and Tausk,* New York: Alfred A. Knopf.

— (1975). *Freud and His Followers*, New York: Meridian.

— (1985). *Helene Deutsch: A Psychoanalyst's Life*, New York: Doubleday.

— (1991). 'Jung and Anti-Semitism', in *Lingering Shadows: Jungians, Freudians, and Anti-Semitism*, ed. Aryeh Maidenbaum and Steven A. Martin, Boston: Shambala.

— (1992). 'The Historiography of Psychoanalysis', in *Psychoanalysis in Its Cultural Context*, ed. Edward Timms and Ritchie Robertson, Edinburgh: Edinburgh University Press.

— (1993). *Meeting Freud's Family*, Amherst: University of Massachusetts Press.

— (1995). *How Freud Worked: First-Hand Accounts of Patients*, Northvale, NJ: Jason Aronson.

Roazen, Paul and Bluma Swerdloff (1995). *Heresy: Sándor Rado and the Psychoanalytic Movement*, Northvale, NJ: Jason Aronson.

Roback, A. A. (1954). *Destiny and Motivation in Language: Studies in Psycholinguistics and Glossodynamics*, Cambridge, MA: Harvard University Press.

Roudinesco, Elisabeth (1990). *Jacques Lacan & Co.: A History of Psychoanalysis in France, 1925–1985*, trans. Jeffrey Mehlman, Chicago: University of Chicago Press.

Roustang, François (1982). *Dire Mastery: Discipleship From Freud to Lacan*, trans. Ned Lukacher, Baltimore: Johns Hopkins University Press.

— (1983). *Psychoanalysis Never Lets Go*, trans. Ned Lukacher, Baltimore: Johns Hopkins Press.

Ruitenbeek, Hendrik M. (1973). 'The Professor', in *Freud As We Knew Him*, Detroit: Wayne State University Press.

Sachs, Hanns (1945). *Freud, Master and Friend*, London: Imago.

Schneiderman, Stuart (1983). *Jacques Lacan: The Death of an Intellectual Hero*, Cambridge, MA: Harvard University Press.

Schrodt, Barbara (1988). 'Figure Skating', in *The Canadian Encyclopedia*, Edmonton: Hurtig.

Schur, Max (1972). *Freud: Living and Dying*, New York: International Universities Press.

Shorter, Edward (1992). *From Paralysis to Fatigue: A History of Psychosomatic Illness in the Modern Era*, New York: Free Press.

— (1997). 'What Was The Matter With Anna O.: A Definitive Analysis', in *Freud Under Analysis*, ed. T. Dufresne, Northvale, NJ: Jason Aronson.

Sterba, Richard (1982). *Reminiscences of a Viennese Psychoanalyst*, Detroit: Wayne State University Press.

Stevenson, Robert Louis (1886). *The Strange Case of Dr. Jekyll and Mr. Hyde*, Lincoln: University of Nebraska Press, 1990.

Strümpell, Adolf von (1896). [review of Breuer and Freud], *Deutsche Zeitschrift für Nervenheilkunde*, 8: 159–61.

Swales, Peter (1989a). 'Freud, Johann Weier, and the Status of Seduction: The Role of the Witch in the Conception of Fantasy', in *Sigmund Freud: Critical Assessments*, vol. 1, ed. L. Spurling, London: Routledge: 331–58.

— (1989b). 'Freud, Krafft-Ebing, and the Witches: The Role of Krafft-Ebing in Freud's Flight Into Fantasy', in *Sigmund Freud: Critical Assessments*, vol. 1, ed. L. Spurling, London: Routledge: 359–65.

Szasz, Thomas (1976). *Karl Kraus and the Soul Doctors: A Pioneer Critic and His Criticism of Psychiatry and Psychoanalysis*, Baton Rouge: Louisiana State University Press.

Ulmer, Gregory (1985). *Applied Grammatology: Post(e) Pedagogy From Jacques Derrida to Joseph Beuys*, Baltimore: Johns Hopkins University Press.

Vichyn, Bertrand (1993). 'La psychanalyse entre l'archéologie et l'histoire', *Revue internationale d'Histoire de la Psychanalyse*, 6: 127–41.

Weber, Samuel (1990). 'Psychoanalysis, Literary Criticism, and the Problem of Authority', in *Psychoanalysis And . . .*, ed. Richard Feldstein and Henry Sussman, New York: Routledge.

Webster, Richard (1995). *Why Freud Was Wrong: Sin, Science, and Psychoanalysis*, New York: Basic Books.

Weiss, Edoardo (1991). *Sigmund Freud as a Consultant: Recollections of a Pioneer in Psychoanalysis*, New Brunswick, NJ: Transaction.

Weizsaecker, Viktor von (1957). 'Reminiscences of Freud and Jung', in *Freud and the 20th Century*, ed. Benjamin Nelson, New York: Meridian.

Wortis, Joseph (1940). 'Fragments of a Freudian Analysis', *American Journal of Orthopsychiatry*, 10: 843–9.

— (1954). *Fragments of an Analysis With Freud*, Northvale, NJ: Jason Aronson, 1984.

Index

Adler, Alfred   94, 165, 166
Alexander, Franz   166
Andreas-Salome, Lou   147
Anna O.   2, 4–25 *passim*, 31, 33–4, 136
Aristotle   9
Ayer, A. J.   36

Bakan, David   82
Balibar, Etienne   91
Benedict, Ruth   166
Benedikt, Moritz   7, 8, 27, 28
Bergson, Henri   8
Bernays, Jacob   9
Bernays, Minna   86, 143
Bernheim, Hippolyte   6, 16–18, 26, 34, 38, 39
   see also Nancy School
Bijur, Angelika   45–6
Billington, James H.   87
Binet, Alfred   19, 31
birth of psychoanalysis   40, 63, 150
Bleuler, Eugen   38
Blum, Harold   88, 89
Bonaparte, Marie   144–6, 193 n.423
Borch-Jacobsen, Mikkel   7, 9, 16–23
   passim, 35, 38–41, 43, 45, 70, 77, 85, 88–9, 91, 158, 160
Bougnoux, Daniel   95
Bragg, William   121

Braid, James   13
Brentano, Franz   8
Breuer, Josef   3, 4–25 *passim*, 26–34
   passim, 38
Brill, A. A.   67
Brome, Vincent   116
Browning, Robert   114
Brunswick, Ruth   107
Burlingham, Dorothy   143

Carnegie, Dale   5, 16, 25
catharsis   ix, 4–9 *passim*, 17, 19, 24, 182 n.106
Ceiman, Alberto   62, 63
Cervantes   136
Chamberlain, Neville   121
Charcot, Jean-Martin   6, 8, 13–22
   passim, 26–8, 38, 39, 64
Cioffi, Frank   35–48 *passim*, 88, 92, 159, 160
Clarke, John Mitchell   17, 38
Collingwood, R. G.   55, 158, 159
Copley-Graves, Lynn   115
Crabtree, Adam   7
Crews, Frederick   viii, 35, 37, 41, 43, 44, 45, 47, 88, 91, 92, 152–4, 159
critical Freud studies   viii, 3, 37, 39, 47, 52, 159

death drive   vii–viii, 72, 75, 78, 147,
    161
deconstruction   51, 54, 61, 70,
    72–83
Delboeuf, Joseph   16, 19
Derrida, Jacques   51, 59, 61, 72–83,
    153, 156, 157, 175
    see also deconstruction
Descartes, René   33, 74, 156, 166
Deutsch, Felix   147
Deutsch, Helene   116
Doolittle, Hilda   66, 139, 141, 142,
    143
Dostoevsky, Fyodor   112

Edinger, Dora   22
Edmunds, Lavina   45
Eilberg-Schwartz, Howard   82
Eissler, Kurt   44, 144, 170
Eitingon, Max   144
Ellenberger, Henri   7, 19, 21, 35
Ellis, Havelock   58, 63, 70
Erikson, Erik   166
Esterson, Allen   35, 44, 88

Farrell, John   45
Fechner, Gustav Theodore   7
Feldstein, Richard   98
Ferenczi, Sándor   36, 66, 109, 154,
    165
Feyerabend, Paul   153
Fish, Stanley   37, 44
Fliess, Wilhelm   39, 41, 42, 43, 55,
    57, 62, 100
Forrester, John   56, 88
Foucault, Michel   67, 79, 153, 156
free association   43–4, 174
Freud, Anna   67, 101, 121, 143, 145,
    166

'Freud basher'   2, 37, 52, 173
    see also psychoanalysis and criticism
Freud, Ernst   74
Freud, Martha   20, 143
Freud, Martin   140, 141, 143
Freud, Sigmund
    as a clinician   39, 46, 66–7, 140–4
    see also psychoanalysis
    works
        'Analysis Terminable and Inter-
            minable'   62
        An Autobiographical Study   164
        An Outline of Psychoanalysis   57
        Beyond the Pleasure Principle   72,
            73, 78, 94
        Civilization and Its Discontents
            60, 137, 172
        Future of an Illusion   137
        Interpretation of Dreams   59, 129
        'Preliminary Communication'   5,
            13, 26, 27, 29, 30
        Psychopathology of Everyday Life
            43
        Studies on Hysteria   3, 4–25
            passim, 26–34 passim, 40
        Three Essays on the Theory of
            Sexuality   42
Freud, Sophie   88
Frink, Horace   45–6, 59
Fromm, Erich   vii, 36, 66, 165,
    171–72

Gay, Peter   20, 21, 62, 70, 88, 89,
    125, 126
Gellner, Ernest   45
Genosko, Gary   142
Goethe, Johann Wolfgang von   18
Goldwin, Samuel   94
Goodman, Nelson   153

gossip 20–2, 52, 56, 57, 59, 84–6
Grinker, Roy 107, 140
Groddeck, Georg 65
Grosskurth, Phyllis 88
Groves, Judy 93
Grünbaum, Adolf 36, 41, 43, 88, 92

Habermas, Jürgen 80
Hansen, Carl 7, 10
Harari, Roberto 85, 86
Hartmann, Heinz 165
Hegel, Georg Wilhelm Friedrich 73,
   74, 95
Heidegger, Martin 74, 83
Henie, Sonja 121
Hirschmüller, Albrecht 11, 19, 20,
   21
Hitler, Adolf 169
Hoare, Samuel 121
Holt, Robert 88
Horkheimer, Max ix
Horney, Karen 144, 165
Hulten, Vivi-Anne 121
hypnosis 5–15, *passim*, 23, 24, 38,
   58
   see also suggestion
hysteria 6–21 *passim*, 26–34, 38, 41,
   and biology 13–17, 18, 26–34, 38

Janet, Pierre 19, 31, 32
Jesus 64
Jones, Ernest xii, 6, 35, 36, 45, 58,
   65, 94, 98, 101–10, 112,
   114–35, 136, 143, 144, 145
Jones, Katherine 107, 118, 120
Jones, Mervyn 116, 117, 118, 119,
   121
Jones, Robert 115, 125
Jones, Sybil 127

Jung, Carl 45, 65, 69, 94, 139, 165,
   166

Kann, Loe 104, 109
Kant, Immanuel 83
Kardiner, Abram 59, 166
Kavanaugh, Patrick 175
Kermode, Frank 81
Klein, Melanie 67, 166, 192 n.372
Kofman, Sarah 77
Krafft-Ebing, Richard von 11, 15, 40
Kraus, Karl 17, 57, 61
Krell, David Farell 77
Kris, Ernst 67
Kris, Marianne 67
Kristeva, Julia 91

Lacan, Jacques x, 51, 52, 58, 63, 84,
   85, 93–100, 101, 108, 133,
   144, 157, 160, 164, 166, 168
Laplanche, Jean 91
Laupus, Dr 7, 19, 20
Leader, Darian 93, 97–9
Library of Congress 37, 52, 87–92,
   183 n.128
Lionells, Mary-Lou 167
Loewenstein, Rudolph 99, 165
Lyotard, Jean-François 153

Macmillan, Malcolm 35, 88
Mann, Thomas 172
Marcus, Steven 56, 64
Marcuse, Herbert vii, 157, 171
Masson, Jeffrey M. 41
McLuhan, Marshall 173
Mesmer, Franz Anton 5, 9, 25
Miller, Jacques-Alain 84, 96–9
Möbius, Julius 8, 27–31
Molnar, Michael 88

Morphy, Paul   122, 132
Morselli, Enrico   80
Münchow, Michael   77

Nancy School, the   14, 16, 26, 27, 38
   see also Bernheim
Nietzsche, Friedrich   50, 55, 60, 64,
   70, 153, 166

Pankejeff, Sergius (aka Wolfman)   44
Pannetier, Odette   141
Papini, Giovanni   107
Pappenheim, Bertha   see Anna O.
Paris School, the   26, 27, 38
   see also Charcot
Phillips, Adam   134
Plato   32–4, 65, 74, 96
Pontalis, Jean-Bertrand   91
Popper, Karl   41
post-structuralism   51, 53, 60, 151,
   153, 155–9, 166, 167
psychoanalysis
   and chess   112, 117, 122, 132, 190
      n.328
   and criticism   2, 7, 36, 90–2,
      151–62 passim, 167, 175
   decline of   ix, xi, 35–48 passim,
      150–78 passim
   politics of   x, xi, 2, 19–23, 36, 37,
      44, 45–6, 50–1, 64–5, 68–9,
      76–8, 80–3, 87–92 passim,
      96–9, 138–9, 150–2
   as science   40, 41, 44, 64, 79, 95,
      153–54
Puységur, Marquis de   9

Rabelais, François   138
Rachman, Stanley   44
Rado, Sandor   143, 174

Rank, Otto   36, 165
Reich, Wilhelm   57, 165, 166
Reik, Theodor   35, 70
repression   24
Rice, Emanuel   82
Richardson, T. D.   116, 134, 135
Richet, Charles   8
Roazen, Paul   36, 51, 53, 54, 56, 61,
   67, 68, 70, 116, 139
Roth, Michael   88, 89, 90, 91
Roudinesco, Elisabeth   77, 90, 91,
   98–9
Roustang, François   35, 45, 55, 59,
   68

Sachs, Hanns   65
Sacks, Oliver   92
Schneiderman, Stuart   58
Schur, Max   147
Seduction Theory   38–42, 44, 55, 86,
   159
sexuality   20, 21, 41, 42
Shakespeare, William   26, 145
Shamdasani, Sonu   58
Sheridan, Alan   97
Shorter, Edward   10, 19
Silberstein, Eduard   136
Simmel, Ernst   140
Socrates   96, 153
split subjects   6, 10, 24, 31, 60–1, 68
Stannard, David E.   44
Stekel, Wilhelm   107
Sterba, Richard   139
Stevenson, Robert Louis   6
Stricker, Salomon   136
Strümpell, Adolf von   12, 27–8, 38
suggestion   3, 13–17 passim, 39, 41,
   42, 43, 58
   see also hypnosis

Sullivan, Harry Stack 165
Sulloway, Frank 35, 41, 43, 44, 88, 160, 165
Swales, Peter 35, 37, 43, 84, 88, 89, 91, 183 n.128
Szasz, Thomas 68

talking cure 4–25 *passim*
Tandler, Julius 67, 134
Tausk, Victor 86
theory, culture of viii, x, 74, 155–7, 165–6, 175–6, 194 n.454
see also psychoanalysis, politics of
therapeutic culture viii, x, 9, 40, 44–6, 66, 90, 174
Thomas, D. M. 51
Timpanaro, Sabastiano 43–4
Tourette, Gilles de la 64
training analysis 64–5
transference 20, 57–9, 62, 68, 91, 140, 142, 144, 152

unconscious, theory of 4–5, 9, 23, 24, 25, 39, 55, 141
Unwin, Sir Stanley 121
Updike, John vii

Valéry, Paul 8
Vinci, Leonardo da 112
Voltaire 147

Webster, Richard 21, 22
Wells, Richard 77
Wilson, Woodrow 112
Wolpe, Joseph 44
Wortis, Joseph 58, 63, 107, 140, 141
Wundt, Wilhelm 7

Yerushalmi, Yosef Hayim 79–82

Žižek, Slavoj 98
Zweig, Arnold 54